Practical English Language Teaching

DAVID NUNAN
EDITOR

Mc
Graw
Hill

Practical English Language Teaching, First Edition

Published by McGraw-Hill/Contemporary, a business unit of The McGraw-Hill Companies, Inc., 1221 Avenue of the Americas, New York, NY 10020. Copyright © 2003 by The McGraw-Hill Companies, Inc. All rights reserved. No part of this publication may be reproduced or distributed in any form or by any means, or stored in a database or retrieval system, without the prior written consent of The McGraw-Hill Companies, Inc., including, but not limited to, in any network or other electronic storage or transmission, or broadcast for distance learning.

 This book is printed on recycled, acid-free paper containing 10% postconsumer waste.

3 4 5 6 7 8 9 0 DOC/DOC 0 9 8 7 6 5

ISBN 0-07-282062-4

Editorial director: *Tina B. Carver*
Senior managing editor: *Erik Gundersen*
Developmental editor: *Linda O'Roke*
Director of North American marketing: *Thomas P. Dare*
Director of international sales & marketing: *Kate Oakes*
Production manager: *Genevieve Kelley*
Cover designer: *NE Studio*
Copyeditor: *Sophia Wisener*
Indexer: *Do Mi Stauber Indexing Services*

www.mhcontemporary.com

The **McGraw·Hill** Companies

Table of Contents

Foreword v

Section **One**

1 Exploring skills **1**

Chapter **1**	Methodology – David Nunan	**3**
Chapter **2**	Listening – Marc Helgesen	**23**
Chapter **3**	Speaking – Kathleen M. Bailey	**47**
Chapter **4**	Reading – Neil Anderson	**67**
Chapter **5**	Writing – Maggie Sokolik	**87**

Section **Two**

2 Exploring language **109**

Chapter **6**	Pronunciation – John Murphy	**111**
Chapter **7**	Vocabulary – I.S.P. Nation	**129**
Chapter **8**	Grammar – David Nunan	**153**
Chapter **9**	Discourse – Michael McCarthy and Steve Walsh	**173**

Section **Three**

3 Supporting the learning process **197**

Chapter **10**	Content-based instruction – Donna Brinton	**199**
Chapter **11**	Coursebooks – Kathleen Graves	**225**
Chapter **12**	Computer-assisted language learning – Ken Beatty	**247**
Chapter **13**	Learning styles and strategies – Mary Ann Christison	**267**
Chapter **14**	Learner autonomy in the classroom – Phil Benson	**289**
Chapter **15**	Classroom-based assessment – Geoff Brindley	**309**

Glossary **329**

Index **337**

Credits **342**

Foreword

Vision and purpose

Practical English Language Teaching is designed for the practicing teacher who may or may not have had formal training in teaching English as a second or foreign language (ESL/EFL). Methodology texts currently available make too many assumptions about the background knowledge of their readership. The authors of the chapters in this book keep such assumptions to a minimum. This is not to say that the concepts underlying the chapters are dealt with in a trivial manner. Rather they are given an accessible treatment which is richly supported by teaching materials and ideas, and illustrative extracts from a wide range of classrooms.

Practical English Language Teaching consists of three sections: Exploring skills, Exploring language, and Supporting the learning process. The first main section, Exploring skills, begins with an introductory chapter that defines and illustrates the concept of methodology. The next four chapters introduce the four key "macroskills" of listening, speaking, reading and writing. In the second section, Exploring language, we look at language from a somewhat different perspective. Here the chapters are organized in terms of the different systems that make up the language: the sound system, the vocabulary system, the grammatical system, and the discourse system which shows how language itself is organized and reflects the communicative purposes that bring it into existence in the first place. The final section, Supporting the learning process, looks at some of the ways in which the learning process can be supported – through teaching styles and strategies, effective use of commercial coursebooks, and by a variety of other means.

Practical English Language Teaching brings together the work of 15 world-class specialists in ESL/EFL. The value of publishing an edited collection, rather that a single-authored volume, is that we have been able to draw on the knowledge and experience of the top specialists in our field.

One of the problems with most edited collections is that they are uneven in terms of their treatment and approach, and in terms of the assumptions that they make about the reader. This collection has a degree of coherence unusual in edited collections. The coherence has been achieved through a clear chapter-by-chapter framework, and the use of detailed writing guidelines.

The length of each chapter has been controlled for accessibility. Each chapter could have been a book in its own right. However, we wanted to present readers with the essentials in terms of conceptual background, theory, and research. These provide the basis for a series of key teaching principles which are illustrated with pedagogical materials and authentic classroom extracts.

Features

- Critical areas of language teaching are comprehensively addressed with a specific focus on practical techniques, strategies, and tips.
- World-class specialists offer a variety of perspectives on language teaching and the learning process.
- *Reflection* questions invite readers to think about critical issues in language teaching, while *Action* tasks outline strategies for putting new techniques into practice.
- Thoughtful suggestions for books, articles, and Web sites offer resources for additional, up-to-date information.
- Expansive glossary offers short and straightforward definitions of core language teaching terms.

Audience

This book is designed for both experienced teachers and those who have only just entered the profession. It will update the experienced teacher on current theoretical and practical approaches to language teaching. The novice teacher will find step-by-step guidance on the practice of language teaching.

Chapter structure

Each chapter is constructed upon the following format.

1. Introduction: Defines the subject of the chapter.
2. Background: Provides an overview of what theory, research, and practice have to tell us about the subject.
3. Principles: Describes and provides examples of key principles for teaching the subject that forms the basis for the chapter.
4. Classroom techniques and tasks: Provides examples of practical classroom procedures.
5. In the classroom: Takes the reader into a range of classrooms where the principles spelled out earlier are exemplified.
6. Conclusion: Summarizes key parts of the chapter.
   Additional resources:
   - Further reading: Introduces additional sources for exploring the subject in question.
   - Helpful Web sites: Points the reader to relevant Web sites.

A glossary at the end of the book defines the key terms related to language teaching and learning that are introduced in the book. These key language terms are printed in bold in the body of the text. Note that section titles and bulleted lists of items throughout the book also appear in boldface type. The glossary does not necessarily provide definitions for all terms mentioned in these section titles and bulleted lists.

Interspersed throughout each chapter are *Reflection* and *Action* boxes. The *Reflection* boxes pose questions inviting readers to reflect on issues, principles, and techniques in relation to their current or projected teaching situations. *Action* boxes invite the reader to apply the ideas through action-oriented tasks.

Acknowledgements

The editor and publisher would like to thank the anonymous readers for this project who reviewed the Practical English Language Teaching manuscript at various stages of development and whose comments, reviews, and assistance were extremely helpful.

Thanks to Linda O'Roke for all her help. – David Nunan

Contributors

Neil Anderson is on the faculty of the Department of Linguistics and English Language at Brigham Young University in Provo, Utah, USA. His research and teaching interests include second language reading, language learning strategies, and learning and teaching styles. Professor Anderson is a past president of Teachers of English to Speakers of Other Languages, Inc. (TESOL).

Kathleen M. Bailey is Professor of Applied Linguistics in the TESOL-TFL Program at the Monterey Institute of International Studies in Monterey, California, USA. She has taught English in Korea, the U.S., and Hong Kong, and has worked with language teachers in Argentina, Australia, Brazil, Czechoslovakia, Italy, Japan, Poland, Singapore, Thailand, Trinidad, and Uruguay.

Ken Beatty is Senior Lecturer for Information Technology in the Division of Languages at City University of Hong Kong in China, where he has taught for ten years. He previously taught at universities and schools in Canada and China. His publications include English as a second language (ESL) and computer textbooks, Web sites, and CD-ROMs.

Phil Benson is Assistant Professor at the University of Hong Kong in China, where he has taught English and Applied Linguistics for more than ten years. He has also taught English in secondary schools and private institutes in Algeria, Japan, Kuwait, Malaysia, and Seychelles. He has published widely on the subject of autonomy in language learning. His research interests also include the use of information technology in language learning and lexicography.

Geoff Brindley is Associate Professor of Linguistics at Macquarie University, Sydney, Australia. He has worked as an English as a second and foreign language (ESL/EFL) teacher, teacher trainer, researcher, test developer, and administrator. He is the author and editor of a wide variety of publications on language assessment, second language acquisition, and language curriculum development.

Donna Brinton is Lecturer in the Department of Applied Linguistics & TESL at the University of California, Los Angeles, where she also serves as Academic Coordinator of the university's English as a Second Language (ESL) courses. She has co-authored several ESL textbook series, produced multimedia instructional materials, and co-authored or co-edited five professional texts. These texts mirror her areas of academic interest in content-based instruction, English for specific purposes, and practical phonetics. She has also conducted teacher in-services in countries as diverse as Israel, Mozambique, Thailand, and Uzbekistan.

Mary Ann Christison is Professor and Director of Graduate Studies in the Linguistics Department at the University of Utah, Salt Lake City, Utah, USA. She is the author of over 70 published articles on second language teaching and research. She served as International TESOL President from 1997-1998.

Kathleen Graves is a teacher educator at the School for International Training, Brattleboro, Vermont, USA. She is interested in helping teachers develop a reflective practice so they can work in partnership with their learners. She has written two books based on teachers' experiences with developing courses and materials.

Marc Helgesen teaches at Miyagi Gakuin Women's College, Sendai, Japan. He has published widely in the area of listening and, along with Steve Brown, is author of the *Active Listening* series (Cambridge University Press).

Michael McCarthy is Professor of Applied Linguistics at the University of Nottingham, England and Adjunct Professor of Applied Linguistics at Pennsylvania State University, State College, Pennsylvania, USA. He has published widely in the areas of discourse analysis, vocabulary, and the grammar of spoken English.

John Murphy is Associate Professor and Director of Graduate Studies in the Applied Linguistics/ESL department at Georgia State University, Atlanta, Georgia, USA. His recent teacher development book was co-edited with Patricia Byrd and is titled *Understanding the Courses We Teach: Local Perspectives on English Language Teaching* (University of Michigan Press).

I. S. P. Nation is Professor of Applied Linguistics at Victoria University of Wellington, New Zealand. He has taught in Finland, Indonesia, Japan, Thailand, and the U.S. His special interests are language teaching methodology and vocabulary learning.

David Nunan holds concurrent Chairs at the University of Hong Kong, China and Newport Asia Pacific University, Newport Beach, California, USA. He is also Senior Academic Advisor to GlobalEnglish, an Internet based English language provider in San Francisco, California, USA. He has written over 100 books and articles on curriculum development, task-based language learning, teacher education, and classroom-based research.

Maggie Sokolik received her Ph.D. in Applied Linguistics from the University of California, Los Angeles. She currently teaches writing and directs the English as a Second Language Workshop at the University of California, Berkeley, USA. She has written several textbooks on reading and writing, and conducts teacher education workshops in many locations around the world.

Steve Walsh is Director of Teacher Education and Lecturer in ELT at the Queen's University of Belfast, Northern Ireland. He has published in the area of discourse analysis in English Language Teaching.

Exploring skills

T his first section of the book introduces you to language teaching methodology from the perspective of language skills, that is, listening, speaking, reading, and writing. Before looking at the skills in detail, there is an initial chapter on language teaching methodology that provides a framework, not just for the four other chapters in this section, but for the book as a whole.

Each chapter follows a set format. Firstly, the skill dealt with in the chapter is defined. Next comes a section providing background information on the skill. This section provides a brief history of the teaching of the skill, summarizes important research findings, and elaborates on key concepts. Section Three sets out key principles that should guide you when teaching the skill concerned. The next two sections provide examples from published and unpublished materials as well as from direct classroom experience illustrating the principles in action. The chapters conclude with useful follow-up text and resources, including Web sites, to provide you with further information and ideas.

Chapter **One**

Methodology

David Nunan, University of Hong Kong (China)

Goals

At the end of this chapter, you should be able to:

✔ **define** methodology.

✔ **explain** how methodology is related to curriculum development and syllabus design.

✔ **describe** the "methods" debate.

✔ **explain** the basic principles of communicative language teaching, and describe its current importance in language teaching pedagogy.

✔ **discuss** some of the research findings that have influenced language teaching methodology.

✔ **create** instructional sequences that incorporate the pretask, task, and follow-up cycle.

1.   What is methodology?

The field of **curriculum development** is large and complex. It includes all of the planned learning experiences in an educational setting. Curriculum has three main subcomponents: **syllabus** design, **methodology,** and **evaluation.** Syllabus design has to do with selecting, sequencing, and justifying content. Methodology has to do with selecting, sequencing, and justifying learning tasks and experiences. Evaluation has to do with how well students have mastered the objectives of the course and how effectively the course has met their needs. The following diagram shows how these different elements fit together.

Curriculum component	Focus	Defining questions
Syllabus design	Content	What content should we teach? In what order should we teach this content? What is the justification for selecting this content?
Methodology	Classroom techniques and procedures	What exercises, tasks, and activities should we use in the classroom? How should we sequence and integrate these?
Evaluation	Learning outcomes	How well have our students done? How well has our program served our students' needs?

Figure 1 Subcomponents of a curriculum

This book is basically about language teaching methodology. In other words, the focus of the chapters is principally on techniques and procedures for use in the classroom, although most chapters also touch on aspects of content selection and evaluation.

The *Longman Dictionary of Applied Linguistics* defines methodology as …

> **1.**   … the study of the practices and procedures used in teaching, and the principles and beliefs that underlie them.
>
> Methodology includes
>
> **a.** study of the nature of language skills (e.g., reading, writing, speaking, listening, and procedures for teaching them)

> **b.** study of the preparation of lesson plans, materials, and textbooks for teaching language skills
>
> **c.** the evaluation and comparison of language teaching methods (e.g., the audiolingual method)
>
> **2.** such practices, procedures, principles, and beliefs themselves.
>
> (Richards, et al. 1985, p. 177)

From the table of contents you will see that this book addresses most of these areas. Section 1 focuses on the language skills of listening, speaking, reading, and writing. Section 2 looks at aspects of language–discourse, grammar, vocabulary, and pronunciation. Section 3 explores elements that support the learning process, including learning styles and strategies, content-based instruction, using textbooks, using computers, fostering autonomy and independence, and classroom-based assessment and evaluation.

2. Background to language teaching methodology

The "methods" debate

A language teaching **method** is a single set of procedures which teachers are to follow in the classroom. Methods are also usually based on a set of beliefs about the nature of language and learning. For many years, the goal of language pedagogy was to "find the right method"–a methodological magic formula that would work for all learners at all times (Brown, 2002). Methods contrast with **approaches**, which are more general, philosophical orientations such as **communicative language teaching** (see page 6) that can encompass a range of different procedures.

The dominant method for much of the last century was the **grammar-translation** method. This was challenged in the 1950s and 1960s by **audiolingualism**, a method that is still very popular today, and whose influence can be seen in a variety of drill-based techniques and exercises.

Audiolingualism was the first method to be based on a theory of learning–**behaviorism**, which viewed all learning as a process of forming habits, and on a theory of language–**structural linguistics**. Behaviorism and structural linguistics provided the following key characteristics of audiolingualism:

- Priority is given to spoken rather than written language.

- Language learning is basically a matter of developing a set of habits through drilling.

- Teach the language, not *about* the language. (Avoid teaching grammar rules. Get learners to develop their skills through drill and practice–teach through "analogy" not "analysis.") (Moulton, 1963)

In the 1960s, behaviorism and structural linguistics were severely criticized as being inadequate representations of both the learning process and the nature of language. In place of behaviorism, psychologists proposed cognitive psychology while the linguist Chomsky developed a new theory called **transformational-generative grammar**. Both approaches emphasized thinking, comprehension, memory, and the uniqueness of language learning to the human species. Methodologists seized on the theories and developed a method known as **cognitive code learning**. This approach promoted language learning as an active mental process rather than a process of habit formation. Grammar was back in fashion, and classroom activities were designed that encouraged learners to work out grammar rules for themselves through inductive reasoning. (For examples, see Nunan, Chapter 8, this volume.)

In addition to methods based on theories of learning and language, there emerged a number of methods that were based on a humanistic approach to education. These methods emphasized the importance of emotional factors in learning, and proponents of these methods believed that linguistic models and psychological theories were less important to successful language acquisition than emotional or affective factors. They believed that successful learning would take place if learners could be encouraged to adopt the right attitudes and interests in relation to the target language and target culture. The best known of these methods were **the silent way, suggestopedia** and community language learning. The best introduction to humanistic learning within language education is Stevick (1997). Stevick became interested in humanism after he observed both audiolingual and cognitive code learning in action. He found that both methods could either be quite successful or extremely unsuccessful. "How is it," he asked, "that two methods based on radically different assumptions about the nature of language and learning could be successful or unsuccessful, as the case may be?" He concluded that particular classroom techniques mattered less than establishing the right emotional climate for the learners.

Communicative language teaching (CLT)

During the 1970s, a major reappraisal of language occurred. Linguists began to look at language, not as interlocking sets of grammatical, lexical, and phonological rules, but as a tool for expressing meaning. This reconceptualization had a profound effect on language teaching methodology. In the earliest versions of CLT, meaning was emphasized over form, fluency over accuracy. It also led to the development of differentiated courses that reflected the different communicative needs of learners. This needs-based approach also reinforced another trend that was emerging at the time—that of **learner-centered education** (Nunan, 1988).

In recent years, the broad approach known as CLT has been realized methodologically by **task-based language teaching** (TBLT). In TBLT, language lessons are based on learning experiences that have nonlinguistic outcomes, and in which there is a clear connection between the things learners do in class and the things they will ultimately need to do outside of the classroom. Such tasks might include listening to a weather forecast and deciding what to wear, ordering a meal, planning a party, finding one's way around town and so on. In these tasks, language is used to achieve nonlanguage outcomes. For example, the ultimate aim of ordering a meal is not to use correctly formed wh-questions, but to get food and drink on the table.

Research

During the "what's the best method?" phase of language teaching, several studies were carried out to settle the question empirically. For example, Swaffar, Arens and Morgan (1982) set out to decide which was superior, audiolingualism or cognitive code learning. The results were inconclusive, and it appeared that, at the level of classroom teaching, few teachers adhered rigidly to one method rather than the other. Instead, they evolved a range of practices that reflected their own personal teaching styles. Among other things, it was studies such as these that gradually led people to abandon the search for the "right method."

In the 1970s, a series of investigations were carried out that had (and continue to have) a great deal of influence on methodology. These came to be known as the **morpheme order studies**. These investigations set out to examine the order in which certain items of grammar were acquired. (For a more detailed description, see Nunan, Chapter 8, this volume.) The researchers concluded from their investigations three significant points: one, that there was a "natural order" in which grammar was acquired; two, that this order did not reflect the order in which items were taught; and three, that the natural order could not be altered by instruction. According to one of the researchers, the implications for the classroom were clear: it was not necessary to drill grammar (Krashen, 1981, 1982). All that was needed in order to teach another language was to engage learners in "natural" communicative tasks that were roughly pitched at their level of proficiency (Krashen and Terrell, 1983).

As you will see in the chapter on grammar, subsequent research has demonstrated that a grammar focus in class *does* seem to be beneficial for most learners. However, the insights provided by Krashen and others did help to advance the field, and many of his suggestions have found their way into current methodological approaches.

Out of the research just cited grew the question: What kinds of communicative tasks seem most beneficial for second language acquisition? A great deal of research has gone into this question in the last fifteen years. (For a review see Nunan, 1999, particularly Chapter 2.) While results from this research are varied, one characteristic that seems particularly beneficial is required information exchange tasks. These are tasks in which two or more learners, working in pairs or small groups, have access to different information. This information needs to be shared in order for the task to be completed successfully. (An example of a required information exchange task is provided below.) It is hypothesized that required information exchange tasks force students to negotiate with each other, and this is healthy for language development because it "pushes" the learners to reformulate and extend their language.

3. Principles for language teaching methodology

1. Focus on the learner.

A learner-centered classroom is one in which learners are actively involved in their own learning processes. There are two dimensions to this learner involvement. The first of these is the involvement of learners in making decisions about what to learn, how to learn, and how to be evaluated. The second is in maximizing the class time in which the learners, rather than the teacher, do the work.

Reflection

1. What do you think some of the objections to the two dimensions of learner involvement outlined above might be?
2. Brainstorm possible solutions to these objections.

In relation to the first dimension, it is sometimes argued that most learners do not have the knowledge or experience to make informed decisions about what to learn, how to learn, and how to be assessed. According to this view, the teacher is the boss, and it is the professional responsibility of the teacher to make these decisions. A countervailing view is that ultimately it is the learner who has to do the learning.

One possible solution to this dilemma is for the teacher to make most of the decisions at the beginning of the learning process. Then gradually, through a process of learner training, begin developing in the learners the skills they need in order to begin taking control of their own learning processes. (See Christison, Chapter 13, this volume.)

In fact, it is not an "all or nothing" issue in which either the teacher or the learner makes all of the decisions. In most classrooms it is somewhere in between, with teacher and students negotiating things such as when to submit assignments, whether to do a task in small groups or pairs, whether to do a reading task before a listening task or vice-versa, and so on. However, a teacher who is committed to this principle will look for opportunities to involve learners in becoming more reflective and in making more decisions about their own learning.

Here are some ways of getting learners more involved in their own learning process and to gradually take control of that process. Each step entails greater and greater involvement of learners in their own learning processes.

Involving learners in the learning process

1. Make instructional goals clear to learners.

2. Help learners to create their own goals.

3. Encourage learners to use their second language outside of the classroom.

4. Help learners to become more aware of learning processes and strategies.

5. Show learners how to identify their own preferred styles and strategies.

6. Give learners opportunities to make choices between different options in the classroom.

7. Teach learners how to create their own learning tasks.

8. Provide learners with opportunities to master some aspect of their second language and then teach it to others.

9. Create contexts in which learners investigate language and become their own researchers of language.

   (For examples of how to make these ideas work in the classroom, see Nunan, 1999.)

Figure 2 Involving learners in the learning process

2. Develop your own personal methodology.

As we saw in the background section of this chapter, the search for the "one best method" was elusive and ultimately proved to be futile. When researchers looked at what teachers actually did in the classroom as opposed to what proponents of one method or another said they ought to do, they found that teachers had a range of practices that were widely used regardless of the method that any given teacher was supposed to follow. The major difference lies, not in the tasks themselves, but in the ordering and prioritizing of the tasks. In other words, in terms of actual classroom practices the same techniques might be used, but their ordering and emphasis would be different.

Another related observation is that just as learners have their own learning styles, so teachers have their own teaching styles. They are derived from their professional training and experience as well as their own experiences as learners. While one teacher might correct errors overtly, others might do it through modeling the correct utterance. These two styles are exemplified in the following examples.

Example 1

> **Student:** I go home at three o'clock, yesterday.
> **Teacher A:** No. Remember Luis, the past tense of go is went.

Example 2

> **Student:** I go home at three o'clock, yesterday.
> **Teacher B:** Oh, you went home at three, did you Luis?

Similarly, one teacher may prefer to give explicit explanation and practice of a new grammar point before getting students to use it in a communicative activity. Another teacher may prefer to introduce the grammar point in the form of a contextualized dialogue and only draw the attention of the student to the grammatical form after they have used it communicatively or pseudocommunicatively.

What is important, then, is that teachers develop their own preferred classroom practices based on what works best for them in their own particular situation and circumstances and given the learners they have at the time. As circumstances, students, and levels of experience change, so will the practices. (If you are teaching large classes, it may not be feasible to do much pair or group work, no matter how highly you think of them.)

This is not to say that all practices are equally valid for all learners. Experiment with different practices. Try out new ideas. Record your lessons, observe your teaching, if possible have a peer observe your teaching, and above all reflect on what happens in your classroom. If you have time, keep a reflective journal and set out observations, questions, challenges, and puzzles. Even if you have relatively little experience, you will be surprised at how much you can learn about processes of teaching and learning by systematically reflecting on what happens in your classroom.

Principle 2 (pages 10-11) mentions self-observation, peer observation, and reflective journals. Brainstorm other ways of obtaining information and feedback on your teaching. Design a plan for getting feedback on your teaching.

3. Build instructional sequences based on a pretask, task, and follow-up cycle.

Successful instructional sequences share certain things in common, regardless of the methodological principles or approaches that drive them. First of all, the main task, whether it be a drill, a role-play, or a listening comprehension, is set up through one or more pretasks. Pretasks have several functions: to create interest, help build students' **schema** in relation to the topic, introduce key vocabulary, revise a grammatical point, etc.

Following the pretasks comes the task itself. This will usually consist of several steps or subtasks. In the communicative classroom, the teacher will seek to maximize the time that the students are processing the language or interacting with each other (although, of course, this will depend on the rationale for the instructional sequence). The teacher will also carefully monitor the students to ensure that they know what they are supposed to do and are carrying out the tasks correctly.

Following the task proper, there should be some sort of follow-up. This also has a number of functions: to elicit feedback from the students about their experience, to provide feedback to the students on how they had done, to correct errors that the teacher might have noticed in the course of the instructional sequence, and to get students to reflect on the tasks and engage in self-evaluation.

Select a language-learning task from a textbook or other source and design a pretask and follow-up to it.

4. Classroom techniques and tasks

In this section, we look at some of the techniques and ideas that have been introduced in the preceding sections. There are so many of these that I have had to be highly selective. I have chosen to organize this section in terms of pretask, task, and follow-up.

Pretask As we have seen, pretasks have several functions: to create interest, help build students' schema in relation to the topic, introduce key vocabulary, and revise grammar items prior to the introduction of the task proper. There is almost no limit to the number of things that can be done at the pretask stage. Here are some examples:

Have students

- look at a list of comprehension questions and try to predict the answers before carrying out a listening task;
- classify a set of words for describing emotions as "positive," "negative," and "neutral" before reading a magazine article about emotions;
- practice a model conversation and then introduce their own variations before doing a role-play;
- study a picture of a group of people at a party and try to guess which people are married/going out with each other before hearing a conversation about the couples;
- brainstorm ways in which cities of the future will be different from now before writing a newspaper article;
- match newspaper headlines and photos before reading articles;
- check off words in a vocabulary list that are associated with living in a foreign culture before listening to a person recounting their experiences of living abroad;
- rank from most to least important a list of factors predicting if a relationship will last before listening to a minilecture on the subject;
- discuss the best year they ever had before taking part in an information gap exercise;
- look at pictures taken from advertisements and guess what the ads are trying to sell before listening to the ads.

Task The number of tasks that can be used to activate language in the classroom is also large. Some of the more popular task types in the communicative classroom include: role-plays, simulations, problem-solving, listening to authentic audio/video material, discussions, decision-making, and information gaps. Information gap tasks in which two or more students have access to different information that they have to share in order to complete the task are popular because

- they work well with learners at most levels of proficiency from post-beginner to advanced;
- students participate actively;

- all students have to take part if the task is to work;
- they work well with mixed level groups.

Here is an example of an information gap task. This task is personalized in that the students create their own information gap based on content from their own lives.

Example

Make a note of the things you have to do this week. Leave two spaces free.

	Monday	Tuesday	Wednesday	Thursday	Friday
Afternoon					
Evening					

Now work with two other students. Arrange a time to see a movie. You might have to change your schedule.

Reflection

1. What level of proficiency do you think the task above is designed for?
2. What language do you imagine that students will need to use?
3. What language functions are the students practicing?

Action Design your own information gap task. Specify the vocabulary, grammar, and structures that you think the students will need in order to complete the task.

Follow-up As already indicated, the follow-up phase also provides lots of scope. The teacher can give feedback to the students, debrief them on some aspect of the preceding task, or encourage them to reflect on what they learned and how well they are doing.

Here are some examples of reflection tasks.

1. Write down five new words you learned in today's lesson. Write sentences using three of these new words. Write down three new sentences or questions you learned.

2. Review the language functions you practiced in this lesson. Circle your answers.

Can you...

| talk about past events? | Yes | A little | Not yet |
| give and receive messages? | Yes | A little | Not yet |

3. What would you say?

Your best friend invites you to his/her birthday party, but you can't make it.
You say ⸻

You want someone to get you a book from the library.
You say ⸻

4. Review the language we practiced today. In groups, brainstorm ways to use this language out of class. Imagine you are visiting an English-speaking country. Where and when might you need this language?

5. Methodology in the classroom

Reflection

What is going on in Extract 1 (page 15–16)? Is the extract taken from a pretask, task, or follow-up? What is the purpose of the instructional sequence?

T stands for teacher. *S* represents a particular student. *Ss* stands for students.

S1: Tourist, visitor, traveler, student.

S2: Student.

S1: Yeah.

S2: *Must be that one, yeah.*

T: *Why do you think—why is* student *the odd one out?*

S2: *Oh,* tourist, visitor, traveler … *They are moving.*

S3: Yeah.

S1: *They are going.*

S2: *They have something in common, no?*

T: *Yeah, yeah. But I'd like you to say what it is that they have in common, you know? How would you describe it?*

S3: *OK, second.* Investigate, determine, explore, inquire. *I think, determine …*

S1: Determine.

S3: *Yeah, because* investigate, inquire, explore *is …*

S1: *Synonymous, synonymous.*

S3: *…means to know something. Mmm. OK.*

S1: *Third.* Elderly, intelligent, stupidly, *and* talkative. Intelligent *and* stupidly, *you know. I think they have, er, some relations between because there is the opposite meanings.*

S3: *How about, er,* elderly *and* talkative?

S2: Talkative—*what means* talkative?

S1: *Yeah, too much.*

S2: Talkative.

S1: *How about the* elderly?

S3: *Adjective.*

S1: *Had a more experience and they get the more …*

S3: Intelligent, stupidly—*maybe that the part of the human being … which is, I think … OK. Oh…*

S1: *Wait. Wait a minute. OK, this is, this is different ad … kind of adjective that the ….*

S2: *OK, all right.*

T: *So, which one did you decide?*

Ss: Elderly, elderly.

T: Why's that?

S2: Because, er, it's quite different this, because this match with your age, with your age, and the other one is with your... kind of person that you are.

T: Personality.

S2: Personality, yeah.

S1: Er, utilize, uncover, reveal, disclose. *Yeah, this is* utilize. Uncover, reveal, disclose—*all of them the same meaning.* Uncover, reveal, disclose.

S2: Uncover? *What's* uncover?

S1: *You know, cover and uncover (gestures).*

S2: Oh. Reveal. *OK.*

S3: *Good.*

T: But how would you define ... how would you define those three words? What is ... what would be the dictionary definition of those three words?

S3: *You mean the* uncover *and* reveal?

T: Reveal *and* disclose. *What is the ... what is the meaning that they share?*

S2: *To find something and to...*

S1: Uncover, revealed.

S3: *And the other one doesn't have anything to do with find. The other one means the opposite of doing something.*

Commentary The sequence is taken from a pretask designed to present and review some key vocabulary that the students would encounter in the task proper–a selective listening task.

Here is the handout they were working from:

Spot the "odd word out." [The word that doesn't belong in each list.]

Example: (radio,) computer, video, television

Discuss the following words. Put a circle around the odd word out and say why it is the odd word.

1. tourist, visitor, traveler, student
2. investigate, determine, explore, inquire
3. elderly, intelligent, stupidly, talkative
4. utilize, uncover, reveal, disclose

Extract 1 is interesting from a number of perspectives. The students negotiate and collaborate well to complete the task. The teacher also does a good job of keeping the students on track and pushing them to describe what the words have in common.

In the extract, the two participants have heard two different interviewing committees discussing the relative merits of three applicants for a job. Their task is to share their information and decide which of the three would be the best person for the job.

Extract 2

A: Are you talking about Alan or Geoffrey? Just the first name.

B: Well, I understood I was talking about Geoffrey, yeah? Is that correct?

A: Not at all.

B: Not at all. So I have confused the man, have I? I've made a mistake here. Who … who are you … can you …? What notes do you have on Richards? See if we can get this sorted out first.

A: We're talking about Geoffrey, right? And he's certainly the man that had a very good report. He knows the job, and I don't see why we should at all discuss this because it is so obvious to me.

B: Well, it could very well be that I'm confusing the names of the people involved, so let's make sure we're talking about the same people.

A: How about Alan?

B: But he's a foreman rather than a supervisor, I understand, and this is basically a union job … I mean I … my information is that all these people are occupying more or less the same rank.

A: Yes, but I mean, er, I agree, they are all, erm, foremen. Supervisor, by the way, is the same to me. Isn't it to you?

B: Um, no, it's not quite the same thing to me. A foreman is, uh, somewhat lower on the range, right?

Reflection

In Extract 2, the learners seem confused about the identities of the individuals. In what ways does this help their language development? In what ways does it hurt it?

Commentary At first sight, it appears that the teacher in Extract 2 has probably not set up this task very well. There is considerable confusion over the identity of the individuals being interviewed. However, this was exactly the purpose of the task. Both students had different, and slightly conflicting, information on the three participants, and this led to considerable negotiation between the two students. As we saw in the background section, such negotiation is hypothesized to be healthy for language acquisition.

Reflection

Extract 3 is a feedback session following a task. What do you think the task was? What do you notice about the way the teacher conducts the session? What is the purpose of the follow-up?

Extract 3

T: OK, let's check your responses. At school?

Ss: Yes, yes.

T: At a party?

S: Yes.

S: No.

T: Never been to a party? Oh, you poor thing. *(laughter)* At the movies?

Ss: No, no.

T: No? Why not?

Ss: *(Inaudible comments and laughter.)*

T: What about at a shopping center?

Ss: No.

T: Sports event?

Ss: Yes. No.

T: Why?

S: Not at sports event.

S: What sports event?

S: Baseball game. Stadium.

S: Stadium. Stadium. Yes.

T: You mean watching?

S: Watching, yeah.

S: *Or playing tennis.*

(There is some confused discussion among the students.)

T: *OK, difference of opinion there. What about at a concert?*

S: *No.*

T: *No?*

(Laughter)

T: *What about at a friend's house?*

Ss: *Yes. Yes.*

S: *No.* (Laughter)

T: *No as well. Don't you have any friends either?*

S: *I didn't meet new people.*

T: *New people. OK. What other, what other places can you meet?*

S: *Part-time job.*

T: *Part-time job.*

(Excited murmuring)

T: *Yeah! Good one. Yeah. Any more?*

S: *Church.*

T: *Church.*

(Scattered Laughter)

S: *Travel, travel, traveling.*

T: *Traveling.*

S: *Some people meet new people at beach or, er, swimming pool.*

T: *OK.*

(Laughter and teasing of student making this remark.)

T: *Is this where you meet new people?* (Laughter)

S: *Huh?*

T: *Is this where you meet new people?*

S: *Yeah.* (Laughter)

T: *Any others?*

S: *Er... organizations.*

T: *Organizations? What kind?*

S: *Oh, like, er, environmental group or...*

T: *Environmental groups—that's good. OK. I think I'll have to put some of these on my list because they're very interesting.*

Commentary In this section, the teacher is conducting a debriefing and eliciting feedback from the students. Students had completed a reading task about how and where single men and women in the United States meet each other and then took part in a pair and group work task based on the following worksheet.

Pair work. In your country, where can you meet new people?		
	Yes	**No**
At school		
At a party		
At the movies		
At a shopping center		
At a sports event		
At a concert		
At a friend's home		
Your idea:		
Your idea:		
Your idea:		

6. Conclusion

In this section, I have provided a basic introduction to language teaching methodology, sketching out how the field has evolved over the last forty years, and then looked at contemporary approaches within the context of a communicative approach to language teaching. This had to be a selective introduction. A comprehensive text on language teaching methodology would be hundreds of pages in length. I hope, however, that it provides a platform you can build on when you read the rest of the chapters in this volume.

Further readings

Celce-Murcia, M. (ed.) 2001. *Teaching English as a Second or Foreign Language.* Third Edition. Boston, MA: Heinle & Heinle.

> This edited volume is one of the standard works in the field. It covers all aspects of language teaching methodology, and many chapters would be excellent follow-up reading to the chapters in this volume.

Nunan, D. 1999. *Second Language Teaching and Learning.* Boston, MA: Heinle & Heinle.

> This book provides an introduction, rationale, research basis, and classroom procedures for task-based language teaching.

Richards J. and W. Renandya (eds.) 2002. *Methodology in Language Teaching.* Cambridge: Cambridge University Press.

> An edited collection of reprints on all aspects of methodology, this volume provides an overview of current approaches, issues, and practices in teaching English to speakers of other languages.

Helpful Web site

Center for Applied Linguistics, Washington DC (http://www.cal.org/ericcll)

> This Web site has many useful resources, including papers, bibliographies, and links to other Web sites of relevance to language teaching methodology.

References

Brown, H. D. 2002. English Language Teaching in the "Post-Methods" Era: Towards better diagnosis, treatment, and assessment. In Richards, J. and W. Renandya (eds.) *Methodology in Language Teaching.* Cambridge: Cambridge University Press.

Krashen, S. 1981. *Second Language Acquisition and Second Language Learning.* Oxford: Pergamon.

Krashen, S. 1982. *Principles and Practice in Second Language Acquisition.* Oxford: Pergamon.

Krashen, S. and T. Terrell 1983. *The Natural Approach*. Oxford: Pergamon.

Moulton, W. 1963. Linguistics and Language Teaching in the United States 1940–1960, *IRAL*, 1(21): 41.

Nunan, D. 1988. *The Learner-Centered Curriculum*. Cambridge: Cambridge University Press.

Nunan, D. 1999. *Second Language Teaching and Learning*. Boston, MA: Heinle & Heinle.

Richards, J., J. Platt, and H. Weber 1985. *The Longman Dictionary of Applied Linguistics*. London: Longman.

Stevick, E. 1997. *Memory, Meaning and Method* (Second Edition). Boston, MA: Heinle & Heinle.

Swaffar, J., K. Arens, and M. Morgan 1982. Teacher Classroom Practices: Redefining method as task hierarchy. *Modern Language Journal*, 66:24–32.

Chapter **Two**

Listening

Marc Helgesen, Miyagi Gakuin Women's College (Japan)

1. What is listening?

Every day we listen to many different things in many different ways. Whether it is conversation with a colleague, the TV news, or a new music CD, we listen. In our native language at least, we seem to automatically know "how to listen" and "what we are listening for." To language learners, listening is far more challenging. In this chapter, we will explore how listening works and ways to help learners become more effective listeners.

Listening is an active, purposeful process of making sense of what we hear. Language skills are often categorized as *receptive* or *productive*. Speaking and writing are the **productive** skills. Listening, along with reading, is a **receptive** skill. That is, it requires a person to receive and understand incoming information (input). Because listening is receptive, we can listen to and understand things at a higher level than we can produce. For this reason, people sometimes think of it as a passive skill. Nothing could be farther from the truth. Listening is very active. As people listen, they process not only what they hear but also connect it to other information they already know. Since listeners combine what they hear with their own ideas and experiences, in a very real sense they are "creating the meaning" in their own minds. As Buck (1995) points out, the assumption that listeners simply decode messages is mistaken, "(M)eaning is not in the **text** (text = whatever is being listened to)–but is something that is constructed by listeners based on a number of different knowledge sources." Among those sources are knowledge of language, of what has already been said, of context, and general background knowledge. Listening is meaning based. When we listen, we are normally doing so for a purpose. You might even say we don't listen to words, we listen to the meaning behind the words.

Listening is often compared to reading, the other receptive skill. While the two do share some similarities, two major differences should be noted from the start. Firstly, listening usually happens in real time. That is, people listen and have to comprehend what they hear immediately. There is no time to go back and review, look up unknown words, etc. Secondly, although listening is receptive, it very often happens in the midst of a conversation–something which requires productive, spoken responses.

To understand how listening works and how to teach it more effectively, start by thinking about your own listening.

Action

What have you listened to today? Write at least eight things. Try to think of different types of things you have listened to.

-
-
-

As you go through this chapter, think about how the ideas presented relate what you were doing when listening to each of the items you listed.

2. Background to the teaching of listening

Historically, learning a foreign language meant learning to read and write. Listening was virtually ignored. Then, in the late 1800s, interest in using children's learning of their first language as a model for foreign language teaching grew. One of the results was Gouin's series method. It featured action and oral presentation of new language in which the teacher would make a series of statements (thus the name of the method), and would carry out the actions so that students could map what they saw on to what they heard.

"I walk to the door.	I walk.
I draw near to the door.	I draw near.
I draw nearer to the door.	I draw nearer.
I get to the door.	I get to.
I stop at the door.	I stop."

(Titone, 1968, cited in Richards and Rodgers, 2001)

This is important since it represents the first time listening played a key role in language teaching methodology. Later, the reform movement promoted ideas such as the teaching of spoken, as opposed to written, language and that learners should hear language before seeing it in written form. Still later, the direct method, often associated with Charles Berlitz, promoted the teaching of listening comprehension and the idea that new teaching points should be introduced orally.

In the years following World War II, the **audiolingual** method came to dominate foreign language teaching. The method, which was heavily influenced by the behavioral psychology of the day, emphasized MIM/MEM (mimicry/memorization) of new structures. As in the direct method, these were presented orally, before the learner saw the written form. The popularity of the audiolingual method paralleled the establishment of language laboratories for dialogue and pattern practice drills. (For a description of the audio/lingual class, see Nunan, Chapter 8, this volume.)

In the 1970s and early 1980s, the introduction of **communicative language teaching**–the idea the student learns though the act of communication–increased the role of listening. During this period, Stephen Krashen's **input hypothesis** made a major impact on language teaching. The input hypothesis says that, "for language learning to occur, it is necessary for the learner to understand input language which contains linguistic items that are slightly beyond the learner's present linguistic competence. Learners understand such language using cues in the situation." (Richards, et al., 1985) Put simply, we acquire language by meeting language that is a bit higher than our current level. Listening was seen as a major source of comprehensible **input**. Language learning textbooks began including listening activities that were not simply presentation of language to be produced. They were listening activities for input, the beginning of the kinds of listening tasks common in books today.

Reflection

1. Think of your experience studying languages. Which of the ideas mentioned in the methods above seem to have influenced your teachers?

2. Which of the ideas do you believe in? Why?

3. Principles for teaching listening

1. Expose students to different ways of processing information: bottom-up vs. top-down.

To understand how people make sense of the stream of sound we all hear, it is helpful to think about how we process the input. A useful metaphor often used to explain reading but equally applicable to listening is "**bottom-up** vs. **top-down processing**," proposed by Rumelhart and Ortony (1977) and expanded upon by Chaudron and Richards (1986), Richards (1990), and others. The distinction is based on the way learners attempt to understand what they read or hear. With bottom-up processing, students start with the component parts: words, grammar, and the like. Top-down processing is the opposite. Learners start from their background knowledge, either content **schema** (general information based on previous learning and life experience) or textual schema (awareness of the kinds of information used in a given situation) (See Long, 1989).

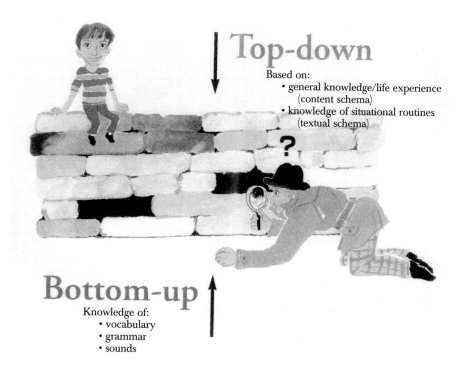

Figure 1 Bottom-up and top-down processing

The idea shown in Figure 1 is, perhaps, better understood by a metaphor.

Imagine a brick wall. If you are standing at the bottom studying the wall brick by brick, you can easily see the details. It is difficult, however, to get an overall view of the wall. If, on the other hand, you're sitting on the top of the wall, you can easily see the landscape. However, because of distance, you will miss some details. And, of course, the view is very different.

Many students—especially those with years of "school English"—have learned via methods that stress the "parts" of English: vocabulary and grammatical structures. It is not surprising, therefore, that these learners try to process English from the bottom up.

It can be difficult to experience what beginning-level learners go through. It is especially challenging to understand what they experience when listening to an article which you are reading. However, a reading task can be used to understand the nature of bottom-up processing. From there you can imagine the initial challenge of trying to make meaning out of aural input. Try reading the following *from right to left*.

> you as, time a at word one ,slowly English process you When
> individual each of meaning the catch to easy is it ,now doing are
> the of meaning overall the understand to difficult very is it ,However. word
> . passage

You understood the paragraph: When you process English slowly, one word at a time, as you are doing now, it is easy to catch the meaning of each individual word. However, it is very difficult to understand the overall meaning of the passage.

While reading, however, it is likely you felt the frustration of "bottom-up" processing; you had to get each individual part before you could make sense of it. This is similar to what our students experience—and they're having to wrestle with the meaning in a foreign language. Their previous training in language learning—this bottom-up processing habit—gets in the way of effective listening.

The opposite type of processing, "top-down," begins with the listener's life knowledge. Brown (2000) gives this example from a personal experience of buying postcards at an Austrian museum:

> I speak no German, but walked up to the counter after having calculated that the postcards would cost sixteen schillings. I gave the clerk a twenty-schilling note, she opened the till, looked in it, and said something in German. As a reflex, I dug in my pocket and produced a one-schilling coin and gave it to her. She smiled and handed me "a five." I managed the transaction based on my prior knowledge of how one deals with change at a store. In some sense, I didn't need German. I just needed my life experience.

He had no "bottom-up" resources (vocabulary, grammar) in German, but by making use of previous knowledge, he was able to work out the likely meaning. Schema are abstract notions we possess based on experiences.

It is not possible to replace bottom-up with top-down, and it wouldn't be desirable to do so even if we could. We need to help learners integrate the two. The following is my own real life example of how top-down and bottom-up processing can integrate: Visiting Rome, I was in the courtyard in front of St. Peter's Basilica. A woman came up and asked me something in Italian, a language I don't know. I looked at her with a puzzled expression. She asked a question again, this time simplifying it to one word: "Cappella?" I didn't know what it meant but repeated, "Cappella?" She asked again, "Sistine Cappella?" Then I understood that she wanted to know if the big church in front of us was the Sistine Chapel. I replied, "No, San Pietro." (I did know the Italian name of St. Peter's.) I pointed to a building on the right side of the courtyard and said, "Sistine." She said, "Grazie," and walked off toward the Sistine Chapel.

What happened in this short interaction was a combination of bottom-up and top-down processing. Recognizing the single word *Sistine* told me that *cappella* must mean *chapel*. We were standing in front of buildings. She was asking a question about a place. My top-down knowledge of what people might talk about—especially to strangers—said that she must be asking for directions. With a friend, you might comment on the size of the buildings or their beauty or something else, but with a stranger asking for directions or asking someone to take a picture seemed the only likely topics. Using both bottom-up data (the word, "Sistine") and the top-down data (likely language function), I was able to understand what she wanted.

In my case, this top-down/bottom-up integration happened by accident. In the classroom, prelistening activities are a good way to make sure it happens. Before listening, learners can, for example, brainstorm vocabulary related to a topic or invent a short dialogue relevant to functions such as giving directions or shopping. In the process, they base their information on their knowledge of life (top-down information) as they generate vocabulary and sentences (bottom-up data). The result is a more integrated attempt at processing. The learners are activating their previous knowledge. This use of the combination of top-down and bottom-up data is also called **interactive processing** (Peterson, 2001).

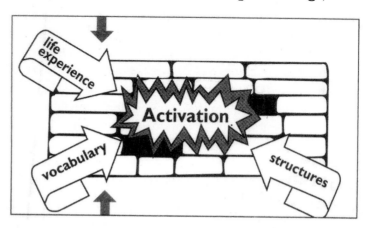

Figure 2 Interactive processing

As useful and important as prelistening activities are, Buck (1995) criticizes books that "provide twenty minutes of prelistening activities for about three minutes of listening practice. This is unbalanced. We need prelistening activities to do two things: provide a context for interpretation and activate the background knowledge which will help interpretation. Give them enough to do that, and then let them listen."

A second word of caution is suggested by Tsui and Fullilove (1998). Learners need to make use of their top-down knowledge but keep reevaluating information. If they lock into an interpretation too early, they may miss information that contradicts it.

Using an example of a news story in which firefighters were aided in saving a housing estate by the direction a wind was blowing, they used a passage that started, "Firemen had to work fast ..." Learners needed to answer the following comprehension question: What saved the estate from burning down?

Although the wind was the key to what saved the estate, many learners relied on their top-down schema (Firefighters put out fires.) and the fact that the story started with the mention of firemen working fast. They incorrectly identified the firefighters as the answer. Tsui and Fullilove suggest that learners need specific work on bottom-up processing to become less reliant on guessing from context.

Reflection

Go back to the list you wrote on page 24. Choose one example of something you listened to.

1. What types of background information (both top-down and bottom-up data) helped you make sense of the information?

2. Would a person just learning your language have been able to understand the things you heard? If you had been using a recording of those listening items in a language class, what kind of prelistening task could your students have done to activate their top-down and bottom-up schema?

3. Think about the examples of buying postcards in Austria and giving directions in Italy. Have you had a similar experience, either in a foreign language or in an unfamiliar situation in your own country?

2. Expose students to different types of listening.

There's an adage in teaching listening that says: It's not just what they are listening *to*. It's what they are listening *for*. Listeners need to consider their purpose. They also need to experience listening for different reasons.

Any discussion of listening tasks has to include a consideration of types of listening. We will consider tasks as well as texts. When discussing listening, **text** refers to whatever the students are listening to, often a recording. For the purpose of this discussion, consider the following text:

Example 1

A: Let's go outside. We could go for a walk. Maybe play tennis.

B: Look out the window. It's raining.

A: Raining. Oh, no.

(Helgesen & Brown, 1994)

This is a simple conversation. Even near beginners would probably understand the meaning. What they understand, however, depends on what they need to know and do.

The most common type of listening exercise in many textbooks is listening for specific information. This usually involves catching concrete information including names, time, specific language forms, etc. In our "Let's go outside" example, asking the students to report on the type of weather is a simple "listening for specific information task."

At other times, students try to understand in a more general way. This is **global** or **gist listening**. In the classroom, this often involves tasks such as identifying main ideas, noting a sequence of events and the like. In our example, it could involve a very general question such as, "What's the main topic?" or, if more task support is needed, giving the learners a few choices (friends, sports, the weather) and having them choose the main topic.

Listening for specific information and listening for gist are two important types of listening, but, of course, they don't exist in isolation. We move between the two. For example, many students have been subjected to long, less than exciting lectures. They listen globally to follow what the speaker is talking about. Then they hear something that seems important ("This sounds like it will be on the test!") and focus in to get the specific information.

Another critical type of listening is inference. This is "listening between the lines"–that is, listening for meaning that is implied but not stated directly. In our "Let's go outside" example, we can ask, "Do the speakers go outside or not?" Of course they don't. It's raining. The text doesn't say that directly. It doesn't need to. Learners can infer the information. Inference is different from gist and specific information listening in that it often occurs at the same time as some other types of listening. The learners' main task might well be to catch specifics or to understand a text generally when they come across information that isn't stated directly. Because inference requires somewhat abstract thinking, it is a higher level skill. However, it is a mistake to put off working on inference until learners are at an intermediate level or above. Indeed, it is often at the beginning level when students lack much vocabulary, grammar, and functional routines that students tend to infer the most.

3. Teach a variety of tasks.

If learners need experience with different types of listening texts, they also need to work with a variety of tasks. Since learners do the tasks as they listen, it is important that the task itself doesn't demand too much production of the learner. If, for example, a beginning level learner hears a story and is asked to write a summary in English, it could well be that the learner understood the story but is not yet at the level to be able to write the summary. Tasks that require too much production can't be done or can't be done in real time—and if students get the answer wrong, you don't know if they really didn't understand, or if they did understand but didn't know how to respond, or if they understood at the time but forgot by the time they got to the exercise.

In this example of a summary task based on a story, it may be better to have a task such as choosing the correct summary from two or three choices. Alternatively, the learner could number pictures or events in the order they occurred or identify pictures that match the text.

Another reason for short, focused tasks is that listening weighs on a person's working memory. According to Just and Carpenter's capacity hypothesis (1992), when people are listening in a second or foreign language, they are having to process not only the meaning of what they are listening to but also the language itself. This can lead to an overload. You may have seen the well-known Far Side cartoon that shows a schoolboy raising his hand and asking the teacher, "May I be excused? My brain is full." What he is experiencing is running out of memory capacity. If the task itself makes the listening even more complex, the learners are simply unable to understand, remember, and do what they need to do. (See Lynch, 1998.)

All of this doesn't mean, however, that we need to limit ourselves and our students to only a few receptive "check the box" and "number the pictures" exercise types. As mentioned before, half of the time people are speaking is spent listening. At times, students need experience with production tasks. Our students need exposure to a wide range of tasks in order for them to deal with different types of texts and respond in different ways. Incorporating different tasks also increases the students' interest. If listening work in class follows too narrow a pattern, it is easy for the learners–and the teacher–to lose interest.

Reflection

Go back to the things you listed on page 24.

1. What types of listening were you doing? (specific information, gist, inference)
2. What was your task for each item? What did you need to do? How did you need to respond?

4. Consider text, difficulty, and authenticity.

In addition to the task, the text itself determines how easy or difficult something is to understand. Spoken language is very different from written language. It is more redundant, full of false starts, rephrasing, and elaborations. Incomplete sentences, pauses, and overlaps are common. Learners need exposure to and practice with natural sounding language.

When learners talk about text difficulty, the first thing many mention is speed. Indeed, that can be a problem. But the solution is usually not to give them unnaturally slow, clear recordings. Those can actually distort the way the language sounds. A more useful technique is to simply put pauses between phrases or sentences. As Rost (2002, p. 145) points out, "By pausing the spoken input (the tape or the teacher) and allowing some quick intervention and response, we in effect slow down the listening process to allow the listeners to monitor their listening more closely."

Speed, of course, is not the only variable. Brown (1995) talks about "cognitive load" and describes six factors that increase or decrease the ease of understanding:

- The number of individuals or objects in a text (e.g., More voices increase difficulty.)

- How clearly the individuals or objects are distinct from one another (e.g., A recording with a male voice and a female voice is easier than one with two similar male voices or two similar female voices.)

- Simple, specific spatial relationships are easier to understand than complex ones. (e.g., In a recording giving directions, information like *turn right at the bank* is easier to understand than *go a little way on that street*.)

- The order of events (e.g., It is easier when the information given follows the order it happened in, as opposed to a story that includes a flashback about events that happened earlier.)

- The number of inferences needed (e.g., Fewer are easier than more.)

- The information is consistent with what the listener already knows (e.g., Hearing someone talk about a film you have seen is easier to understand than hearing the same type of conversation about one you haven't seen.)

Any discussion of listening text probably needs to deal with the issue of **authentic texts**. Virtually no one would disagree that texts students work with should be realistic. However, some suggest that everything that students work with should be authentic. Day and Bamford (1998, p. 53) go so far as to refer to this as "the cult of authenticity." However, the issue of authenticity isn't as simple as it sounds. Most of the recordings that accompany textbooks are made in recording studios. And recordings not made in the studio are often not of a usable quality.

You could ask what is authentic and natural anyway? We have already touched on the issue of speed. What is natural speed? Some people speak quickly, some more slowly. The average for native speakers of English seems to be 165-180 words per minute (wpm), but sometimes it jumps to 275 wpm. Even native speakers can get lost at that speed (Rubin, 1994).

With children learning their first language, we simplify (*motherese*). The advocates of "authentic only" would seem to deny this comprehensible input to foreign language learners, who, in many cases, lack that comprehension/acquisition rich environment that L1 learners enjoy.

When people think about authenticity in listening materials, they are usually considering the input. Brown and Menasche (1993) suggest looking at two aspects of authenticity: the task and the input.

They suggest this breakdown:

1. **Task authenticity**

   - **simulated:** modeled after a real-life; nonacademic task such as filling in a form
   - **minimal/incidental:** checks understanding, but in a way that isn't usually done outside of the classroom; numbering pictures to show a sequence of events or identifying the way something is said are examples

2. **Input authenticity**

   - **genuine:** created only for the realm of real life, not for classroom, but used in language teaching
   - **altered:** no meaning change, but the original is no longer as it was (glossing, visual resetting, pictures or colors adapted)
   - **adapted:** created for real life (words and grammatical structures changed to simplify the text)
   - **simulated:** written by the author as if the material is genuine; many genuine characteristics
   - **minimal/incidental:** created for the classroom; no attempt to make the material seem genuine

Reflection

1. In your experience as a language learner, what kinds of listening have you found easy? What has made it easy?
2. What has been difficult? Why?
3. What listening have you done that was authentic? What wasn't?
4. What listening activities have been authentic? Which ones haven't been?
5. Children read kids' books. They are "authentic" children's literature but very different from what adults read. Does this idea apply to listening materials in a foreign language? What is authentic? For whom?

5. Teach listening strategies.

Learning strategies are covered elsewhere in this book. However, in considering listening, it is useful to note the items Rost (2002, p. 155) identifies as strategies that are used by successful listeners.

- **Predicting:** Effective listeners think about what they will hear. This fits into the ideas about prelistening mentioned earlier.
- **Inferring:** It is useful for learners to "listen between the lines."
- **Monitoring:** Good listeners notice what they do and don't understand.
- **Clarifying:** Efficient learners ask questions (*What does ___ mean? You mean ___ ?*) and give feedback (*I don't understand yet.*) to the speaker.
- **Responding:** Learners react to what they hear.
- **Evaluating:** They check on how well they have understood.

1. Go back to your list on page 24. Choose one example of something you listened to. Imagine that you were using a recording of that in a classroom listening lesson. Give five ways that learners could include the ideas on Rost's list of strategies of successful listeners.

2. Think of your own experience as a language learner. What listening strategies have you used? List them. Which have been effective? Which haven't?

4. Classroom techniques and tasks

In this section, we will consider classroom activities and a variety of textbook exercises that make use of the above principles. We will also look at ways to modify textbook activities that don't already include the ideas.

Dictation with a difference For many teachers, listening for specific information means dictation. Dictation as it is usually done presents some problems because it is almost completely bottom-up–students need to catch every word. In our native language we don't process every word. So dictation is often asking students to do something in a foreign language that is unnatural and very difficult even in the first language. A related problem is that, since dictation is a "word level" exercise, the learners don't need to think about overall meaning.

The following exercise attempts to deal with those problems. Read the following and, in your mind, imagine the story.

Step 1

A road went though a forest. A woman was walking down the road. Suddenly she saw a man. He was wearing a shirt, pants, and a hat. He smiled and said something.

In class, students hear the passage and imagine the story. Then they listen again, but this time, at several points, they hear a bell. As they listen, they fill in a **cloze** (fill in the blanks) dictation sheet. Each time they hear the bell, they write any word that fits the story as they imagined it. The imagined words go in the boxes.

The student task appears in Figure 3.

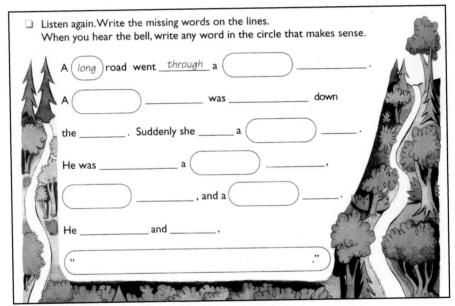

Figure 3 *Listen In* (Thomson Learning, 1998)

The script, as they hear it this time is as follows. The dots (•) show the points where the learners hear the bell.

Step 2

A • road went though a • forest. A • woman was walking down the road. Suddenly she saw a • man. He was wearing a • shirt, • pants and a • hat. He smiled and said•.

(Helgesen and Brown, 1995)

While the students have the accuracy work of the dictation–writing the missing words (forest, woman, walking, etc.)–they are also getting the top-down experience of imagining the story and describing their version of it. Some see a *dark forest*. Some see it as *green, old, a rainforest,* etc.

Since everyone's image of the story will be somewhat different, it provides a good reason for them to compare stories after they finish their writing. This, of course, means they continue listening–this time to their partners.

Do-it-yourself: Modifying materials to add "listening for specific information" While listening for specifics is the most common type of listening in textbooks, teachers sometimes want to add their own activities. This could be to provide an additional listening task–letting the students listen to the same recording for a different purpose. You might want to add different tasks just for variety if your textbook overuses a small number of task types. The following are some ways of modifying listening tasks to add or increase listening for specifics.

- **Micro-listening** (usually done after they know the main topic of the recording, but before they have begun the main listening task) Choose a few target items that occur several times on the recording. Examples might be names of colors, people, places, etc. In class, tell the students the topic of the recording. Ask them to listen for the target items. Each time they hear one, they should raise their hands. Play the recording. Students listen and raise their hands. The showing of hands is a good way for those who caught the items to give a cue to those who didn't.

- **Bits and pieces** (before the main task) Tell the students what the topic will be. In small groups or as a whole class, they brainstorm vocabulary likely to come up on the recording. Each learner makes a list. Then they listen to the recording and circle the words they hear.

- **What do I want to know?** (before the main task) Tell the students the topic and enough about what they will hear for them to imagine the situations. In pairs or small groups, they write two or three questions about the information they think will be given. Then they listen and see how many of the questions they are able to answer.

- **Dictation and cloze** Many books feature cloze (fill in the blanks) dictation as listening. Very often these are not actually listening tasks since learners can find the answer by reading. If you are using a book that has such exercises, have the students try to fill in the blanks before they listen. They read the passage and make their best guesses. Then when they listen to the text, they have an actual listening task: to see if they were right. (See Nunan, Chapter 8, this volume.)

What are they talking about?: Listening for gist Listening in a global way, trying to understand the main ideas, is an essential kind of listening. In the classroom, we should give our learners a lot of experience with this activity, both as a task in itself and as a "way in" to other types of listening with the same recording.

Look at Figure 4. For the first task, the students are asked to listen for the general meaning of five conversations (conversations between a doctor and a patient and conversations not between a doctor and a patient). For the second task, the students are asked to listen to the conversations again and to write key words that helped them distinguish between the two types of conversations. This is an excellent follow-up task since it moves from a general understanding of the gist to a narrower, more specific understanding of what was said. At the same time, it asks the learners to ask themselves, "How did I know the gist?" This type of task increases awareness of their own learning.

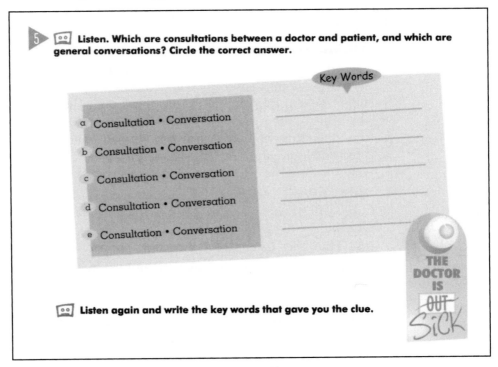

Figure 4 *Speak Out* (Heinle/Thomson, 1998)

Do-it-yourself: Adding gist tasks Even though many textbooks concentrate on "listening for specific information" exercises, sometimes transforming them into global listening tasks are as simple as asking, "What are they talking about? What words gave you the hints?" Here are some other ways to add gist listening.

- **Main ideas** Write the main idea for the recording on the board, along with three or four distracters. Often, subpoints within the conversation make good distracters. In the second example above, the main point is "she feels sick" and the distracters could be *rotten day, go to bed,* and *take some aspirin.* Students listen and identify the main idea.

- **What is the order?** When the listening text is a story, list five or six events from the story. Students listen and put the items in order. It is often useful to tell them which item is number one to help them get started. It is also useful to have at least one item as a distracter that isn't used. Otherwise, the last item is obvious without listening.

- **Which picture?** If pictures are available (e.g., one from the particular listening page of your textbook and distracters from elsewhere in the book) students can listen and identify the one that goes with what they are hearing.

Listening between the lines: Inference tasks As mentioned earlier, students often find inferring meaning challenging because it requires abstract processing. Consider the following task:

- Stay to the left   • Elevator

> **Example**
>
> Look at this sign. What do you think it means?
>
> Listen to the dialogue, then circle your answer.
>
>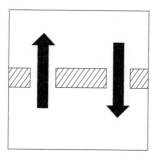
>
> Now read the script to see if you were right.
>
> *Man:* So the office is, what, on the fifth floor?
>
> *Woman:* That's right, fifth floor. Room 503.
>
> *Man:* Where's the—oh, there it is. Well, shall we go up?
>
> *Woman:* Yeah, let's go.
>
> (Helgesen & Brown, 1994)

As you can tell from the script, the sign means there is an elevator. However, neither speaker ever says the word "elevator." They don't need to. By their talking about the floor the office is on and talking about going up, the listener is able to understand what they are talking about and consequently what the sign means. For that reason, asking the learners, "How did you know?" is probably just as important as whether or not they got the correct answer. It makes them aware of the clues that gave them the meaning. It also provides information and an example for students who may not have gotten the correct answer.

Do-it-yourself inference Unfortunately, it isn't possible to provide "recipes" for adding inference the way it is for gist and specific information listening. This is because inference depends as much on the text—what is being said—as it does on the task. However, as teachers, we can try to be aware of inference and look for opportunities to work with it. The following are two places to start:

- **Focus on emotions**. How do the speakers feel? How do you know that?
- **Look for background information**. Has one or more of the speakers been here/done that/tried this before? Why do you think so?

Action

Think of a listening lesson you have taught or experienced, or a time you had to listen to and understand something in another language or culture. Identify the following:

1. What was the task? What did the students (or you) need to do?

2. Was there a prelistening task? If there was, did it integrate top-down and bottom-up processing? If not, how could you have changed it to do so? If there wasn't a prelistening task, how could one be added?

3. What type of listening was it (specific information, gist, inference, a combination)? How could you have changed the type of listening using the same text (recording), but a different task?

4. Think about how you would teach the lesson differently. If possible, explain your new plan to a partner. If that is not possible, just imagine yourself teaching the new plan. Write it out, step-by-step.

5. Listening in the classroom

In this section, we will return to the activities profiled earlier in this chapter and look specifically at how they are used in the classroom. In the process, we will note a few extra techniques teachers sometimes employ.

In each case, the listening task itself is the second step in the activity. The learners do a prelistening, which serves to activate the top-down and bottom-up schema. Each activity is followed with a speaking activity. As mentioned earlier, although listening is a different skill than speaking, they often go hand-in-hand. Also, students often come to our classes to learn to speak. Listening can be a good way to preview a speaking activity and speaking, in turn, can be useful to expand on what they've listened to. A balance of listening and speaking activities (and, depending on the class, reading and writing) can be important to maintain learner engagement.

In the "Your story" dictation activity, the students will be working with adjectives. The prelistening task is to have the students work in pairs. The teacher gives them a series of adjectives that could have more than one opposite. For example, the opposite of "right" could be either "wrong" or "left." Other adjectives with more than one antonym include "hard," "smart," "sweet," "straight," "free," etc. Learners see how many opposites they can think of. Providing the adjectives gives them support—as opposed to just saying, "How many adjectives can you think of?" It also focuses them on meaning, rather than just grammar. They are thinking about descriptions—just what they will need to do in the main task. The follow-up speaking activity for "Your story" is clear. Students, having created their own version of the story, usually want to compare their images with their partners.

The prelistening task for the doctor/patient activity both elicits information from the students and presents new information. The students see a cartoon of several obviously ill people in a doctor's waiting room. They identify what is wrong with the people. Then they are presented with a list of several symptoms and illnesses that the students may not know in English (appendicitis, rash, etc.). They look up the words they don't know, then match the symptoms to the illnesses. This is a useful example of activating their background knowledge while preteaching vocabulary at the same time.

Once the students have completed the main task in their books, the teacher might elicit answers from the students and write them on the board. At this point, the teacher may want to have the learners choose their own level of support of a final listening:

Teacher: *OK, we'll listen to this one more time. Please choose* how *you want to listen.*

If this was kind of difficult, watch me. I'll point to the answers just before they say them (on the recording).

Or if you don't need my help spotting the answers, watch your book. Try to catch the answers as they say them.

Or if it wasn't difficult at all, close your eyes. Listen. Imagine the people. What do they look like? Where are they? Watch the "movie" in your mind.

This final listening serves several purposes. It gives students a new task—albeit a simple one—and thus a new reason to listen. It also lets them choose the amount of support they want or don't want. Finally, for those who choose the third option, it encourages imagination.

The doctor/patient listening activity is followed by group work in which learners brainstorm a list of things they do to stay healthy. Then they exchange lists with another group and compare. This activity allows them to make use of the ideas and language from the warm-up and the listening, and to personalize the task by relating the information to their own lives.

In the sign activity, learners guess the meaning before they listen. By doing so, they are activating their previous (top-down) knowledge: the likely meaning of the sign based on other signs they know. It also puts them in touch with vocabulary and phrases, bottom-up information. And the fact that they have to commit to an answer often increases student interest. It's like they make a bet with themselves about the meaning. They listen to see if they win the bet.

As they listen, the teacher could suggest pair work, either to the whole class or to lower-level students.

It was pointed out earlier that "How did you know?" is just as important as getting the correct answer on inference activities. By working in pairs, students are more likely to take the time to analyze their listening process. Another reason for doing the activity in pairs has to do with making the task easier. Students tend to focus on different parts of the listening and listen in different ways. By working in pairs, they tend to understand the listening more quickly. This idea can be used with nearly any sort of listening where there are specific correct answers.

In considering these activities in the classroom, the flow suggested below is often a useful way to structure a lesson plan to include listening:

1. A warm-up activity that integrates top-down and bottom-up data
2. A main listening task
3. A speaking task related to the previous task

Over the length of a course, the listening tasks should be balanced to include a variety of listening types and tasks. It is often useful to decide on the listening task before planning the warm-up. Often, the task itself will determine the kind of information you want to elicit or preteach through the warm-up. Student speaking tasks often take place in pairs or small groups and require learners to listen and respond to each other.

Action

Go back to your list on page 24.

Choose one example of something you listened to. Imagine that you have a recording of it that you want to use for a lesson.

1. What would the task be? What would the students do as they listened?
2. Design a lesson plan. What kind of prelistening task would you use? What kind of information would it target?
3. How would you follow it up with a speaking task?

6. Conclusion

This chapter started by emphasizing listening as an active, purposeful process. It involved processing information based on both overall top-down schema and the bottom-up "building blocks" of language such as vocabulary and grammar. Prelistening tasks are suggested as ways to integrate a learner's processing. I also considered text difficulty, authenticity, and the use of strategies.

Exposing learners to a variety of tasks, as well as different types of listening, is helpful in enabling them to become more skillful listeners. To that end, examples of how to incorporate these ideas into the classroom and ways to modify textbook tasks are provided. If we do these things, our learners can become more effective, active listeners.

Further readings

Davis, P. and M. Rinvolucri 1988. *Dictation: New methods, new possibilities.* Cambridge: Cambridge University Press.

> This book is a classic exploration of communicative possibilities for dictation.

Mendelsohn, D. and J. Rubin (eds.) 1995. *A Guide for the Teaching of Second Language Listening.* San Diego, CA: Dominie Press.

> This is a very accessible overview of listening.

Murphey, T. 1992. *Music & Song. (Resource Books for Teachers).* Oxford: Oxford University Press.

> Murphey offers creative ways of using music in the classroom.

Nunan, D. and L. Miller (eds.) 1995. *New Ways in Teaching Listening.* Washington, DC: TESOL.

> This is a "cookbook" of nearly 150 "recipes" (lesson plans/ ideas) for teaching listening contributed by teachers around the world.

Rost, M. 2002. *Teaching and Researching Listening.* Harlow: Pearson Education/ Longman.

> This is a very thorough handbook for both teachers and researchers, representing state-of-the-art teaching and learning to listen.

White, G. 1998. *Listening (Resource Books for Teachers).* Oxford: Oxford University Press.

> White provides many ideas including using authentic texts and having students create their own texts.

Helpful Web sites

University of Oregon American English Institute Intensive English Program-Study Resources for Students (http://aei.uoregon.edu/iep/iep.htm)

> This site links to language learning pages for listening and other language skills.

Randall's Cyber Listening Lab (http://www.esl-lab.com)

> An extensive set of listening tasks are arranged by level of difficulty (easy, medium, difficult).

University of Illinois Intensive English Institute Interactive Listening Comprehension Practice Page (http://www.iei.uiuc.edu/LCRA/)

This site has listening tasks based on texts from sources such as National Public Radio.

References

Brown, G. 1995. Dimensions in difficulty in listening comprehension. In Mendelsohn, D. and J. Rubin (eds.) *A Guide for the Teaching of Second Language Listening*. San Diego, CA: Dominie Press.

Brown, S. and L. Menasche 1993. *Authenticity in Materials Design*. TESOL Convention. Atlanta.

Brown, S. 2000. *Listening at the Turn of the Century*. Three Rivers TESOL Fall Conference. Pittsburgh.

Buck, G. 1995. How to Become a Good Listening Teacher. In D. Mendelsohn and J. Rubin (eds.) *A Guide for the Teaching of Second Language Listening*. San Diego, CA: Dominie Press.

Chaudron, C. and J. Richards 1986. The Effect of Discourse Markers on the Comprehension of Lectures. *Applied Linguistics.* 7(2):113–127.

Day, R. and J. Bamford 1998. *Extensive Reading in the Second Language Classroom.* Cambridge: Cambridge University Press.

Helgesen, M. and S. Brown 1994. *Active Listening 1: Introducing skills for understanding.* New York: Cambridge University Press.

Helgesen, M. and S. Brown 1994. *Active Listening 2: Building skills for understanding.* New York: Cambridge University Press.

Just, M. and P. Carpenter 1992. A Capacity Hypothesis of Comprehension; Individual differences in working memory. *Psychological Review.* 99:122–149.

Long, D. 1989. Second Language Listening Comprehension: A schema-theoretic perspective. *Modern Language Journal.* 73:32–40.

Lynch, T. 1998. Theoretical Perspectives on Listening. *Annual Review of Applied Linguistics.* 18:3–19.

Nunan, D. 1998. *Listen in 2.* Singapore: Thomson Asia ELT.

Peterson, P. W. 2001. Skills and Strategies for Proficient Listening. In M. Celce-Murcia (ed.) *Teaching English as a Second or Foreign Language*. Boston, MA: Heinle & Heinle.

Richards, J., J. Platt, and H. Weber 1985. *Longman Dictionary of Applied Linguistics.* London: Longman.

Richards, J. and T. Rodgers 2001. *Approaches and Methods in Language Teaching* Second Edition. New York, NY: Cambridge University Press.

Rost, M. 2001. *Teaching and Researching Listening,* Harlow: Pearson Education/ Longman.

Rubin, J. 1994. A Review of Second Language Listening Comprehension Research. *The Modern Language Journal,* 78:199-221.

Rumelhart, D.E. and A. Ortony 1977. The Representation of Knowledge in Memory. In R.C. Anderson, R.J. Sprio, and W.E. Montagues (eds.) *Schooling and the Acquisition of Knowledge.* Hillsdale, NJ: Lawrence Erlbaum.

Richards, J. 1990. *The Language Teaching Matrix.* Cambridge: Cambridge University Press.

Titone, R. 1968. *Teaching foreign languages: An Historical Sketch.* Washington, D.C.: Georgetown University Press.

Tsui, A. and J. Fullilove 1998. Bottom-Up or Top-Down Processing as a Discriminator of L2 Listening Performance. *Applied Linguistics,* 19(4):432–451.

3

Chapter **Three**

Speaking

Kathleen M. Bailey, Monterey Institute of International Studies (USA)

Goals

At the end of this chapter, you should be able to:

✔ **identify** the "levels" of spoken language and explain their relationships.

✔ **explain** the main differences between the audiolingual method and communicative language teaching.

✔ **describe** some differences between spoken language and written language.

✔ **demonstrate** familiarity with all the techniques discussed in this chapter.

1. What is speaking?

If you have learned a language other than your own, which of the four skills–listening, speaking, reading, or writing–did you find to be the hardest? Many people feel that speaking in a new language is harder than reading, writing, or listening for two reasons. First, unlike reading or writing, speaking happens in *real time:* usually the person you are talking to is waiting for you to speak right then. Second, when you speak, you cannot edit and revise what you wish to say, as you can if you are writing.

In language teaching, the four skills are described in terms of their direction. Language generated by the learner (in speech or writing) is referred to as **productive.** Language directed at the learner (in reading or listening) is called **receptive.** Another important idea is the **channel,** which refers to the medium of the message (aural/oral or written). Thus, speaking is the productive aural/oral skill. It consists of producing systematic verbal **utterances** to convey meaning.

Teaching speaking is sometimes considered a simple process. Commercial language schools around the world hire people with no training to teach conversation. Although speaking is totally natural, speaking in a language other than our own is anything but simple.

Spoken language and written language differ in many significant ways. Here are some key contrasts (van Lier, 1995, p. 88):

Spoken language	Written language
Auditory	Visual
Temporary; immediate reception	Permanent; delayed reception
Prosody (rhythm, stress intonation)	Punctuation
Immediate feedback	Delayed or no feedback
Planning and editing limited by channel	Unlimited planning, editing, revision

Given these differences between writing and speech, you can see why people who learn a foreign language largely from textbooks often sound bookish when they speak.

2. Background to teaching speaking

For many years people taught speaking by having students repeat sentences and recite memorized textbook dialogues. **Audiolingual** repetition drills were designed to familiarize students with the sounds and structural patterns of the **target language** (the language which learners are aiming to learn). People supposedly learned to speak by practicing grammatical structures and then later using them in conversation. So an audiolingual speaking lesson might involve an interaction like Example 1. *T* stands for teacher and *S* represents a particular student. *Ss* stands for students. (Textbook lines are in quotation marks.)

Example 1

T: Repeat please: "Good morning, Maria."

Ss: "Good morning, Maria."

T: "Where are you going?"

Ss: "Where are you going?"

T: Good. "I'm going to the library."

Ss: "I going to libary."

T: Listen: "I'm going to THE library."

Ss: "I going to THE libary."

T: Listen again. "Li-BRA-ry." Rrr. "Librrrary."

Ss: "Librrrary."

T: "To the library."

Ss: "To the library."

T: "Going to the library."

Ss: "Going to the library."

T: "I'm going to the library."

Ss: "I going to the library."

T: Good! Now the next part.

The concept of habit formation, of **behaviorism,** is the theoretical basis of the audiolingual method. Since learners needed to form good habits, lessons involved a great deal of repetition. Students were not supposed to form bad habits, so teachers treated spoken errors quickly. Teachers worried that if errors were left untreated, the students might learn those erroneous forms.

For many years, teaching speaking involved providing students with the components of the language, in hopes that they would eventually put them all together and speak. So students might spend several semesters repeating after the teacher, studying grammar rules, reciting dialogues, and learning vocabulary. Unfortunately, actual conversations didn't sound like the textbook dialogues, and if you really met someone like Maria, she was seldom going to the library.

Find a dialogue in an ESL/EFL or foreign language textbook. Ask someone who speaks that language well to see if people might have actually had that conversation. Does the language sound natural? If not, why not?

During the late twentieth century, language acquisition research made us reconsider some long-standing beliefs about how people learn to speak. Several studies led to the conclusion that we had gotten the basic idea backwards: People don't learn the pieces of the language and then put them together to make conversations. Instead, infants acquiring their first language and people acquiring second languages learn the pieces by interacting with other people.

This realization has several interesting implications. If we believe that people learn languages by interacting, then learners should interact during lessons. As a result, a method called **communicative language teaching** arose. Two versions of communicative language teaching emerged. The weak version says teachers should teach the components of language but include communication activities. The strong version says since students learn through interacting, lessons should consist of opportunities to communicate in the target language. In this method, teachers often downplay accuracy and emphasize how students communicate when they speak the target language.

However, in order to communicate well in another language, we must make ourselves understood by the people we are speaking with, and this is not an easy task—especially at the beginning and intermediate levels. There is some need to be accurate in speaking the target language. This is tricky because, as we saw in the speaking-writing contrast, there is limited time for planning and editing speech during conversations. And for less-than-proficient speakers, managing the components of language that must work together when we speak is very demanding indeed.

Figure 1 on page 51 depicts the many linguistic elements involved in speaking. The left column lists four areas of linguistic analysis, but it is the center column which concerns us as teachers. It labels the units of spoken language.

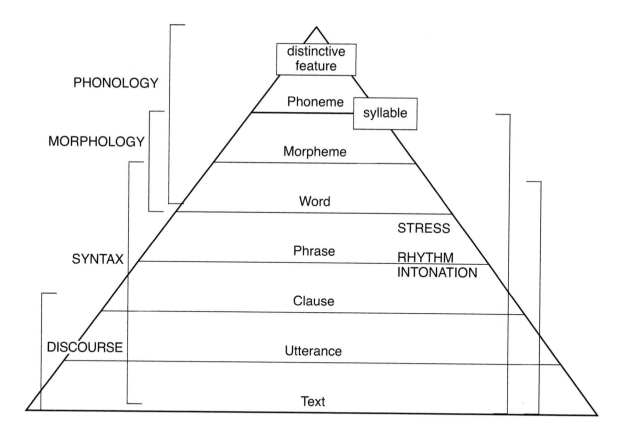

Figure 1: *Interaction in the Language Curriculum: Awareness, Autonomy, and Authenticity* (Longman, 1996)

Beginning at the pyramid's base, text means stretches of language of an undetermined length. Spoken texts are composed of utterances. An utterance is something someone says. It may not be a full sentence, as the concept is used in writing. For example, in asking a friend about what to eat, you might ask, "Would you like pizza?" This utterance is a fully formed grammatical sentence. But if you are both thinking about what to eat, you might just ask your friend, "Pizza?" Although this is not a grammatical sentence, it is an utterance.

Action

Eavesdrop on two people having a conversation. Do they use complete sentences or are their turns composed of shorter utterances? Share your answer with your classmates.

The next two levels, **clauses** and **phrases,** are often confused. A phrase is two or more words which function as a unit but don't have a subject or a verb marked for tense. These include prepositional phrases (*to the store or after breakfast*) and infinitive phrases (*to eat* or *to look up*). Clauses are two or more words that do contain a verb marked for tense. These may be full sentences (*John ate the cake.*) or something less than a full sentence (*While John was eating the cake…*). Such clauses and phrases don't usually appear alone in formal writing, but they are quite common in speech. Both clauses and phrases can be utterances, as can words, the next level in the pyramid.

A word is called a free **morpheme**—a unit of language which can stand on its own and have meaning (*hat, flee, already,* etc.). There are also bound morphemes, which are always connected to words. These include prefixes, such as *un-* or *pre-,* as well as suffixes, such as *-tion* or *-s* or *-ed*. Sometimes during the pressure of speaking, it is difficult for English learners to use the necessary suffixes—especially if words in their own language don't usually end in consonants.

Action

Identify the free and bound morphemes in this list:

ski jumpers   inappropriately   dysfunctional   nonrefundable

The top levels of the pyramid on page 51 deal with the sound system of the language. Pronunciation is covered elsewhere (Murphy, Chapter 6, this volume), so only a few related issues will be mentioned here.

In Figure 1, the word *syllable* overlaps the levels of morphemes and **phonemes.** A phoneme is a unit of sound in a language that distinguishes meaning. Phonemes can be either consonants (like /p/ or /b/ in the words *pit* and *bit*) or vowels (like /I/ and /æ/ in *bit* and *bat*).

Action

Think of five pairs of words where the phonemic distinctions are consonants (as in *pit* and *bit*). Now think of five pairs where the phonemic difference is based on vowel sounds (as in *bit* and *bat*).

Consonants and vowels are **segmental** phonemes. Sometimes a spoken syllable consists of one phoneme (/o/ in *okay*). But syllables also consist of combined sounds (the second syllable of *okay*), and of both free and bound morphemes. For instance, the free morpheme *hat* consists of three phonemes but only one syllable. The word *disheartened* has three syllables, four morphemes (*dis + heart + en + ed*), and eight phonemes.

An even smaller unit, a **distinctive feature,** relates to how or where a sound is produced when we speak. The distinctive feature which makes /b/ and /p/ separate phonemes in English is voicing: when /b/ is pronounced the vocal cords are vibrating, but when /p/ is pronounced, the vocal cords are not vibrating. These minute contrasts contribute to a speaker's accent. (One of my Arabic-speaking students who didn't distinguish between /b/ and /p/ told me he'd had "green bee soup" for lunch!)

On the right side of the pyramid there are three other labels. Stress, rhythm, and intonation are called the **suprasegmental** phonemes, because when we speak, they carry meaning differences but they operate "above" the segmental phonemes. To illustrate that the suprasegmental phonemes carry meaning, consider the sentence, "I think I know." It can convey four different meanings, depending on the stress:

I think I know.   I think *I* know.   I *think* I know.   I think I *know.*

In these four utterances, the bold italic typeface shows which word is stressed. If you say these sentences aloud, you will hear the sound and meaning differences among them. The differences are related to the context where the utterances occur. Consider these interpretations:

I think I know. (You may not think I know the answer, but I'm pretty sure I do.)

I *think* I know. (I'm not entirely sure, but I think I know the answer.)

I think *I* know. (You may not know the answer, but I think I do.)

I think I *know.* (I am not unsure—I am quite confident that I know the answer.)

Action

Ask a friend to explain the difference in meanings in the following utterances:

- It *was* Jane who missed the bus.
- It was Jane who *missed* the bus.
- It was *Jane* who missed the bus.
- It was Jane who missed the *bus*.

See if your friend's interpretations match your predictions.

Now that we have reached the top of the pyramid, you can see that all the levels of language operate when we speak, and conversation is not really simple at all. It is important for language teachers to understand these units of language and how they work together. Given this background information, we will now consider five principles for teaching speaking.

3. Principles for teaching speaking

1. Be aware of the differences between second language and foreign language learning contexts.

Speaking is learned in two broad contexts: foreign language and second language situations. The challenges you face as a teacher are determined partly by the target language context.

A **foreign language (FL) context** is one where the target language is not the language of communication in the society (e.g., learning English in Japan or studying French in Australia). Learning speaking skills is very challenging for students in FL contexts, because they have very few opportunities to use the target language outside the classroom. Sometimes foreign language learners traveling in countries where their target languages are spoken find that they can neither understand native speakers nor be understood. There is an old story of the college freshman who struggled with introductory French and then with intermediate French. When he finally passed that course, his parents were so proud they sent him on a trip to Paris. When he got to Paris, he discovered that no one there speaks or understands intermediate French!

A **second language (SL) context** is one where the target language is the language of communication in the society (such as English in the UK or Spanish in Mexico). Second language learners include refugees, international students, and immigrants. Some second language learners (especially those who arrive in their new country as children) achieve notable speaking skills, but many others progress to a certain proficiency level and then go no further. Their speech seems to stop developing at a point where it still contains noticeable, patterned errors. These can be errors in grammar, vocabulary, pronunciation, or any combination of problems that affect the learners' ability to communicate by speaking.

Reflection

Do you have experience learning a foreign language and then trying to use it with people who speak that language natively? Or have you learned a new language when you moved to a new country? If so, did you have any problems making yourself understood? What problems did you have? (If you had no problems, ask some friends with different backgrounds.)

2. Give students practice with both fluency and accuracy.

Accuracy is the extent to which students' speech matches what people actually say when they use the target language. **Fluency** is the extent to which speakers use the language quickly and confidently, with few hesitations or unnatural pauses, false starts, word searches, etc.

In language lessons—especially at the beginning and intermediate levels—learners must be given opportunities to develop both their fluency and their accuracy. They cannot develop fluency if the teacher is constantly interrupting them to correct their oral errors. Teachers must provide students with fluency-building practice and realize that making mistakes is a natural part of learning a new language.

Reflection

Think about when you have tried to learn a new language. How did you develop your fluency? How did you develop your accuracy? Think of an effective strategy for helping learners developing fluency and one for developing accuracy.

3. Provide opportunities for students to talk by using group work or pair work, and limiting teacher talk.

Research has repeatedly demonstrated that teachers do approximately 50 to 80 percent of the talking in classrooms. It is important for us as language teachers to be aware of how much we are talking in class so we don't take up all the time the students could be talking.

Pair work and group work activities can be used to increase the amount of time that learners get to speak in the target language during lessons. One further interesting point is that when the teacher is removed from the conversation, the learners take on diverse speaking roles that are normally filled by the teacher (such as posing questions or offering clarification).

4. Plan speaking tasks that involve negotiation for meaning.

Research suggests that learners make progress by communicating in the target language because interaction necessarily involves trying to understand and make yourself understood. This process is called **negotiating for meaning**. It involves checking to see if you've understood what someone has said, clarifying your understanding, and confirming that someone has understood your meaning. By asking for clarification, repetition, or explanations during conversations, learners get the people they are speaking with to address them with language at a level they can learn from and understand.

5. Design classroom activities that involve guidance and practice in both transactional and interactional speaking.

When we talk with someone outside the classroom, we usually do so for interactional or transactional purposes. **Interactional speech** is communicating with someone for social purposes. It includes both establishing and maintaining social relationships. **Transactional speech** involves communicating to get something done, including the exchange of goods and/or services.

Most spoken interactions "can be placed on a continuum from relatively predictable to relatively unpredictable" (Nunan, 1991, p. 42). Conversations are relatively unpredictable and can range over many topics, with the participants taking turns and commenting freely. In contrast, Nunan states that "transactional encounters of a fairly restricted kind will usually contain highly predictable patterns" (1991, p. 42), and he gives the example of telephoning for a taxi. According to Nunan, interactional speech is much more fluid and unpredictable than transactional speech. Speaking activities inside the classroom need to embody both interactional and transactional purposes, since language learners will have to speak the target language in both transactional and interactional settings.

4. Classroom techniques and tasks

Information gap is a useful activity in which one person has information that the other lacks. They must use the target language to share that information. For instance, one student has the directions to a party and must give them to a classmate.

Jigsaw activities are a bidirectional or multidirectional information gap. Each person in a pair or group has some information the other persons need. For example, one student could have a timetable for train travel in Canada. Another could have a map of Canada. Without showing each other the visual information, they must speak English to plan a one-week trip.

Many information gap and jigsaw activities can be done with simple props, such as coins. First, make sure each student in a class has a penny, a quarter, a nickel, and dime (or the coins of your country). Next, hide your coins so the students can't see what you are doing. The students then follow your instructions as you do the actions you are describing: "Place the quarter with the man's picture facing up. Put the penny on the quarter. Put the dime below the quarter but not touching it. Put the nickel next to the dime on the right." Finally, reveal the design you have made with your coins so the students can see if their patterns match yours.

In the teacher-led version of this task, the students are primarily listening. But you can have them do the activity in pairs, where they take turns speaking. One natural information gap task—especially if the students don't know each other well—is to have one learner describe his family to another, while his partner draws a family tree diagram and labels it with names and information about the speaker's family. This activity promotes a great deal of negotiation for meaning, as one student asks another, "Wait—who lives in Madrid? Your aunt or, how you say, your cousin?"

You can have the students use **tango seating** to work in pairs. In tango seating one student's right shoulder is next to the other student's right shoulder and they are facing opposite directions. This arrangement allows them to hear one another but not see what is being drawn or constructed on their partner's desk.

Try an information gap activity with tango seating. Using simple objects, give a friend instructions about how to arrange the items as you are doing the same thing with yours. (You and your partner must have identical sets of objects.) When you have finished, compare the results.

Role-plays are also excellent activities for speaking in the relatively safe environment of the classroom. In a **role-play,** students are given particular roles in the target language. For example, one student plays a tourist telephoning the police to report his wallet stolen. The other plays the role of a police officer trying to help the tourist file a report. Role-plays give learners practice speaking the target language before they must do so in a real environment.

Simulations are more elaborate than role-plays. In a **simulation,** props and documents provide a somewhat realistic environment for language practice. So for instance, in a language lesson about the grocery store, a teacher might bring in "products" for the students to buy (a box of crackers, coffee, a jar of jam) and even play money for making their purchases. A check-out counter would be set up for the students to practice transactional speaking with the cashier.

Plan a role-play activity for a language lesson. The task should involve two people (for instance, a tourist and a waiter in a café). Write brief instructions on index cards. Try the role-play with a friend.

Contact assignments involve sending students out of the classroom with a stated purpose to talk to people in the target language. In a second language environment, you can send students on an information treasure hunt in a nearby business district. Provide a worksheet which the students complete by asking merchants questions. For instance, at a grocery store, they would have to ask how soon a shipment of fresh fruit would be delivered.

You can also use **contact assignments** in FL contexts if there are tourists, exchange students, or international businesspersons for your students to talk to in the target language. In a train station or at a ferry terminal, for example, students can interview tourists. Afterwards the students compile the results of the class survey and report what they learned.

In designing a contact assignment, be sure the required information cannot be gotten by reading available written information. The point is to get the students to speak with people using the target language.

5. Speaking in the classroom

Research has demonstrated that teacher-dominated classroom talk is one type of **unequal power discourse.** That is, the teacher usually has the power to determine the topics, distribute the turns, give feedback, and ask most of the questions, among other things.

Extract 1 (Long, 1980, p. 16) provides an example of teacher-controlled classroom discourse. It is based on an audio-tape of an intermediate vocabulary lesson for young adult EFL students. In the extract, indented lines mean one person's turn overlapped another person's. For example, in line 24, S3 says "Jeans" when the teacher is saying "Say the ...". In this segment the teacher was finishing with the vocabulary item *chemical pollution* and moving on to *trousers,* when S4 (Carlos) yawned loudly.

> **Extract 1**
>
> **"Carlos's Trousers" transcript**
>
> 1. *T:* *...Okay? Chemical pollution. Okay.*
> 2. *S4:* *(Yawning) O-o-o.*
> 3. *T:* *Trousers! All right, Carlos (S4), do you wear trousers?*
> 4. *S4:* *Always ... All my life.*
> 5. *S:* *(Laughter)*
> 6. *T:* *Always. You've worn, I have ...*
> 7. *S4:* *Eh, wear wear (inaudible).*

8. *T: I have … well, do you wear trousers?*

9. *S4: I wear.*

10. *S: I wear, I wear.*

11. *S4: Yes, I I do.*

12. *T: Yes, you do. What's, how do you say that word?*

13. *S4: Trousers.*

14. *T: Trousers.*

15. *S4: Trou<u>sers</u>.*

16. *T: <u>Tro</u>users.*

17. *S4: <u>Trou</u>sers.*

18. *S3: Trousers.*

19. *T: Mn-hm. Have you got trousers on?*

20. *S3: Yes, I have.*

21. *T: What kind?*

22. *S3: Jeans.*

23. *T: Jeans. Say the word jeans. Jeans.*

24. *S3: Jeans.*

25. *T: Jeans.*

26. *S2: Jeans.*

27. *T: Jeans.*

28. *S1: Jeans.*

29. *T: Okay. Okay. Huh! …*

Reflection

In Extract 1, how many turns does the teacher take? How many turns do the students take? What do you think the students learned about speaking English during this segment of this lesson?

It is difficult to imagine, by reading a printed transcript, what the intonation contours, volume, and stress patterns add to the meaning conveyed in the spoken discourse. This particular segment of a lesson involves some tightly controlled turn taking in which most of the students' utterances involve repeating what the teacher has just said.

Extract 2 is from an adult ESL lesson. In the extract "FS" stands for an unidentified female student and "xx" means the tape recording was not clear enough to transcribe what was said at that point. Words or phrases in parentheses indicate that the transcriber wasn't completely sure about what was said. Once again, indented lines indicate overlapping turns. Square brackets give the researcher's interpretation, based on the notes taken by an observer who was present during the lesson.

In this case, although the lesson is teacher-fronted, the learners had greater freedom to participate actively than did those in the lesson about Carlos's trousers. As you read this transcript, notice its conversational nature and the many times the students and the teacher work together to negotiate for meaning.

Extract 2

T: *Here's, here's another useful word.* (Writing on the blackboard.) *Have you ever heard of a flasher?*

S3: *Yeah, yeah.*

FS: *Yeah, I (/heda/) (= heard of) flasher.*

(One or two students laughing.)

T: *(S8's name), what's a flasher?*

S8: *It's like a flash. (Laughter.)*

T: *What's a flasher?*

S8: *(Flasher?)*

S1: *Somebody takes pictures.*

T: *No. (Laughter.)*

S3: *No.*

T: *xx. What's a flasher? You ever seen one? You ever seen a flasher?*

S3: *Somebody that flash.*

FS: *No.*

In the lines of transcript you just read, the teacher asks the class, "What's a flasher?" Student 1 guesses, "somebody [that] takes pictures" and Student 3 says, "somebody that flash." Both students use their knowledge of English morphemes as they analyze the word's bound and free components. The teacher then asks the classroom aide to explain the slang term to the students:

> **T:** OK. (Aide's name), you know. (Aide laughs.) (You) want to tell them xx
>
> **A:** Somebody who shows off, uh, all the parts of his body.
>
> **S6:** (Gasps.) Oh, xx!
>
> **T:** A flasher, a flasher is like a person who has nothing on and maybe a raincoat.
>
> **S3:** Nude?
>
> **S7:** Exhibitionist?
>
> **T:** OK, flash is uh flash is a quick movement, right?
>
> **S3:** Streaker?
>
> **S6:** A strea-   A streaker?
>
> **T:** xx OK, well. A streaker has absolutely nothing on. A flasher shows himself for a second or two.
>
> **S7:** Exhibitionist.
>
> (Laughter.)

Reflection

Extract 1 about Carlos's trousers takes 29 lines. Count the number of turns taken by the teacher and students in the first 29 lines of Extract 2. How do the two extracts compare? What do you think the students learned about speaking during this segment of the lesson?

> **T:** xx Like he'll, (above laughter) he may have a raincoat on or something or a coat and he comes up to
>
> **S3:** Why?
>
> **T:** you and he goes (Shows movement of someone opening a coat quickly.)
>
> **S3:** Why? (Laughing. General laughter.)
>
> **T:** And then he runs away, OK?
>
> **S3:** He should be out of his mind.

(Some laughing continues.)

FS: *xx.............................xx*

T: *That's a, that's a flasher. Anyway.*

S3: *xx*

(Some whispering.)

T: *Oh, dear. OK.*

S3: *It's a job? It's a job?*

T: *Pardon. It's a job? No, it's not a paying job. No.*

S3: *It's a job? Flasher.*

(S3 laughs. Mumbling continues.)

(Allwright and Bailey, 1991, pp. 58-59)

Reflection

Extracts 1 and 2 are both based on tape recordings made in classes for adult language learners. When you compare the two extracts, which lesson would you prefer if you were a student? Why?

Speaking includes the oral production of many different genres. Reciting poetry, participating in debates, engaging in class discussions, and leaving messages on answering machines are all different types of speaking. Perhaps the most common type of speaking is conversing.

Reflection

What is the difference between *speaking* and *conversing*? In other words, what are the defining characteristics of conversation?

In Extract 2 the interaction is highly conversational even though the teacher is managing the discourse. One key characteristic of true conversations is that their outcome is not predetermined or wholly governed by any one participant. Extract 3 shows three learners interacting together, without a teacher participating in the discussion. This in-class conversation is particularly interesting because the three learners are discussing the circumstances in which they can understand conversations in their second language. Notice how the learners negotiate for meaning (for example, when L1 pronounces "theme" as "seem"). In these lines the use of a colon (:) indicates that a sound is lengthened.

> **Extract 3**
>
> | 1. | L1 | *Can you fo- can you follow any conversation? Any people?* |
> |---|---|---|
> | 2. | L2 | *Sometime yes, but ah … many times I can't.* |
> | 3. | L1 | *(hm::* |
> | 4. | L1 | *And what about you?* |
> | 5. | L3 | *The same but depend of (who) the conversation, no?* |
> | 6. | L2 | *Yah* |
> | 7. | L3 | *Or the point, because sometimes is point very very easy, but the::: depend of the theme* |
> | 8. | L1 | *(si:m)* |
> | 9. | L3 | *Theme* |
> | 10. | L1 | *(si:m)* |
> | 11. | L2 | *The topic* |
> | 12. | L1 | *(si:m) ah! (si:m) ah yes (si:m)… yeah yes=* |
> | 13. | L2 | *(((chuckle)) ((unintelligible)) topic   = yes (si:m) tee- aitch- ((spells))…theme…theme* |
> | 14. | L3 | *(yes* |
> | 15. | L2 | *(yeah* |
> | 16. | L3 | *Yeah, theme* |
> | 17. | L2 | *Okay … next thing* |
>
> (van Lier, 1996, pp. 176–177)

In conversations among equals, people are normally free to take turns, ask questions, and change topics. If you are teaching speaking, it is important to plan activities for small groups or pairs in language classrooms so the learners have a chance to practice these conversational skills without the teacher dominating the discussion.

6. Conclusion

In this chapter, we learned that speaking is the productive oral skill, and we contrasted speech with writing. We noted that speaking a second or foreign language is far from simple. In fact, speaking–especially in a language other than our own–is quite a complex undertaking which involves using all the different levels of language.

This chapter focused on five principles for planning speaking lessons in language classrooms. We examined three transcripts from actual language lessons, ranging from tightly teacher-controlled, to teacher-fronted but conversational, to highly conversational and not under a teacher's control. We also saw that some classroom discourse and some teaching materials do not sound very much like real conversations outside of classrooms. Several teaching strategies were suggested that can be used to help language learners gain practice in speaking in the target language.

Further readings

Bailey, K. M. and L. Savage (eds.) 1994. *New Ways in Teaching Speaking.* Alexandria, VA: TESOL.

This book, written by teachers, provides practical activities for teaching speaking.

Brown, G. and G. Yule 1983. *Teaching the Spoken Language: An Approach Based on the Analysis of Conversational English.* Cambridge: Cambridge University Press.

This book helps teachers understand authentic speech. It has fine chapters about teaching speaking and assessing language learners' progress.

Celce-Murcia, M. and E. Olshtain 2000. *Discourse and Context in Language Teaching: A Guide for Language Teachers.* Cambridge: Cambridge University Press.

> This book has chapters on phonology and on speaking. The text is clearly written and does not require a background in linguistics.

Curtis, A. and K. M. Bailey 2001. Picture Your Students Talking: Using pictures in the Language Classroom. *ESL Magazine, July/August:10–12.*

> This brief article gives many practical ideas for using pictures to get language learners to speak.

Legutke, M. and H. Thomas 1991. *Process and Experience in the Language Classroom.* London: Longman.

> This book has several good ideas about interaction in classrooms. Chapter 6 discusses role-plays and many other communicative tasks.

Nunan, D. 1999. *Second Language Teaching and Learning.* Boston, MA: Heinle & Heinle.

> This book is a good source of principles for understanding how to teach speaking. Chapter 8 elaborates on many of the ideas presented here.

Helpful Web sites

TESOL (http://www.tesol.org)

> Visit this site to learn more about teaching English to speakers of other languages. The international TESOL association produces the TESOL Quarterly and the TESOL Journal, both of which should be helpful for teaching speaking classes.

English Language Teaching Journal (http://www.oup.com/elt)

> Find abstracts for articles published in this journal, which is both practical and highly readable.

Amerispeak (http://www.amerispeak.com)

> This Web site was designed to help non-native speaking professionals communicate successfully in English.

References

Allwright, D. and K. M. Bailey 1991. *Focus on the Language Classroom: An Introduction to Classroom Research for Language Teachers.* Cambridge: Cambridge University Press.

Long, M. H. 1980. Inside the 'Black Box': Methodological Issues in Classroom Research on Language Learning. *Language Learning.* 30:16. Reprinted in H.W. Seliger & M.H. Long (eds.) *Classroom Oriented Research in Second Language Acquisition.* 1983. Rowley, MA: Newbury House.

Nunan, D. 1991. *Language Teaching Methodology: A Textbook for Teachers.* New York, NY: Prentice Hall.

van Lier, L. 1995. *Introducing Language Awareness.* London: Penguin English.

van Lier, L. 1996. *Interaction in the Language Curriculum: Awareness, Autonomy and Authenticity.* London: Longman.

Chapter **Four**

Reading

Neil Anderson, Brigham Young University (USA)

Goals

At the end of this chapter, you should be able to:

 define the following concepts central to an understanding of reading: silent reading, interactive models of reading, reading fluency, extensive reading, and intensive reading.

 identify and explain seven key principles related to second language reading.

 demonstrate familiarity with practical classroom techniques for teaching reading.

 set goals for improving your ability to teach reading.

1. What is reading?

Reading is a fluent process of readers combining information from a text and their own background knowledge to build meaning. The goal of reading is comprehension. **Strategic reading** is defined as the ability of the reader to use a wide variety of reading strategies to accomplish a purpose for reading. Good readers know what to do when they encounter difficulties. **Fluent reading** is defined as the ability to read at an appropriate rate with adequate comprehension. Meaning does not rest in the reader nor does it rest in the text. The reader's background knowledge integrates with the text to create the meaning. The text, the reader, fluency, and strategies combined together define the act of reading. See Figure 1 for a representation of the definition of reading.

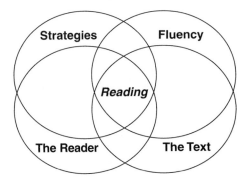

Figure 1 Definition of reading

Notice the overlapping circles. The intersection of all four circles represents reading. This is the point where meaningful reading happens. Grabe (1991) points out the complexity of even defining reading by stating that "a description of reading has to account for the notions that fluent reading is rapid, purposeful, interactive, comprehending, flexible, and gradually developing" (p. 378).

Teaching reading usually has at least two aspects. First, it can refer to teaching learners who are learning to read for the very first time. A second aspect of teaching reading refers to teaching learners who already have reading skills in their first language. You only learn to read once. Once you have learned how to read in one language, you do not learn how to read again in a second/foreign language, but rather you learn how to transfer skills that you have already learned to the new reading context in a new language.

This chapter will focus on the second of these aspects. We will review pedagogical techniques that second language teachers can use to teach learners who are already literate in at least one other language and are learning how to read in a second (or third) language. The ideas presented here can be adapted for children, teenagers, or adults. Your role as the teacher will be to enhance the learners' reading skills by teaching them to read in their second language.

Reflection

1. Reading is defined as being composed of four elements. What are the four elements?
2. Do you agree with this definition of reading? Why or why not?
3. What are other elements of reading that may have been overlooked?

2. Background to the teaching of reading

Reading is an essential skill for learners of English as a second language. For most of these learners it is the most important skill to master in order to ensure success not only in learning English, but also in learning in any content class where reading in English is required. With strengthened reading skills, learners will make greater progress and development in all other areas of learning.

What is involved in reading? How do we make sense of printed material? These are questions I have had to answer as I prepared to teach ESL/EFL reading. I believe that it is important for me to understand the process of reading so that I can then be better prepared to facilitate the learning of this skill.

Silent reading

Reading is primarily a silent activity. The majority of reading that we do will be done silently. In Western cultures oral reading was the primary practice until the nineteenth century. In about 1880 a debate began on the advantages of silent reading versus oral reading (Allington, 1984). Huey (1908) compiled a summary of the early studies on oral versus silent reading and came out strongly in favor of silent reading. However, today many teachers still believe that oral reading is the best approach for teaching. Let me emphasize here that reading is primarily a *silent* activity. Classroom approaches to teaching reading should emphasize the silent nature of this skill and avoid overemphasis on oral reading.

Different strategies are used when reading orally than when reading silently. Since comprehension is the goal of reading, your primary focus in the classroom should be on getting meaning from print. Make silent reading the goal in your classroom instead of using oral reading.

Reading processes

Understanding the process of reading has been the focus of much research over the past 125 years. Models of how the printed word is understood have emerged from this research (Goodman, 1976; Stanovich, 1980). Understanding what happens from the moment our eyes meet the page to the "click of comprehension" (Samuels & Kamil, 1984, p. 185) has only been researched for the past 50 years. The models can be divided into three categories: bottom-up models, top-down models, and interactive models.

Bottom-up models typically consist of lower-level reading processes. Students start with the fundamental basics of letter and sound recognition, which in turn allows for morpheme recognition followed by word recognition, building up to the identification of grammatical structures, sentences, and longer texts. Letters, letter clusters, words, phrases, sentences, longer text, and finally meaning is the order in achieving comprehension.

A **phonics approach** to teaching reading supports a bottom-up model. This approach is used in many reading series. Many teachers and researchers suggest that for readers to be successful they must be able to break a word down into its smallest parts, the individual sounds. When a reader comes to an unknown word he or she can sound out the word because of the knowledge of the individual units that make up the word. The blending together of the various sounds allows the reader to then move toward comprehension. Teachers must remember that phonics is a method, *not* the goal for teaching reading.

One element of a bottom-up approach to reading is that the pedagogy recommends a graded reader approach. All reading material is carefully reviewed so that students are not exposed to vocabulary that is too difficult or that contains sounds that they have not yet been introduced to.

Figure 2 is a graphic representation of a bottom-up approach to reading. (See Helgesen, Chapter 2, this volume.) The reader begins with the smallest elements and builds up to comprehension of what is being read.

Comprehension

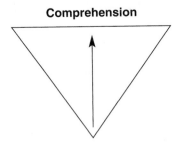

Figure 2 Bottom-up approach to reading

Within a bottom-up approach to reading, the most typical classroom focus is on what we call **intensive reading**. Intensive reading involves a short reading passage followed by textbook activities to develop comprehension and/or a particular reading skill. Most textbooks used to teach first and second language reading using an intensive reading approach.

Top-down models, on the other hand, begin with the idea that comprehension resides in the reader. The reader uses background knowledge, makes predictions, and searches the text to confirm or reject the predictions that are made. A passage can thus be understood even if all of the individual words are not understood. Within a top-down approach to reading the teacher should focus on meaning generating activities rather than on mastery of word recognition.

Goodman (1976), a strong advocate of top-down models of reading, criticizes bottom-up models because the readers become "word callers" who can read the words on the page but do not understand what they have read. Goodman (1976) believes that teachers make learning to read difficult "by breaking whole (natural) language into bite-sized, abstract little pieces" (p. 7). I agree somewhat with him. For example, I can read Spanish and pronounce all of the words that I'm reading, and yet, depending on what I am reading, I may have no comprehension of what I have read.

A meaning-based approach or a whole language approach to reading is supportive of top-down models of reading. Four key features highlight a meaning-based or whole language approach to teaching reading. First, it is a literature-based approach. Books are used which contain authentic language. Readers are exposed to a wide range of vocabulary. Next, whole language is student-centered; the focus is on the individual reader choosing what he or she wants to read. Third, reading is integrated with writing. Classes work on both skills simultaneously. Finally, emphasis is on constructing meaning. The focus should be on meaning and keeping the language whole, as opposed to breaking it down into smaller units. Whole language is a method, *not* the goal.

Figure 3 is a graphic representation of a top-down approach to reading. (See Helgesen, Chapter 2, this volume.) The reader begins with the largest elements and works down towards smaller elements to build comprehension of what is being read.

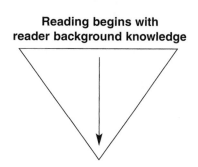

Figure 3 Top-down approach to reading

Extensive reading plays a key role in top-down approaches to reading. Extensive reading can be contrasted with intensive reading. Extensive reading means reading many books (or longer segments of text) without a focus on classroom exercises that may test comprehension skills.

Interactive models of reading

The models that are accepted as the most comprehensive description of the reading process are **interactive models**. This third type combines elements of both bottom-up and top-down models assuming "that a pattern is synthesized based on information provided simultaneously from several knowledge sources" (Stanovich, 1980, p. 35). Murtagh (1989) stresses that the best second language readers are those who can "efficiently integrate" both bottom-up and top-down processes (p. 102).

Figure 4 is a graphic representation of an interactive approach to reading. The reader combines elements of both bottom-up and top-down models of reading to reach comprehension.

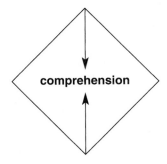

Figure 4 Interactive approach to reading

An interactive approach to reading would include aspects of both intensive and extensive reading. We need to provide learners with shorter passages to teach specific reading skills and strategies explicitly. We also need to encourage learners to read longer texts without an emphasis on testing their skills. Extensive reading provides opportunities to practice strategies introduced during intensive reading instruction.

Teachers should be aware that a single classroom textbook will not meet the needs for both intensive and extensive instruction. Materials will need to be selected that engage the learners in both types of reading.

When I observe my students, I can see that an interactive model is the best description of what happens when we read. Second language readers do many bottom-up things when they read (decode unfamiliar vocabulary, struggle with poor print quality, wonder about a part of speech of a particular word) and they do many top-down things when they read (anticipate what is coming next in the text, draw on their previous experience). My teaching has improved as I have come to understand that reading is an interactive process of both bottom-up and top-down processes.

Reflection

1. Describe the characteristics of a bottom-up reader.
2. Describe the characteristics of a top-down approach to reading.
3. Why is an interactive approach to reading the best description of what happens when we read?

Action

1. There is a problem with the text below. Notice that at the end of each line the last few letters of each word have been left off. In spite of this problem, read and figure out what the passage is about.

Preparing your resume

So, you want to find a job? You're getting close to completing your uni
studies and you are ready to begin the search for employment. Caref
preparation of your resume is the key to successfully landing the job o
your dreams. A resume is a short summary of your skills and abilities. A potential em
reviews your resume to determine whether you are the appropriate pers
hire. Most university graduates do not understand the importance of prep
resume that will present themselves in the best possible light. You must
remember that the resume is the tool that you have to sell yourself as the b
possible candidate for a job opening.

2. What were the top-down and bottom-up strategies you used in the above reading task? Share your answer with others in your class.

3. Principles for teaching reading

1. Exploit the reader's background knowledge.

A reader's background knowledge can influence reading comprehension (Carrell, 1983, Carrell and Connor, 1991). Background knowledge includes all of the experiences that a reader brings to a text: life experiences, educational experiences, knowledge of how texts can be organized rhetorically, knowledge of how one's first language works, knowledge of how the second language works, and cultural background and knowledge. Reading comprehension can be significantly enhanced if background knowledge can be activated by setting goals, asking questions, making predictions, teaching text structure, and so on. If students are reading on an unfamiliar topic, you may need to begin the reading process by building up background knowledge.

An interesting concept to consider related to the role of background knowledge is the negative influence it may have. Incorrect background knowledge can hinder comprehension. For example, some readers may have misconceptions about how AIDS is contracted. Some may believe that you can get AIDS by kissing or swimming in a pool. These misconceptions may interfere with a reading passage on AIDS, and you may have to correct the background knowledge through a prereading activity before reading comprehension can be achieved.

2. Build a strong vocabulary base.

Recent research emphasized the importance of vocabulary to successful reading. (See Nation, Chapter 7, this volume.) As I have developed my own philosophy of the role of vocabulary in reading instruction, I have decided that basic vocabulary should be explicitly taught and L2 readers should be taught to use context to effectively guess the meanings of less frequent vocabulary. I have arrived at my philosophy, in part, by reviewing the research on vocabulary acquisition. Levine and Reves (1990) have found that "it is easier for the reader of academic texts to cope with special terminology than with general vocabulary" (p. 37). They stress the great need for a teaching program that builds general, basic vocabulary.

I have found my own vocabulary instruction enhanced by asking these three questions from Nation (1990, p. 4):

1. What vocabulary do my learners need to know?
2. How will they learn this vocabulary?
3. How can I best test to see what they need to know and what they now know?

3. Teach for comprehension.

In many reading instruction programs, more emphasis and time may be placed on *testing* reading comprehension than on *teaching* readers how to comprehend. Monitoring comprehension is essential to successful reading. Part of that monitoring process includes verifying that the predictions being made are correct and checking that the reader is making the necessary adjustments when meaning is not obtained.

Cognition can be defined as thinking. Metacognition can be defined as thinking about our thinking. In order to teach for comprehension, it is my belief that readers must monitor their comprehension processes and be able to discuss with the teacher and/or fellow readers what strategies they use to comprehend. By doing this, the readers use both their cognitive and metacognitive skills.

Questioning the author, developed by Beck, McKeown, Hamilton, and Kucan (1997), is an excellent technique for engaging students in meaningful cognitive and metacognitive interactions with text and for assisting students in the process of constructing meaning from text. Beck et al. emphasize that this activity is to be done *during* the reading process, *not after* reading. The approach requires that the teacher model the reading behavior of asking questions in order to make sense of what is being read. Students learn to engage with meaning and develop ideas rather than retrieve information from the text. This particular technique is the kind of activity that teachers of reading should engage the class in, rather than asking them to read a passage and then testing reading comprehension of the material. Use of this approach engages the teacher and readers in queries about the text as the material is being read. Examples of queries include "What is the author trying to say here? What is the author's message? What is the author talking about? What does the author mean here? Does the author explain this clearly?" (Beck et al., 1997, pp. 34, 37).

4. Work on increasing reading rate.

One great difficulty in the second language reading classroom is that even when language learners can read, much of their reading is not fluent. Often, in our efforts to assist students in increasing their reading rate, teachers overemphasize accuracy which impedes fluency. The teacher must work towards finding a balance between assisting students to improve their reading rate *and* developing reading comprehension skills. It is very important to understand that the focus is not to develop *speed* readers, but *fluent* readers. I define a fluent reader as one who reads at a rate of 200 words-per-minute with at least 70 percent comprehension.

One focus here is to teach readers to reduce their dependence on a dictionary. Skills such as scanning, skimming, predicting, and identifying main ideas get students to approach reading in different ways. Readers should spend more time analyzing and synthesizing the content of the reading, and not focusing on moving through the passage one word at a time. Part of the joy of reading is being able to pick up a book and comprehend it, without having to struggle through the task of reading.

5. Teach reading strategies.

Strategies are "the tools for active, self-directed involvement that is necessary for developing communicative ability. Strategies are not a single event, but rather a creative sequence of events that learners actively use" (Oxford, 1996). This definition underscores the active role that readers take in strategic reading. To achieve the desired results, students need to learn how to use a range of reading strategies that match their purposes for reading. Teaching them how to do this should be a prime consideration in the reading classroom (Anderson, 1991; Chamot and O'Malley, 1994).

Some of the research that I have done indicates that "there is no single set of processing strategies that significantly contributes to success ..." in second language reading tasks. Strategic reading means not only knowing what strategy to use, but knowing how to use and integrate a range of strategies (Anderson, 1991).

A good technique to sensitize students to the strategies they use is to get them to verbalize (or talk about) their thought processes as they read. Readers can listen to the verbal report of another reader who has just read the same material, and it is often revealing to hear what other readers have done to get meaning from a passage. I use this technique in my reading classes to get students to become more aware of their reading strategies and to be able to describe what those strategies are.

6. Encourage readers to transform strategies into skills.

An important distinction can be made between strategies and skills (Kawai, Oxford, and Iran-Nejad, 2000). Strategies can be defined as conscious actions that learners take to achieve desired goals or objectives, while a skill is a strategy that has become automatic. This characterization underscores the active role that readers play in strategic reading. As learners consciously learn and practice specific reading strategies, the strategies move from conscious to unconscious; from strategy to skill.

For example, guessing the meaning of unknown vocabulary from context can be listed as both a strategy and a skill in reading texts. When a reader is first introduced to this concept and is practicing how to use context to guess the meaning of unfamiliar vocabulary he or she is using a strategy. The use of the strategy is conscious during the learning and practice stages. As the ability to guess unfamiliar vocabulary from context becomes automatic, the reader moves from using a conscious strategy to using an unconscious skill. The use of the skill takes place outside the direct consciousness of the reader. The goal for explicit strategy instruction is to move readers from conscious control of reading strategies to unconscious use of reading skills.

7. Build assessment and evaluation into your teaching.

Assessing growth and development in reading skills from both a formal and an informal perspective requires time and training. Both quantitative and qualitative assessment activities should be included in the reading classroom. Quantitative assessment will include information from reading comprehension tests as well as reading rate data. Qualitative information can include reading journal responses, reading interest surveys, and responses to reading strategy checklists. (See Brindley, Chapter 15, this volume.)

8. Strive for continuous improvement as a reading teacher.

The quality of the individual teacher is integral to success of second/foreign language readers. Reading teachers need to be passionate about their work. They should view themselves as facilitators, helping each reader discover what works best. Integrating the key principles discussed above can lead to more effective reading instruction in the second language classroom. While research studies conducted as early as the 1960s failed to support a single approach to teaching reading as better than others, it did support the central role of the teacher in students' success in learning to read (Farstrup, 2002). The good reading teacher actively teaches students what to do. To succeed, you need more than classroom tips and techniques: you need to understand the nature of the reading process (Anders, Hoffman, and Duffy, 2000).

The International Reading Association gathers input from reading educators around the world each year on what the "hot topics" are in reading. For 2002 a hot topic that appeared on the list for the first time was teacher education for reading (Cassidy and Cassidy, 2002). Just because you are a reader does not mean that you are prepared to be a teacher of reading. Aebersold and Field (1997) have entitled their text for teacher education in reading, *From Reader to Reading Teacher*. What a nice title for each of us as we seek to improve our ability to teach reading!

Reflection

1. Which of the principles mentioned in Section 3 are you the most familiar with already? Which are you least familiar with?
2. What is the difference between the terms *strategies* and *skills*?
3. Why does the teacher play such a central role to the success in a reading classroom?

Action

1. Are you aware of a reading passage with which readers may have misconceptions in their background knowledge that would need to be corrected prior to reading? Describe the passage and why readers may have incorrect **schemata**.

2. Select an appropriate reading passage and practice the technique of *questioning the author* on page 75. What do you learn about your own comprehension processes as you read?

3. Read for five minutes and estimate your reading rate. What do you learn about your own rate from this activity?

4. Classroom techniques and tasks

As a new reading teacher over twenty years ago, I struggled to know how to implement reading theory in the reading classroom. I would read chapters like this one that presented a variety of ideas and information on teaching reading. Knowing how to integrate the theory of reading into appropriate classroom practice was my challenge. As I thought about the key elements of reading, I organized a teaching system for reading around the word ACTIVE:

A: Activate prior knowledge

C: Cultivate vocabulary

T: Teach for comprehension

I: Increase reading rate

V: Verify reading strategies

E: Evaluate progress

Activate prior knowledge Prior to each reading passage, it is beneficial to engage the readers in an activity that gets them thinking about what they already know about the topic of the reading. One activity that you could use is called an anticipation guide. The purpose of the anticipation guide is to learn what the readers already know about the topic of the reading. You can ask five key questions about the content of a reading passage based on the reading skill you are trying to develop. For example, if you are trying to develop the readers' ability to make inferences, prepare five inference questions. Before the students read the passage, they read the inference statements and determine whether they agree or disagree with the statement. The students then read the passage and respond a second time to the same inference statements. We expect that the students will not be able to respond correctly to the inference statements before reading the passage. But, after reading the passage, we expect that they will be able to answer the statements correctly. Figure 6 contains a blank anticipation guide that you can use as a model.

Instructions: Respond to each statement twice, once *before* you begin this unit and *again* at the conclusion of the unit.

(Continued on page 80)

Write *A* if you agree with the statement.

Write *D* if you disagree with the statement.

Response before reading	Topic:	Response after reading
	1.	
	2.	
	3.	
	4.	
	5.	

Figure 5 Anticipation guide

Cultivate vocabulary Word webs are a very good activity for building students' vocabulary skills. Begin by writing a key concept in the middle of the chalkboard. Choose a concept that is central to the reading you are about to do. Have the students work individually, in small groups, or as a class in building from the center of the word web by adding other vocabulary that is related to the key word. For example, if the key word is music, students could create a word web similar to the one in Figure 8.

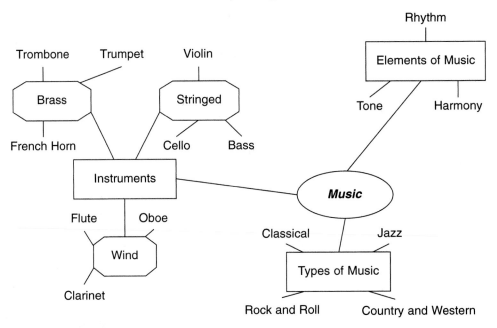

Figure 6 Word web

Teach for comprehension Instead of asking the students comprehension questions after reading a passage, a teacher can model with the class how comprehension is reached. The class reads together and discusses how they are understanding what is written. One of my favorite activities to use is teaching students how to make inferences. The teacher selects a passage that lends itself to making inferences. One of my favorite short stories to use for this activity is *Charles* by Shirley Jackson. The class reads a portion together and the teacher models the inferences that can be made while reading. As the class continues reading together, the teacher asks the students to verbalize the inferences that they are making. Instead of waiting to test students' ability to make inferences after they read, the class works together at making inferences while reading. Short mystery stories lend themselves well to teaching inferences.

Increase reading rate One successful activity is called repeated reading. Students read a short passage over and over again until they achieve criterion levels of reading rate and comprehension. For example, students may try to read a short 100-word paragraph four times in two minutes. As learners participate in repeated reading exercises, they come to realize how this activity is also a tool for improving reading comprehension. They understand more when reading something twice at a faster reading rate than reading it slowly only one time. This activity helps empower second language readers and strengthens their metacognitive awareness of the value of reading rate.

Verify reading strategies Think-aloud protocols in a guided format get learners to identify the strategies that they use while reading. I ask readers to respond verbally to five questions. (1) What are you trying to accomplish? (2) What strategy(ies) are you using? (3) Why did you select this/these strategy(ies)? (4) How well is/are the strategy(ies) working? (5) What other strategy(ies) could you use to accomplish your purpose?

Responses to these five questions allow the readers to share with each other a wide range of strategies available for comprehending reading material. The teacher does not have to generate the list of all appropriate reading strategies. Students can work together under the direction of the teacher in sharing and evaluating strategy use.

Evaluate progress Reading journals are an effective way to evaluate reading progress. Students make a journal entry each day. They respond to different questions based on different areas of focus they are working on in class. One day I may ask the students to engage in a repeated reading activity and then record in their reading journal what they have learned about their reading rate after doing the activity. On another day I may ask the students to do a written protocol and record the strategies they have used while reading during a homework assignment. The reading journal helps the students see the progress they are making in class.

1. Why do you think that word webs strengthen vocabulary skills?
2. What is the difference between *teaching* comprehension skills and *testing* comprehension skills?
3. In what ways are journals a tool for evaluating reading development?

Action

1. Create an anticipation guide for a short reading selection of your choosing. Share your work with others in the class.
2. Engage in a repeated reading activity. Mark off a chunk of text of approximately 100 words. Read this chunk four times in two minutes. If you're able to do this, you are reading approximately 200 words per minute.
3. Read a short passage and engage in a think-aloud protocol.

5. Reading in the classroom

Let's now consider how these concepts take effect in the classroom. The reading that follows is a passage from *ACTIVE Skills for Reading, Book 1* (Anderson, 2002). This material is intended for high-beginning level readers in a non-US context.

Before the teacher asks the students to read the passage, the following five true/false questions are addressed (*activate prior knowledge*):

Step 1

1. Chicken soup is a good remedy for a cold. _____ T _____ F
2. Eating chocolate can cause skin problems. _____ T _____ F
3. A vegetarian diet is low in protein. _____ T _____ F
4. Coffee is better for you than tea. _____ T _____ F
5. Bread and potatoes are not fattening foods. _____ T _____ F

The readers then practice the reading skill of scanning the passage to see if their responses to the true/false questions were correct. Readers are taught that: *When we read to find information, we move our eyes very quickly across the text. We don't read every word. We don't stop reading when we see a word we don't understand. We look for the information we want to find. This is called 'scanning'.* This reading skill is taught to make sure that readers know how to use the skill of scanning (*teach for comprehension*).

Step 2

Around the world, people have beliefs about certain foods and drinks. Some people think that chicken soup is good for a cold. Others believe that it is unhealthy not to eat meat. The question is, are any of these beliefs true?

Belief: *Chicken soup helps to fight a cold.*

Fact: *For centuries, people have believed that chicken soup is a good cold remedy. Chicken soup contains a special chemical that stops a cold from getting worse. Also, heat from the soup can make a person feel better.*

Belief: *A vegetarian diet is unhealthy.*

Fact: *Meat, especially red meat, contains protein that the body needs. A person who doesn't eat meat can get enough protein and be healthy by eating tofu, eggs, nuts, and certain vegetables.*

Belief: *Chocolate causes pimples.*

Fact: *This is a common belief that is not true! Many researchers say that eating chocolate does* not *cause pimples. More often, the cause is stress or not getting enough sleep.*

Belief: *Tea is better than coffee.*

Fact: *A study in 2002 showed that black or green tea contains substances that can protect your heart, fight cancer, and lower fat in your body. Coffee does not do this.*

Belief: *Foods like bread and potatoes are fattening.*

Fact: *Bread and potatoes do not contain much fat or many calories. Eating too much and not exercising can cause us to gain weight. Also, adding butter or other fattening things to bread and potatoes can raise the number of calories we eat. Now, doctors say that this belief may not be true.*

6. Conclusion

This chapter set out to accomplish four goals. I believe that we have accomplished three of these four goals. We have discussed seven key concepts related to second language reading. You can define the following concepts central to an understanding of reading: silent reading, interactive reading, reading fluency, extensive reading, and intensive reading. You can demonstrate familiarity with practical classroom techniques for teaching reading. The single goal that we have not yet accomplished is having you set goals for improving your ability to teach reading.

What goals do you now have to improve your ability to teach second language reading in the classroom? Reflect back over the content of this chapter and set two to three specific, measurable goals for yourself. These should be goals that you believe could be accomplished within the next six to nine months. Write the goals in a teaching journal you will have regular access to. Share these goals with a colleague, one that you trust and one that you know will help remind you of your commitment to become a better teacher of reading. Use the references listed in the Further Readings section as well as those listed in the References to provide you with background reading on the topics of your goals.

Perhaps the best piece of advice that I can give you as you set goals to improve your teaching of reading is to enjoy what you are doing in the classroom. As ESL/EFL teachers of learners we have opportunities every day to interact with the learners in our classrooms. We can learn more from them than they will ever learn from us. Good luck on your adventure to improve your teaching of reading.

Further readings

Anderson, N. J. 1999. *Exploring Second Language Reading: Issues and strategies.* Boston, MA: Heinle & Heinle.

The ACTIVE reading framework described in this chapter is outlined in greater detail in this book.

Day, R. R. 1993. *New Ways in Teaching Reading.* Alexandria, VA: TESOL.

This book provides over 100 reading activities appropriate for use in the classroom.

Day, R. R. and J. Bamford 1998. *Extensive Reading in the Second Language Classroom.* New York, NY: Cambridge University Press.

Day and Bamford discuss the importance of extensive reading and describe how teachers can encourage students to do more free reading.

Grabe, W. and F. Stoller 2001. Reading for Academic Purposes: Guidelines for the ESL/EFL teacher. In M. Celce-Murcia (ed.) *Teaching English as a Second or Foreign Language*. Boston, MA: Heinle & Heinle.

> Many teachers need to prepare students to read academic material. This chapter describes how to approach the teaching of academic reading.

Wallace, C. 2001. Reading. In R. Carter and D. Nunan (eds.), *The Cambridge Guide to Teaching English to Speakers of Other Languages*. New York, NY: Cambridge University Press.

> This chapter provides additional insights on how to approach the teaching of reading.

Helpful Web sites

Kyoto University Extensive Reading Site (http://www.kyoto-su.ac.jp/information/er)

> A helpful site for teachers interested in using extensive reading in their class.

The Reading Matrix (http://www.readingmatrix.com)

> An on-line reading journal of interest to teachers.

References

Aebersold, J. A. and M. L. Field 1997. *From Reader to Reading Teacher: Issues and Strategies for Second Language Classrooms*. New York: Cambridge University Press.

Allington, R. L. 1984. Oral Reading. In P.D. Pearson (ed.), *Handbook of Reading Research*. New York: Longman.

Anders, P. L., J. V. Hoffman, and G. G. Duffy 2000. Teaching Teachers to Teach Reading: Paradigm shifts, persistent problems, and challenges. In M.L. Kamil, P.B. Mosenthal, P.B. Pearson, and R. Barr (eds.) *Handbook of Reading Research,* vol. 3. Mahwah, NJ: Lawrence Erlbaum.

Anderson, N. J. 1991. Individual Differences in Strategy Use in Second Language Reading and Testing. *Modern Language Journal*, 75:460–472.

Beck, I.L., M. G. McKeown, R. L. Hamilton, and L. Kucan 1997. *Questioning the Author: An approach for enhancing student engagement with text.* Newark, DE: International Reading Association.

Carrell, P. L. 1983. Background Knowledge in Second Language Comprehension. *Language Learning & Communication*, 2: 25–34.

Carrell, P. L. and U. Connor 1991. Reading & Writing Different Genres. Paper presented at the twenty-fifth annual conference of TESOL, New York.

Cassidy, J. and D. Cassidy 2002. What's Hot, What's Not for 2002. *Reading Today,* 19(1):18–19.

Chamot, A. U. and J. M. O'Malley 1994. *The CALLA Handbook.* Reading, MA: Addison-Wesley.

Farstrup, A. E. 2002. There is More to Effective Reading Instruction Than Research. In A. E. Farstrup and S. J. Samuels (eds.), *What Research has to Say about Reading Instruction,* Newark, DE: International Reading Association.

Goodman, K. 1976. Reading: A psycholinguistic guessing game. In H. Singer & R. B. Ruddell (eds) *Theoretical Models and Processes of Reading.* Newark, DE: International Reading Association.

Grabe, W. 1991. Current Developments in Second Language Reading Research. *TESOL Quarterly,* 25:375–406.

Huey, E. B. 1908. *The Psychology and Pedagogy of Reading.* New York, NY: Macmillan.

Kawai, Y., R. L. Oxford, and A. Iran-Nejad 2000. Sources of Internal Self-Regulation with a Focus on Language Learning. *The Journal of Mind and Behavior,* 21:45–60.

Levine, A and T. Reves 1990. Does the Method of Vocabulary Presentation Make a Difference? *TESL Canada Journal,* 8:37–51.

Murtagh, L. 1989. Reading in a Second or Foreign Language: Models, processes, and pedagogy. *Language, Culture and Curriculum,* 2:91–105.

Nation, I. S. P. 1990. *Teaching and Learning Vocabulary.* New York, NY: Newbury House.

Oxford, R. L. 1996. *Language Learning Strategies Around the World: Cross-cultural perspectives* (ed.) National Foreign Language Resource Center. Manoa, HI: University of Hawaii Press.

Samuels, S. J. and M. L. Kamil 1984. Models of the Reading Process. In M. L. Kamil, P. B. Mosenthal, P. D. Pearson, and R. Barr (eds.) *Handbook of Reading Research,* vol.1. New York, NY: Longman.

Stanovich, K. E. 1980. Toward an Interactive-Compensatory Model of Individual Differences in the Development of Reading Fluency. *Reading Research Quarterly,* 16:32–71.

Chapter **Five**

Writing

Maggie Sokolik, University of California, Berkeley (USA)

At the end of this chapter, you should be able to:

Goals

 understand the ways in which writing instruction can be built into the ESL/EFL class.

 show confidence in using process approach techniques in the classroom, including quickwriting, brainstorming, word mapping, drafting, and peer review.

identify suitable assessment options, including writing comments on student work and using written guidelines (rubrics).

1.   What is writing?

Writing can be defined by a series of contrasts:

- It is both a *physical* and a *mental* act. At the most basic level, writing is the physical act of committing words or ideas to some medium, whether it is hieroglyphics inked onto parchment or an e-mail message typed into a computer. On the other hand, writing is the mental work of inventing ideas, thinking about how to express them, and organizing them into statements and paragraphs that will be clear to a reader.

- Its purpose is both to *express* and *impress*. Writers typically serve two masters: themselves, and their own desires to express an idea or feeling, and readers, also called the **audience**, who need to have ideas expressed in certain ways. Writers must then choose the best form for their writing–a shopping list, notes from a meeting, a scholarly article, a novel, or poetry are only a few of the choices. Each of these types of writing has a different level of complexity, depending on its purpose.

- It is both a *process* and a *product*. The writer imagines, organizes, drafts, edits, reads, and rereads. This process of writing is often cyclical, and sometimes disorderly. Ultimately, what the audience sees, whether it is an instructor or a wider audience, is a product–an essay, letter, story, or research report.

These contrasts may seem merely like clever or convenient ways to break down the larger concept. In fact, they point to the source of many conflicts and misunderstandings about writing and the teaching of writing.

Reflection

Think about your attitude towards writing. How do you feel when you know you have a writing task to complete? Do you think your attitude towards writing is similar to the attitudes of your students or your future students?

2.   Background to the teaching of writing

Concern with the teaching of writing goes back thousands of years. However, up until the early twentieth century, writing instruction was based on a somewhat rigid set of assumptions: good writing was done from a set of rules and principles, the teacher's duty was to relate these rules, and students then wrote in response to selected written texts, following the rules of good writing. A student essay was then graded for its grammatical accuracy and correct organization as well as its content. This idea is shown clearly in Harvard University's entrance requirements of 1874:

> Each candidate will be required to write a short English composition, correct in spelling, punctuation, grammar, and expression, the subject to be taken from such works of standard authors as shall be announced from time to time. The subject for 1874 will be taken from one of the following works: Shakespeare's *Tempest, Julius Caesar,* and *Merchant of Venice;* Goldsmith's *Vicar of Wakefield;* Scott's *Ivanhoe* and *Lay of the Last Minstrel.* (Cited in Bizzell, Herzberg & Reynolds, 2000.)

In second language writing instruction during this time, as in native language instruction, the "rules of writing" were concerned more with correctness of form over function. In class, students spent a great deal of time in copying models rather than expressing their own ideas creatively. Writing was used to show that students had mastered a particular grammatical rule, rather than had a good idea about the subject matter. In fact, correct spelling, grammar, and overall organization were the most important evidence of second language proficiency. A student's ability to form and write the future perfect tense correctly was seen as evidence of a student's ability to write, and moreover, of the student's overall English ability.

A movement for more progressive writing instruction started in 1911, when the National Council of Teachers of English (NCTE) was founded. The NCTE protested against the American high school curriculum, which they felt was dictated by the large universities, and did not address the needs of the diverse population of high school students across the U.S. However, it wasn't until the 1960s that a broader understanding of writing and the teaching of writing began to take hold in classrooms. Writing instruction began to include the entire process of writing—invention, drafting, feedback, and revision—and not just the **product**.

Second language writing instruction generally included the principles and methods followed in first-language writing classes. However, additional concerns surfaced in the 1960s. ESL/EFL instructors began to recognize that certain writing problems seemed to be related to students' first languages. In 1966 Robert Kaplan introduced the idea of **contrastive rhetoric**, or the comparison of different types of writing in terms of organizational patterns. In his landmark essay, *Cultural Thought Patterns in Intercultural Education,* he claims: "Each language and each culture has a paragraph order unique to itself, and … part of the learning of a particular language is the mastery of its logical system." (Kaplan, 1966, p. 14)

This idea was represented in a drawing (Figure 1), showing the paragraph structures by speakers of different languages: extensive parallel constructions in the Semitic group, an indirect approach in the Oriental group, and repeated digressions in Romance and Slavic groups. This illustration is often criticized for being too simplistic and for assuming the English language writing to be *linear* or *normal*. However, it continues to attract attention, and there is a renewed interest in the influence first language has on an additional language (Connor, 1996).

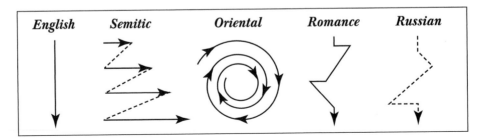

Figure 1 Contrastive rhetoric

Reflection

1. Have you been a student in a writing class? What was your experience like?
2. Could your writing instructors have considered your needs as a learner more effectively? Explain your answer.
3. Do you think Kaplan's contrastive rhetoric model (Figure 1) can help teachers to understand student writing? Explain your answer.

Scholars of first language writing, such as Peter Elbow and Donald Murray, called for teachers to take student writers' needs into consideration. This methodology has been called **expressivism**; in it, students are encouraged to write freely and personally. Writers explore their identities and writing processes in order to take control of their writing. Teachers are seen as "facilitators" who urge students to write without thought to "the rules" of writing. Peter Elbow, for example, encourages a type of writing called **freewriting**, in which students write on any topic they want for a specified period of time (usually about ten minutes), without concern for grammar, spelling, or punctuation. This writing exercise is intended to make students comfortable with the act of writing, and less afraid to make errors and experiment with ideas.

Although many instructors think expressivism has added something important to writing instruction, this approach has had several critics within

ESL/EFL. First of all, in some traditional academic settings, personal writing is discouraged, or at least not required by other disciplines. Students from some cultures will be unfamiliar with this style of writing for school purposes, or see the topics as inappropriate in an academic environment. However, aspects of this process, such as reading responses, journal-keeping, and **quickwriting** (page 97), are more and more common in the ESL/EFL writing classroom.

In the 1970s, interest in cognitive science and the sociology of language broadened writing instruction even further. The psychological processes of composing (see Shaughnessy, 1977), were seen as providing important insights into how students write and learn. In **cognitivism**, critical thinking and problem solving are of greatest importance. In the writing class, students define problems, investigate them thoroughly, and then after presenting their arguments, come to considered and logical conclusions. The cognitivist approach in ESL/EFL classrooms is also evident in aspects of a process approach that encourages brainstorming, drafting, and conferencing among students and with the instructor, in order to work out the substance of writing. Editing and proofreading are seen as a final, and less important stage, in the working out of the written text.

These trends continued into the 1980s and 1990s, when, in ESL settings, concerns for diversity, bilingualism/multilingualism, and political issues informed the teaching of writing. Writers were seen as belonging to "discourse communities," in what was called **social constructionism**. In this view, the language and form of writing arise from the target community. For native speakers in formal educational settings, this often means direct instruction in academic discourse, which in turn integrates them into the academic community. For second-language writers, there is a double burden: to learn the skills that will help them integrate into the new language community as well as into the academic community.

A concrete way in which these concerns took shape was in the formation of Writing Across the Curriculum (WAC) programs. In these programs, students were taught explicitly how to write in different disciplines, understanding that to write an essay for a literature class was a different task, and required a different style and vocabulary, than writing a laboratory report for biology. WAC appeared in second language learning in the form of **adjunct programs**. In these programs, students took "content" courses, such as psychology or political science and also attended adjunct courses, in which the specific writing and language issues related to the content course were addressed.

Most recently, Larsen-Freeman (2000) encourages teachers to adopt some form of **principled eclecticism**. Principled eclecticism encourages instructors to consider carefully the different trends and ideas that have occurred historically, and to choose those that most closely fit the needs of a particular classroom or individual student. In fact, in the writing curriculum, many instructors have done just that for many years.

3. Principles for teaching writing

The following are a few principles that every teacher should consider while planning a course, whether it is a writing course, or a course in which writing will play a part. These principles can (and should) be adapted to the many different learning situations.

1. Understand your students' reasons for writing.

The greatest dissatisfaction with writing instruction comes when the teacher's goals do not match the student's, or when the teacher's goals do not match those of the school or institution in which the student works. It is important to understand both and to convey goals to students in ways that make sense to them. Are the students required to take other courses? If so, which ones? Will those courses require writing? If so, what kind of writing?

This is not to say that your course should only be in service to other courses. However, if your curriculum includes a lot of personal writing, and the students' other courses do not, what is your justification for including this kind of writing? What benefit do you think it has? How do the skills learned in personal writing apply to other types of writing? Answering these questions will help you to find a focus for the writing that is to be done in your class.

Action

1. What are the ways in which you use writing? Make a list (think of everything from shopping lists to research essays) of all the ways in which you use writing.

2. Review your list and think of which could be converted into writing activities. Create one activity related to an item on your list.

2. Provide many opportunities for students to write.

Writing almost always improves with practice. Evaluate your lesson plans: how much time is spent reading or talking about writing, and how much is spent actually writing? My students groan when they see how much writing is required, but I draw an analogy for them: Since writing is in part a physical activity, it is like other physical activities—it requires practice, and lots of it. If someone wanted to become an excellent basketball player, would she read and discuss basketball, or would she go out and shoot some baskets? Just as basketball players play basketball, writers write. However, you can lower the stakes. Not every piece of writing needs to be corrected or graded. You don't keep score when you're practicing free throws, so teachers shouldn't grade "practice writing." When practice writing sessions are integrated regularly into your syllabus, students will become more comfortable with the act of writing.

Practice writing should provide students with different types of writing as well. Short responses to a reading, journal entries, letter writing, summaries, poetry, or any type of writing you find useful in your class should be practiced in class.

3. Make feedback helpful and meaningful.

Students crave feedback on their writing, yet it doesn't always have the intended effect. If you write comments on students' papers, make sure they understand the vocabulary or symbols you use. Take time to discuss them in class. Be cautious about the tone of your comments. The margins of a paper are small and can force you into short comments. When writing short comments, we tend to leave out the words that soften our message. While you may think, "I'm not sure I understand your point here," the limited space may cause you to write simply, "UNCLEAR" or just "?". Students can see comments such as these as unkind and unhelpful. Feedback need not always be written in the margins. You can experiment with different forms: individual conferences, taped responses, typed summary responses, and so forth.

Finally, feedback should not entail "correcting" a student's writing. In order to foster independent writers, you can provide summary comments that instruct students to look for problems and correct them on their own. So, instead of adding an –s to the end of every first person present tense verb, a comment at the end might say, *"There are several verbs that are missing an -s at the end. Try to locate and correct these verbs in the next version of this paper."*

Action

With one of the sample student papers on pages 103-105, experiment with written feedback.

1. Find one good idea the student has, and make an encouraging comment about it.

2. Find a place where the student wasn't clear, and write a comment that will help her/him clarify it.

3. Identify a grammar problem, and make a comment that will help the student see the problem in other places in the paper.

4. Which of these was easiest to do? Which was most difficult?

5. What other issues might you comment on in the paper you chose?

4. Clarify for yourself, and for your students, how their writing will be evaluated.

Students often feel that the evaluation of their writing is completely subjective. Teachers often hear, "I just don't understand what you want." One way to combat that feeling is to first develop a statement for yourself about what is valued in student writing, either in your classroom or in your institution as a whole. Some questions you might ask are:

1. On a scale of 1–10, how important is creativity, or originality of ideas?
2. On a scale of 1–10, how important is following a particular written format (such as a research report, book report, letter, etc.)?
3. On a scale of 1–10, how important is grammatical accuracy?
4. On a scale of 1–10, how important is it that the assignment include recently taught material?
5. On a scale of 1–10, how important is accuracy in spelling and punctuation?

Answering these (and other questions that are relevant to your situation) will help you to develop a **rubric**, a kind of scoring grid that elaborates the elements of writing that are to be evaluated. This rubric should outline the weight of grammar and mechanics in relationship to content and ideas, as well as other features of writing that you find important.

There are three general types of rubrics that you can develop for your assignments:

Non-weighted rubric This type of rubric provides descriptions of writing quality by level across other writing criteria. A brief example of this type of rubric would look like the following:

	Excellent	Adequate	Inadequate
Contents	Description of what would be excellent content	Description of adequate development of content	Description of inadequate content
Organization	Description of superior organization	Description of adequate organization	Description of inadequate organization
Grammar	Statement of level of grammatical accuracy expected	Statement of an adequately grammatical paper	Statement of types of grammatical problems that lead to the paper's inadequacy
Comments: The instructor's general comments on the student's assignment			

Figure 2 Non-weighted rubric

With this type of rubric, the teacher would circle or check the level the student had achieved in each of the three categories, and then provide some written comments on the bottom of the page, or on the student's assignment.

Weighted rubric A weighted rubric is similar to the unweighted one, but it breaks the writing skills into categories and sub-categories. A specific point value is assigned to each. Converting the *organization* element of the non-weighted rubric on page 94 into an element in a weighted rubric might look like this:

Organization: 10 points

- has a clear introduction
- has separate paragraphs
- has a conclusion
- uses transitions to join paragraphs
- uses transitions when needed within paragraphs

For each element listed, for example, the instructor might assign up to two points, for the total of ten.

Holistic rubric A holistic rubric describes in general terms the qualities of excellent, good, fair, and unsatisfactory assignments. These descriptions can be tied to grades or stand on their own. The instructor then chooses the description that fits the assignment. An example of one part of a holistic rubric might look like this:

Grade	Description
B	**The 'B' paper shows:** • an ability to interpret and develop ideas in the writer's own words • a clear organizational pattern • vocabulary that is adequate in expressing ideas • generally correct use of punctuation or spelling, although with occasional errors • grammar that is usually accurate, and does not interfere with the reader's understanding

Figure 3 Holistic rubric

Students can help to form a rubric as well. Take class time to ask them what they value in writing. Ask them what features make writing enjoyable to read and what features distract from that enjoyment. This kind of discussion has two benefits: it not only gives students a voice in the evaluation of their own work, it also provides a common vocabulary with which the entire class can discuss their writing and the writing of others. To assist in this discussion, give students a piece of good writing and a piece of poor writing (from a different class than the one they attend, of course). Ask them to state which is the good and which is the poor piece, with an explanation. Then get them to say *why* one piece is good and the other piece is poor. In this way, they generate the criteria for good writing.

Reflection

1. Who are the learners that you are teaching (or imagine yourself to be teaching)? Consider their ages, first languages, academic training and experience, proficiency level in English, and learning goals, both personal and as defined by the curriculum.
2. Given these learners, how will you select writing activities for the class?

4. Classroom techniques and tasks

This section presents a few techniques and tasks you can use to teach writing. All of these techniques are part of what has been called the process approach or **process writing,** although as Kroll correctly points out:

> [T]he "process approach" serves today as an umbrella term for many types of writing courses… What the term captures is the fact that student writers engage in their writing tasks through a cyclical approach rather than through a single-shot approach (2001, p. 220).

In other words, these activities serve to encourage brainstorming, drafting, writing, feedback, revising, and editing in a cyclical fashion. These types of activities encourage the idea that learning to write is more than creating a final product; it is the learning of a series of skills leading to that product.

Invention techniques: brainstorming, wordmapping, quickwriting
Instructors often feel a tension between providing students a topic for writing and allowing students to formulate their own topics. Whichever you decide upon, students will have to come up with ideas to use in their assignment. These ideas will not come fully formed, so it is helpful to provide activities that allow them to "think on paper." In this way, they can develop their thoughts before spending time writing a more formal essay.

Brainstorming can be done individually or in pairs or groups of students. In a brainstorming session, students list all the ideas they can think of related to a topic, either in writing or aloud, quickly and without much planning. If no topic is given, then the student can brainstorm possible topics.

Give students plenty of time for this activity–the most obvious, and sometimes clichéd ideas, come early in the process. When they have time to get past these ideas, more sophisticated and original ideas often surface. From the lists of brainstormed ideas or topics, students can choose those they are most interested in, or feel they can write most proficiently about.

Reflection

1. What is your writing process? Do you make lists, write drafts, work on paper, a computer, etc.?
2. What is the most effective aspect of your writing technique? What is the least effective?
3. How does your technique change, depending on the task you have to complete?
4. How could you use your insights into your own technique to help students write more effectively?

Wordmapping is a more visual form of brainstorming. When students create wordmaps, they begin with an idea at the top or center of a blank piece of paper. They then think of related ideas or words and draw relationships with a series of boxes, circles, and arrows (See Anderson, Chapter 4, this volume).

Quickwriting is where students begin with a topic, but then write rapidly about it. You can give the students a time limit, usually 10 to 15 minutes, and instruct them not to erase or cross out text, to keep writing without stopping, and to just let the ideas and words come out without concern for spelling, grammar, or punctuation. From their piece of quickwriting, they then identify key ideas or interesting thoughts by underlining them. These ideas are then used in the first draft of their essays.

Writing: drafting, feedback, and revising After students have developed their topics and ideas, it is time for them to write their first draft. Ample time should be given for the first draft, and students should be reminded that at this point, they need to focus on the development of ideas and the organization of those ideas more than the development of perfect grammar, punctuation, or spelling.

After the draft is handed in, the instructor can make comments, but only in keeping with the instructions given to students; make comments more on the ideas and organization than on the grammar and spelling. At this point, the instructor can also utilize peer feedback. Students exchange papers and provide each other with comments on the paper's contents. If peer commentary is used, it is best to use some kind of structured feedback form, such as that found in Figure 4.

Peer Comment written by _____ for _____

Read your partner's paper. Answer these questions:

1. Is the introduction effective? Explain your answer.
2. What is the author's main idea? Restate it here:
3. Does the writer support that idea with evidence? What is that evidence?
4. What evidence is missing, or incomplete?
5. What questions do you have about this writing?
6. Is the conclusion effective? How would you improve it?
7. Do you notice any grammar or word choice errors? Underline them.

Give this sheet back to your partner, and then discuss your answers.

Figure 4 Example feedback form for students

After students have received feedback, they then begin the process of revising their papers. Note that students often mistake the idea of revision with "correcting mistakes" (Sommers, 1980), so you should spend time talking about the process of reorganization, developing ideas, and so forth, as separate from editing for grammar or spelling.

Proofreading and editing Before the final draft is turned in for evaluation, students should, of course, read for mistakes in spelling, grammar, punctuation, and so forth. Students can help each other to proofread and edit, although the instructor should keep his/her involvement to a minimum. In developing independent writers, it is important that students learn to proofread and edit on their own as much as possible. And, a teacher should not correct a student's draft by supplying all the correct forms of words, punctuation, and so forth. Students are often overwhelmed by the large amount of teacher's writing on their papers, and feel paralyzed by what looks like an immense number of "errors."

Although these techniques are presented in a linear fashion, as mentioned in the introduction to this section, any of these steps can and should be performed, or "reperformed" at any stage in the writing process. For example, if a student's essay is not well developed, doing another round of quickwriting or brainstorming may help to further flesh out her/his ideas. And, while spelling and punctuation may not be of prime concern early in the process, students can, and should, make corrections any time they notice them, and not wait until the "last step."

Action

Plan an assignment in which you will ask your students to write a short essay about a favorite musician.

1. Write the steps of the assignment. For example, which of the techniques above will you use to help students through the process?
2. Describe a peer-review and feedback activity.
3. Choose a type of rubric or evaluation method you might use, and explain why you chose that method.

5. Writing in the classroom

In this section, we will look first at exercises from some textbooks that implement the principles described in this chapter. These example exercises come from different levels. We will then look at short samples of student writing, and possible ways to comment on that writing.

Textbook examples

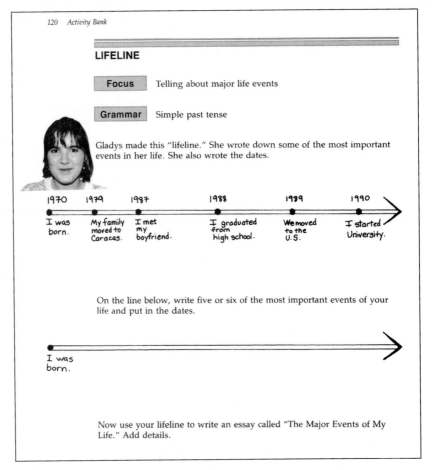

120   *Activity Bank*

LIFELINE

| Focus | Telling about major life events |

| Grammar | Simple past tense |

Gladys made this "lifeline." She wrote down some of the most important events in her life. She also wrote the dates.

```
1970      1979      1987           1988           1989          1990
●─────────●─────────●──────────────●──────────────●─────────────●──────►
I was     My family  I met          I graduated    We moved      I started
born.     moved to   my             from           to the        University.
          Caracas.   boyfriend.     high school.   U.S.
```

On the line below, write five or six of the most important events of your life and put in the dates.

```
●──────────────────────────────────────────────────►
I was
born.
```

Now use your lifeline to write an essay called "The Major Events of My Life." Add details.

Figure 5 *Writing Workout: A Program for New Students of English,* by Jann Huizenga and Maria Thomas-Ruzic, Boston, MA: Heinle & Heinle, 1990, p. 120

Commentary Figure 5 shows how process writing can be integrated into a lower-level class. It uses a variation on brainstorming in which students first create a visual map, in this case a timeline, and write from the details that they first created.

This activity would be best used after the instructions to write an essay. There is also a follow-up activity and the opportunity to rewrite their essay.

Action

Write a follow-up activity that encourages students to revise their "Major Events" essay.

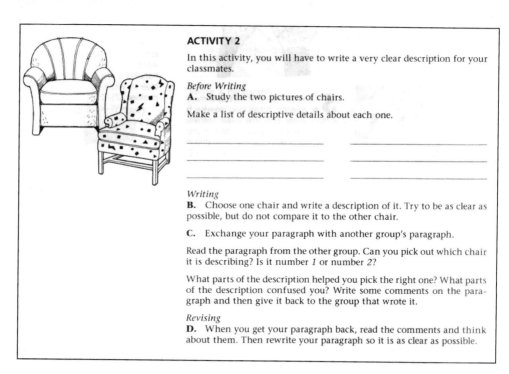

ACTIVITY 2

In this activity, you will have to write a very clear description for your classmates.

Before Writing
A. Study the two pictures of chairs.

Make a list of descriptive details about each one.

_____   _____

_____   _____

_____   _____

Writing
B. Choose one chair and write a description of it. Try to be as clear as possible, but do not compare it to the other chair.

C. Exchange your paragraph with another group's paragraph.

Read the paragraph from the other group. Can you pick out which chair it is describing? Is it number *1* or number *2*?

What parts of the description helped you pick the right one? What parts of the description confused you? Write some comments on the paragraph and then give it back to the group that wrote it.

Revising
D. When you get your paragraph back, read the comments and think about them. Then rewrite your paragraph so it is as clear as possible.

Figure 6 *Ready to Write: A First Composition Text* (Pearson Education Inc., 1994)

Commentary Figure 6 shows again a breaking down of the writing process into steps, beginning with a type of brainstorming list. It also uses peers in the reviewing of the written product. By having a goal, that is, creating a description that someone will be able to use to identify something, there is an added value of having a built-in audience for the writing. Writing projects are often most effective when they have a "real-world" purpose; that is, the audience is authentic. This encourages students to write clearly and with an audience in mind.

1. What *position* will you take toward your subject? Explain your choice.

    - Neutral: A neutral position tells only the facts.

    - Positive: A positive position praises the person for his or her accomplishments.

    - Negative: A negative position condemns the person for the life he or she has led.

    My reasons: _____

    _____

    _____

2. What part (or events or incidents) of the person's life will you write about?

    From _____

    to _____

    Reasons: _____

    _____

    _____

3. What topics will you cover?

    Reasons: _____

    _____

    _____

4. How will you organize your essay?

    - chronologically

    - by theme or main ideas

    - other (explain):

    Reasons: _____

    _____

    _____

5. What other things are you thinking about for your essay?

    Notes: _____

    _____

    _____

Figure 7 *Tapestry Writing 4* (Heinle/Thomson, 2000)

Commentary Figure 7 presents a more advanced activity for students' essays. Here, the assignment asks them to write a biography of a person of their choice. However, again, it breaks down the activity by guiding students through a series of topics and questions that help them formulate their ideas.

Reflection

Consider the three textbook samples in Figures 5-7.

1. In what ways are the activities similar?
2. Which do you find would be easiest to implement? Why?
3. Which do you think you would amend in some way? Explain how you would change each of the activities.

Sample student writing

The following are samples of student writing. All essays are reprinted with the students' permission. The first is a paragraph written in response to the question: *Which room in the house is most important?*

> ### Student Essay 1
>
> The most important room in a home is the living room. Because living room is the place where our family joins together. The living room is the place where family watch TV together. The family can only communicate in the living room, we will have no place to see each other. Because when people got off from work or got off from school, people will go back to their bedroom. People will not see each other unless they come out of the room and go through the hall way at the same time. So living room offers a place that members of the family can have entertainment together, and it offers people in the family was doing on that day or recently. And they won't become strangers as the days pass by.

Action

Make a copy of Student Essay 1 and write marginal comments.

1. Identify one grammar element that the student should focus on (but remember not to "correct" the problem).
2. Comment on the main idea; do you think it's a good one? Can it be improved?

What should the writer focus on when he or she revises this paragraph? Give him/her one piece of advice about revision.

The next two essays are from students writing in response to the question: *Should class attendance be required at the university level?*

Student Essay 2

Attendance of University

Most people feel more freedom when they attend at University than high school because students at University can have more flexible time than students at high school. One of the biggest problems to freshmen at University is a time management. Usually, their teachers or parents set up the schedule of students at high school. They spend most of day time at school and last of time to do homework or go to preparatory schools. However, the system of University is different with high schools.

In my opinion, students have to go to school. It does not matter if they go to high schools, Universities, or graduate schools. Why do we have to go to school? We need to learn something from professors who are specialist for some areas. It helps us very much to understand something that we do not know but want to know. For example, if there is a student who takes Mathematics and Native American History, and skips those classes a lot. The Mathematics and History classes are connected every class. So, if a student skips classes, it is very hard to catch up next time.

According to theory X of Mcgregor who is economic psychologist in 20 century, 'Most people are lazy, irresponsible, and work hard only when forced to do so.' I agree with his theory because lots of people reluctant to work if they do not have to do.

Study is not really fun all the time except some people. Also, it is true that we can live without studying. It is an option to go to University. People can study by themselves without going to school because there are plenty of books, videotapes, and other sources to learn. However, going to school means attending classes and studying with professors and other students regularly.

Student Essay 3

Attendance

University students should be require to attend class. Those who attend classes every time they have to, they have more possibilities of passing the class and not only that, but also they are exploring into different things to make sure what your major is going to be the same time they are being mature people which shows how serious education is them.

If you attend class, you will follow up on what the whole class is doing. You are able to do what do all of the assignments, take notes for the final exam. Having a good understanding of what is going on the class it will be easier to do a good work and have a good grade on your mid-terms and finals. The grading part is based on assignments, exams, and participation. Do you think you will get a good grade if you are not attending class and participating. Or what are you going to do when you will need to talk to the professor and the professor does not know you because you have not been attending class. Attending to class is not only about going into a room and sit until the class is dismiss, it can be more than that.

When you attend to class you have the chance to know more of what you want to do or just been introduce to a new thing. If you have the class you wanted, you will enjoy it. But if you don't, give it a chance to know what it is about and maybe you will like it. It is good to explore different things because it will help to make sure what you want to study.

Attending to class is one responsibility that you should take care of because at this time it is expect a lot from you. You are on the stage where you start being independent and responsible of your actions.

Probably you might think that is to much work, but in the reality is not. Put it this way, you will have to work more than you are used and do your best. But all of this hard work will be paid of when you see yourself in stage in front of your family and the people getting your diploma and thinking that you have accomplish one of your many goals.

Reflection

1. How would you describe the main problem with each essay?
2. In Student Essay 2, what piece of advice would you give the writer in order to improve her essay?
3. In Student Essay 3, what piece of advice would you give the writer in order to improve his essay?

6. Conclusion

In this chapter, you have read about the many influences on writing instruction and been introduced to general techniques for writing and evaluating student writing. The most important principle, however, is to learn to adapt any of these ideas to the many different situations in which students write.

Many people falsely believe that writing is a talent that is present in the lucky few, and cannot be taught to the rest. Fortunately for both native speakers and non-native speakers alike, writing is a teachable and learnable skill, and the instructor can play an invaluable role in making this skill an enjoyable one. First, the instructor can help the student understand the **context** of their writing assignments by discussing who the audience is, and what their expectations are.

The instructor also aids the students in understanding the purpose of the writing assignment. Is it to demonstrate knowledge of new vocabulary or grammatical structures? Is it to show creativity in thinking? Is it to report events accurately? Defining the purpose for writing assists students in completing assignments in different contexts.

Finally, helping students understand the process of writing by guiding them through the steps of invention, drafting, review, revision, and evaluation will help demystify writing and make it an important part of their learning of English. In addition, by reflecting on your own experience as a writer, and as a student of writing, you can help illuminate the path that your own students will walk as they become proficient writers of English.

Further readings

Campbell, C. 1998. *Teaching Second Language Writing: Interacting with text.* Boston, MA: Heinle & Heinle.

> Part of the TeacherSource series, this volume tells of the author's development as a teacher of writing. It addresses major issues in the field of writing and leads readers into an examination of their own practices. Teaching Second Language Writing has an accessible style and a strong teaching focus.

Ferris, D. and J. S. Hedgcock 1998. *Teaching ESL Composition: Purpose, process, and practice.* Mahwah, NJ: Lawrence Erlbaum.

> Teaching ESL Composition is a practical guide for designing handouts, revision plans, and writing portfolio assessment. It is designed to serve a wide audience of teachers and researchers.

Kroll, B. 2001. Second Language Writing: Research insights for the classroom. In M. Celce-Murcia (ed.) *Teaching English as a Second or Foreign Language.* Boston, MA: Heinle & Heinle.

> This collection of articles covers the main issues writing teachers face in teaching ESL/EFL writing. Topics include the composing process, variables in writing performance, instructor response to student writing and student processing of feedback, assessment, and the reading/writing connection.

Leki, I. 1992. *Understanding ESL Writers: A Guide for Teachers.* Portsmouth, NH: Boynton Cook.

> This text focuses on the ESL writer as well as the writing product. It examines: the educational and linguistic contexts, the writing behaviors of ESL students, and types of assignments.

Reid, J. M. 1993. *Teaching ESL Writing.* Englewood Cliffs, NJ: Prentice-Hall.

> This book provides a theoretical and historical basis for the field of ESL writing, from planning and implementing of courses to actual writing activities. It includes discussion of: cross-cultural communication, learning styles and strategies, collaborative learning, and response and evaluation techniques for ESL writing.

Helpful Web site

The Journal of Second Language Writing (http://www.jslw.org)

A refereed journal that features reports of research and discussion of issues in second and foreign language writing and writing instruction. Topics include characteristics and attitudes of second language writers, second language writers' composing processes, features of writers' tests, readers' responses to second language writing, assessment/evaluation and other issues of relevance. Although this journal is not specifically devoted to ESL/EFL, a large number of the articles deal with writing issues and English learners.

References

Bizzell, P., B. Herzberg, and N. Reynolds 2000. *The Bedford Bibliography for Teachers of Writing.* Fifth Edition. Boston, MA: Bedford/St. Martin.

Connor, U. 1996. *Contrastive Rhetoric, Cross-Cultural Aspects of Second-Language Learning.* Cambridge: Cambridge University Press.

Kaplan, R. 1966. Cultural Thought Patterns in Intercultural Education. *Language Learning,* 16:1–20.

Kroll, B. 2001. Considerations for Teaching an ESL/EFL Writing Course. In M. Celce-Murcia (ed.) *Teaching English as a Second or Foreign Language.* Boston, MA: Heinle & Heinle.

Larsen-Freeman, D. 2000. *Techniques and Principles in Language Teaching,* Second Edition. Oxford: Oxford University Press.

Shaughnessy, M. P. 1977. *Errors and Expectations: A guide for the teacher of basic writing.* New York, NY: Oxford University Press.

Sommers, N. 1980. Revision Strategies of Student Writers and Experienced Writers. *College Composition and Communication,* 3:46–49.

Exploring language

In this section, we look at four different features of language and how they are taught. These are the different systems of language: the sound system, the vocabulary (or lexical) system, the grammatical system, and finally the discoursal system. The chapters in this section follow the same organizing principle as those in Section 1. The aim of the section is to deepen your understanding of the language systems, as well as to provide practical techniques for teaching pronunciation, vocabulary, grammar, and discourse in the classroom.

You will find a lot of recycling of concepts and ideas within the chapters in this section as well as between this section and Section 1. This is done deliberately to help deepen and enrich your understanding of the ideas and techniques introduced in Sections 1 and 2. Addressing the same ideas from several perspectives mirrors the principle that recycling language items in the classroom enriches second language learners' understanding and mastery of these language items.

Chapter **Six**

Pronunciation

John Murphy, Georgia State University (USA)

At the end of this chapter, you should be able to:

Goals

✔ **provide** your own definition of pronunciation.

✔ **explain** the following concepts: fluency and accuracy, speech intelligibility, segmentals and suprasegmentals, variation in the sound system of English, and influencing factors that impact pronunciation learning.

✔ **demonstrate** familiarity with practical classroom techniques for establishing openness to change, contextualizing minimal pairs, tracking, using drama techniques, analyzing scripted dialogues, and focusing on vowel sounds in context.

✔ **understand** and discuss benefits of using gadgets/props and slow motion speaking in the pronunciation classroom.

1.   What is pronunciation?

Most people think of pronunciation as the sounds we make while speaking. As speakers of a language, we need to be able to understand each other with relative ease. The pronunciation patterns native speakers use reflect those commonly accepted by particular speech communities. Though most of us think in terms of speech production, the *Longman Dictionary of Applied Linguistics* emphasizes "the way sounds are perceived by the hearer" to define pronunciation (Richards, Platt, and Weber, 1992, p. 296). An emphasis on hearers' perceptions is especially relevant. How we pronounce words, phrases, and sentences communicates to others considerable information about who we are, and what we are like, as people. As language teachers, we need to acknowledge that variation is a central feature of English pronunciation since there are many legitimate varieties of English in a large number of English-dominant countries around the world.

Reflection

1. Name as many countries as you can where English is the dominant language.
2. What are examples of words you have noticed that have different pronunciations as produced by speakers of English from different backgrounds?
3. For language teachers, what variety of English pronunciation do you think should be used in classrooms where English is being taught to speakers of other languages?
4. Can you think of an example of a famous second-language speaker of English who seems to have overcome what used to be a strong foreign accent in English?

2.   Background to the teaching of pronunciation

The place of pronunciation teaching in the ESL/EFL classroom has gone through periods of dramatic change over the past 50 years. We can identify at least three primary orientations.

First orientation: 1940s–1950s – "Listen carefully and repeat what I say."

The first orientation depends upon learners' abilities to imitate sounds they hear. Grounded in theories of **behaviorism**, "listen carefully and repeat" lessons challenge learners to mimic, memorize, and in other ways practice language samples to the point of being able to reproduce them automatically. Based upon scripts and dialogues to be memorized, language lessons feature teacher-led presentations of language samples, substitution drills, intensive practice with sentence patterns, and so forth. Throughout these lesson phases, pronunciation practice of language samples serves as a primary medium through which grammar and vocabulary are taught. An implicit feature of such lessons is the expectation that learners will be successful in learning to mimic and approximate their teacher's style of speech.

Reflecting this first orientation, classroom procedures assume that learners with a "good ear" will be able to figure out how to pronounce English through guided exposure to reliable models. A problem is that learners differ in how effectively they are able to really listen to and discern the sound system of a new language. Since beginning learners "hear" the English sound system through the filter of their first language, they may need explicit training in how the sound systems of their first language and of English may differ in both obvious and subtle ways.

Reflection

1. What classroom procedures do instructors use to teach spoken language in foreign language classrooms you are familiar with?
2. What are some of the problems with the assumption that learners with a "good ear" will be able to figure out how to pronounce English well on their own?

Second orientation: 1960s–1970s – "Let's analyze these sounds closely to figure out how to pronounce them more clearly."

The second orientation features explicit presentation, intensive practice with specific sounds, and depends upon learners' mental abilities to make sense of complex descriptions of sounds. Teachers devote considerable time to explicit presentation and practice with the sounds of English, especially individual vowel and consonant sounds. Instruction appeals to learners' analytic abilities to "learn about" speech sounds, compare features of the sound system of English with features of their native languages, and practice new sounds intensively. The teacher may introduce diagrams, charts, and video clips that depict visually particular locations in the mouth where specific sounds are produced. To be able to introduce and practice an inventory of sounds in class, the teacher may familiarize learners with a listing of symbols to represent individual vowels and consonants sounds–for example, the International Phonetic Alphabet (IPA). Once learners are familiar with the symbols introduced, teachers make the most of this knowledge by using symbols to raise learner awareness of new sounds and to provide feedback on pronunciation. It is worth mentioning that the second orientation is not limited to vowels and consonant sounds alone. Similar explicit attention is given to broader aspects of spoken language such as blendings across word boundaries (e.g., Di**d y**ou ea**t y**et?), word stress, rhythm patterns, and intonation.

Reflection

1. If you have ever taken a foreign language class, how did your instructor teach pronunciation?

2. Are you familiar with the IPA or another set of symbols to represent the sounds of English or some other language? Do you think that the time it would take to learn such a system would be worth the effort?

Third orientation: 1980s and beyond (communicative and task-based language teaching) – "Let's start using these sounds in activities as soon as we can while I provide cues and feedback on how well you're doing."

The third orientation may include brief explanations of how sounds are produced, but shifts quickly to interactive classroom activities that are controlled, guided, and increasingly more extemporaneous in nature. Instruction provides opportunities for learners to use specific features of pronunciation with generous amounts of teacher support. It is an experiential orientation that depends in large part on students' abilities to "learn through doing."

Teachers representative of the third orientation highlight the importance of genuine communication in classrooms. The idea is to involve learners in using targeted sounds and sound patterns as quickly and interactively as possible. As in the second orientation, the teacher may describe how specific sounds are produced, but technical explanations are kept short and learners are given increased opportunities to begin conversing with one another while using targeted sounds. Classroom tasks are structured for learners to focus on the expression of meaning while teachers listen in, monitor how well their students are doing, and lend support. In such ways, a normal part of the instructional process challenges learners to incorporate new sounds into more extemporaneous opportunities to speak. This process can be accomplished through a four-stage sequence (adapted from Celce-Murcia, 1987):

1. Identify what sounds or sound patterns might be in need of improvement.
2. Find real-world contexts of natural language use with many natural occurrences of the identified sounds or sound patterns.
3. Design communication-based classroom tasks of genuine language use that incorporate the identified sounds.
4. Develop at least three or four tasks that may be used to recycle the focus for instruction while providing new contexts for practicing the target sound patterns.

A further characteristic of this third orientation is that the domain of teaching is expanded to give even greater attention to other features of the sound system than individual consonant and vowel sounds. Attention to such suprasegmental dimensions as word stress, sentence stress, rhythm, and intonation becomes a priority.

3. Principles for teaching pronunciation

1. Foster intelligibility during spontaneous speech.

In earlier decades, a serious flaw of pronunciation teaching was the tendency to teach speech sounds isolated from meaningful content. Contemporary teachers and learners realize that efforts to communicate meaningfully are even more important than perfect pronunciation. Lessons should engage learners in using sounds in more personalized ways and through more spontaneous ways of speaking. Being able to produce sounds in isolation is a far cry from being able to use them intelligibly in connected streams of speech.

2. Keep affective considerations firmly in mind.

Emotions can run high whenever language learners are asked to develop new pronunciation habits. It is essential to realize that pronunciation practice normally takes place in front of other students and a teacher. There are many learners who have what they believe to be very good reasons to resist a teacher's efforts to modify their ways of pronouncing English. Peer pressure often plays an important a role. A learner may fear rejection from classmates if her or his pronunciation begins to sound better than other students' in the room. This is an area in which teachers need to provide learners with generous degrees of affective support.

Reflection

1. As a teacher how can you best address the affective considerations of your students when teaching pronunciation?
2. Have you ever felt embarrassed by something connected with your pronunciation of a second language that happened in a language classroom?

3. Avoid the teaching of individual sounds in isolation.

It is crucial for teachers to embed whatever sounds or sound patterns are the focus of instruction within connected stretches of speech. Other than very brief lesson segments when teachers may introduce a specific pronunciation point for the first time, it is almost always more effective to illustrate and practice sounds within contexts of whole phrases, short sentences, and interactive classroom tasks. Activities that provide opportunities for learners to communicate meaningfully with each other are more interesting, enjoyable, and memorable. In the long run, such activities have more of an impact on enhancing speech intelligibility.

4. Provide feedback on learner progress.

It is important to provide learners with feedback on how well they are doing. Teachers need to support learners' efforts, guide them, and provide cues for improvement. Otherwise, learners may be unaware where they need to place their energies. Such feedback can be provided by you as the classroom teacher, by peers, and through self-awareness training in conjunction with live analysis, video, and/or audio recordings.

5. Realize that ultimately it is the learner who is in control of changes in pronunciation.

Try as we may, teachers are not able to make the changes necessary for improvement in pronunciation to take place. Teachers can provide guidance and practice opportunities, but learners are the ones who are in charge of making any changes that may ultimately take place. Morley (1994) speaks of the pronunciation teacher as a "language coach" who "supplies information; gives models from time to time; sets high standards; provides a wide variety of practice opportunities; and supports and encourages the learner" (p. 89).

4. Classroom techniques and tasks

Here are a few of the more popular activity types and teaching strategies today's teachers use in order to teach pronunciation.

Openness to change Spending some time building learners' self-confidence and attending to their emotional needs as speakers of a new language is especially important at the start of a course. One way is to give learners opportunities to voice what they believe to be their strengths as speakers of English. Alternatively, teachers can ask learners to discuss problem areas and frustrations. By giving learners a chance to vent their frustrations, a teacher demonstrates concern for emotional needs. Laroy (1995) suggests asking learners to speak in their native languages while mimicking a native English speaker's way of pronouncing their own language. If all students are from the same background, their teacher can hand out a few brief dialogues written in the students' native language. In small groups students may be asked to imitate the speech of an English speaker performing the dialogues. Later, the class can participate in a discussion of what it is like to listen to non-native speech patterns. The point can be made that some of the exaggerations students use to mimic the speech of English speakers in their own language may be put to good effect in learning to pronounce English forms well.

Contextualized minimal pairs One of the oldest techniques in pronunciation instruction is to teach students to distinguish between specifically targeted sounds, stress patterns, or intonation patterns through the use of minimal pairs (for example, two words which differ from each other by only one distinctive sound and which also differ in meaning). Simple pictures or drawings can be designed to provide practice in learning to distinguish such minimal pairs as: pen/pan, man/men, hand/ham, etc. In the most familiar examples the vowel sounds in words such as "bat" and "bet" may be contextualized as follows:

That's a heavy <u>bat</u>. (Show a picture of a baseball player in a baseball stadium.)

That's a heavy <u>bet</u>. (Show a picture of a gambler in a gambling casino.)

Using the examples provided above as models, compose five additional sets of minimal pair words. For each set, also include accompanying descriptions of pictures for distinguishing each member of the five sets.

Gadgets and props Rubber bands, balls that bounce easily, and kazoos may be used in pronunciation classrooms to call attention to word stress, sentence stress, rhythm patterns, and features of intonation. For stress patterns at either word level or sentence level, students can be taught to stretch rubber bands dramatically to illustrate the prominence of specific syllables. Rubber balls may be used for similar purposes to illustrate words that are stressed at sentence level. By bouncing or tossing a rubber ball from hand to hand, a speaker can call attention to word stress at sentence levels. Kazoos are useful to illustrate some of the distinctive intonation contours of English sentences since "humming" a sentence into a kazzo strips away most linguistic information except the sentence's musical quality. To focus on word stress with the aid of a rubber band, place both index fingers inside the band and stretch its ends apart by pressing your fingers in opposing directions. As depicted below, the four syllable word "education" has primary (or main) stress on the third syllable and just a bit of secondary stress on the first syllable.

Eď u CÁ tion

To illustrate the word's stress pattern, the teacher says the word aloud while simultaneously stretching the rubber band slightly in coordination with the first syllable but much more dramatically for the word's third syllable. Students may be taught to analyze words on their own, and to practice saying words while stretching rubber bands, bouncing rubber balls, or humming into kazoos in coordination with their pronunciation of stressed syllables.

Slow motion speaking A way to build fluency with more accurate pronunciation is through "slow motion speaking" (SMS). To introduce SMS, the teacher models to learners how to deliberately slow down one's speech. Then, learners are given a brief excerpt of scripted language to practice aloud. Once familiar with the sample, they are asked to say it aloud along with their teacher while the teacher pronounces the excerpt in a highly unnaturally slowed-down manner. The idea is for the teacher to be slow, deliberate, and exaggerated in her or his way of slowly moving the tongue and lips while maintaining accurate sound articulation, rhythm, intonation, and pausing patterns. SMS permits learners to view close up, and to imitate, the teacher's way of producing specific sounds in context.

Tracking Tracking begins with students analyzing written transcripts of English—as produced by native speakers—for which video or audio recordings are available. Either commercially produced ESL/EFL materials or transcripts from off-air recordings of television or radio shows may be used. (Transcripts for many TV talk shows are easily available at low cost.) It is important to select a recording covering a topic accessible to learners. Once learners are familiar with the transcript and know the material well, the video or audio recording is played for students and they are asked to say the material aloud while speaking along with the recorded voices. The process of working closely with such materials can continue for as long as learners find the material useful. One of tracking's distinctive features is that language learners are not being asked to repeat after the recorded voices. Rather, their challenge is to try to say the words presented in the transcript concurrent with the voices they are listening to.

Action

1. What are some resources you are aware of that could be used as source materials for tracking activities? While working alone, create a list of five such resources. Then, share your list of five resources with the other members of the class.

2. Make a VCR recording of a television talk show and write away for a transcript of the show. Once you have the transcript, locate a five to ten minute segment that would be suitable for in-class use.

Techniques from drama and theater arts Another source of interesting pronunciation work is working with brief excerpts from popular plays and screenplays. There are numerous scenes from Neil Simon's *The Odd Couple,* Joseph Kesselring's *Arsenic and Old Lace,* and Thornton Wilder's *Our Town* that are useful in pronunciation classrooms. Instruction can be structured in ways similar to how an actor might work during rehearsal for a performance. Teachers can provide tips on body language, tempo of speech, pitch range, and so forth. Handman (1978) and Schulman and Mekler (1984) provide edited collections of scenes from movies and screenplays that are especially helpful when working with ESL/EFL learners. Also, the Internet is a valuable resource since it provides complete screenplays for thousands of movies in the public domain. (See the Web site, http://www.iscriptdb.com.)

5. Pronunciation in the classroom

Dialogue and pattern practice

This extract is taken from an EFL university setting in Latin America. At the time, the students were starting the second semester of a two semester, first-year English course. *T* stands for teacher. *S* represents a particular student. *Ss* stands for students.

Extract 1

(The teacher asks students to read through the following dialogue.)

A: Hi, Sarah. Sorry I haven't called you. I've been really busy.

B: Me, too.

A: How about a game of tennis?

B: I'm afraid I can't play this week. My arm's hurting again.

A: Oh, is it? I thought it was better.

B: Well, it was. But I played on Saturday, and it started hurting again.

A: What a shame!

B: Well, yes, in fact, I've been feeling pretty bad all over. My . . .

A: Well, maybe next week? I've got to run. Bye.

B: Yes, umm. Okay. Bye.

[Dialogue adapted from Richards, Gordon, and Harper, 1987, p. 49.]

(The teacher begins the lesson)

T: Okay, everyone, please close your books. Listen carefully and repeat after me, "Hi, Sarah."

Ss: "Hi, Sarah."

T: "Hi, Sarah."

Ss: "Hi, Sarah."

T: Great, now try this one. "Sorry I haven't called you."

Ss: "Sorry I haven't called you."

T: "haven't called you."

Ss: "haven't called you."

T: "Sorry I haven't called you."

Ss: "Sorry I haven't called you."

TT: Okay, now just the right hand side of the room: "Sorry I haven't called you."

> ***(Ss*** from the right-hand side*): "Sorry I haven't called you."*
>
> **T:** *Now those seated on the left: "Sorry I haven't called you."*
>
> ***(Ss*** from the left-hand side*): "Sorry I haven't called you."*
>
> **T:** *Maria, you try this one: "I've been really busy."*
>
> **Maria:** *"I've been really busy."*
>
> **T:** *…"been really busy"*
>
> **Maria:** *"been really busy"*

These communication patterns continue for about twenty minutes until all of the lines from the dialogue have been practiced repeatedly. The teacher shifts between whole class responses and individual responses. At times, the teacher gestures to divide the class into four quadrants, and alternates work with individual quadrants at a time.

Analyzing the dialogue first

Now let's see how a different EFL classroom with a different teacher in the same general setting teaches the same dialogue material.

Extract 2

> **T:** *Please read through this selection carefully. Pick out any of the words that are of two or more syllables. Try to figure out which of the syllables receives primary stress.*
>
> (Over the next few minutes students identify words such as *busy, about, tennis, afraid, again, Saturday, pretty, maybe.*)
>
> **T:** *Okay, now for each of those words, I want you to work with a partner and try to identify which syllable is the primary-stressed syllable.*
>
> (Students begin to complete this task in small groups of two or three students. Several times, one or more students will ask the teacher to say a word aloud for them to hear while isolating the stressed syllable.)
>
> After about three minutes the teacher says to the whole class:
>
> **T:** *I see most of you are finished. Of the words you identified, which of the two or more syllables receives a primary stress in the individual words?*
>
> **S1:** *"Maybe," on the first, "may"*
>
> **T:** *Yes, good.*
>
> **S2:** *"Saturday," the last, on "day"*
>
> **S3:** *No, not on "day."*
>
> **T:** *Who can show us where on "SATurday"?*
>
> **S1:** *"Sat" "SATurday"*

T: *I agree. Yes, it's on the first syllable.*

(This lesson phase continues for several minutes.)

T: *Now, let's read through the selection together, using slow motion speech.*

(Students and teacher do this together as a whole class.)

T: *Arrange yourselves into pairs. Each of you takes a different part of the dialogue. But when you perform it, I'd like you to whisper only. Do the whole text several times if you can, in a whisper.*

(The whispering activity continues for three minutes.)

T: *Okay, now that you are familiar with the material, I'd like you to take the script and do some more analysis of the language presented there. Take out a pencil and underline any words that you feel should receive some emphasis when the line is delivered. Do this individually, and then we will work in small groups to compare notes in a few minutes. For example, where do you think the emphasis should be placed in the following line? "But I played on Saturday, and it started hurting again."*

(Following the teacher's illustration, students begin to work together. After about ten minutes, the teacher projects the same script on an overhead projector. A whole class discussion begins about sentence-level stress locations.)

Commentary This teacher has used dialogue material in ways quite different from "repeat after me" pattern practice. Students have examined individual words carefully, identified the number of syllables in words, and determined the location of primary-stressed syllables. They have also practiced slow motion speaking, while growing more familiar with the materials. The final task required students to further analyze the language sample, first during individual work, and then within the context of interactive discussion with the whole class.

Focus on vowel sounds

Extract 3 is from an intermediate level ESL classroom at a community college in the United States. It's near the beginning of the course.

(The teacher projects an overhead of Figure 1. Simultaneously he distributes a copy of the same figure to everyone in the class.)

1 <u>see</u> / iy / 2 <u>it</u> / I /		13 <u>two</u> / uw / 12 b<u>oo</u>ks / ʊ /
3 s<u>ay</u> / ey / 4 y<u>es</u> / ɛ /	14 <u>about</u> / ə /	11 n<u>o</u> / ow / 10 b<u>oy</u> / y /
5 f<u>a</u>t / æ /	6 m<u>y</u> /ay/ 8 c<u>ow</u> /aw/ 9 l<u>aw</u> / ɔ / 7 st<u>o</u>p / a /	

Figure 1 Symbols for 14 vowel phonemes with corresponding numbers and key words (Modified from Morley, 1979, p. 116)

T: What you see here is a set of words that depicts the 14 major vowel sounds of English. We will be working with these sounds in a number of different ways throughout the course. For today, I would like you to start tuning your ear to how the various sounds are produced.

S: There are so many. Too many.

T: Well, yes, there are quite a few. But notice that there are only 14. It doesn't go on forever. Listen to me as I say all of the words in order. "See, it, say, yes, fat, my, stop, cow, law, boy, no, books, two, about."

(The teacher does this three times as the students watch and listen.)

T: Okay, now I am going to say a single word, and all I want you to do is to tell me what number it is. "Yes," I love to say "yes" to everyone as often as I can.

Ss: Number 4

T: That's good. How about "see," can you "see" it there?

Ss: Number 1

T: "Boy." Look at that "boy" out there across the street (pointing out the window).

Ss: *10.*

T: *Okay, I think you have the idea. Now, in pairs, try to do what I have just been doing. You can both look at the chart. One of you says one of the words, and puts it into a short sentence. All your partner has to do is to tell you what number goes with that word.*

(Students begin to work in pairs. They follow the teacher's model. This continues for several minutes.)

T: *Let me get everyone's attention. Now this time, I am not going to give you a whole word. Instead, I'll just isolate the individual vowel sound. But your task will be the same. I give you a sound, and perhaps an example word different from the ones on the chart, and you tell me which number on the chart goes with that sound.*

T: */aw/, like in "how"*

S: *number eight*

T: */ɛ/, like in "head"*

S: *number three*

T: *Well, that's close, but it's not three. Can someone else try it?*

S: *number four*

T: *Yes, /ɛ/, like in "head" is number four.*

T: *How about /ɔ/, as in "tall?" That child is very "tall" for his age.*

S: *That's number nine.*

(The teacher continues working with the class, providing individual vowel sounds, example words, and short sentences to contextualize the sounds until all 14 of the vowels have been illustrated at least three times each.)

T: *Now, taking the 14 words you have in the chart, see if you can make phrases or sentences with those words. You can add additional words if you'd like, but your sentences need to have at least two of the words from the chart.*

S: *"Say yes."*

T: *"Say yes," that's a good example. That phrase uses vowel numbers 3 and 4. I like to "say yes" as often as I can. Sometimes you can get into trouble if you "say yes" to things you really do not want to do. Who has another example?*

S: *"See my books."*

T: Hey that's great. "See my books." So those would be vowel sounds 1, 6, and 12. "See my books" over there. Can you bring them to me? Can you "see my books?" 1, 6, 12. How about something else?

S: "See my fat boy."

T: Now you've got four words together. "See my fat boy." I guess that is not a very nice way to talk about a child. "See my fat boy." Those are vowel numbers 1, 6, 5, 10.

S: There's "no law" here.

T: Great! Yes, that is the idea, you can add other words to make a more complete idea. You used numbers 11 and 9, "no" and "law."

S: "Cow boy"

T: Okay, I used to like to watch "cow boy" movies when I was a kid. Do you like "cow boy" movies?

S: No, I like action movies.

T: Which of those words do you think the "act-" in "action" rhymes with?

S: "fat"

T: Good, "fat," so that's number 5.

(This activity continues for a total of twenty minutes as the class grows accustomed to associating vowel sounds with the numeric conventions the teacher presented.)

Commentary This teacher has decided it will be worthwhile to familiarize students with individual vowel sounds and with related phonemic and numeric symbols. Not all teachers of pronunciation make such a commitment. An advantage is that once the system is familiar to students, everyone in the class has a common vocabulary for talking about vowel sounds. Notice that the teacher avoids introducing individual sounds one at a time. Instead, he works with a large inventory of the vowel sounds within a single classroom activity. From the start of the activity, the sounds are embedded in whole words, short phrases, and sentences. The principle is to present sounds in context and to provide opportunities for students to learn sounds in connected streams of speech.

6. Conclusion

In this chapter, I set out to define pronunciation and describe the role it plays in the teaching of English to speakers of other languages. Some teachers assume that learners will learn to pronounce English well with little or no direct instruction. Other teachers give extensive attention to aspects of pronunciation teaching. The best of contemporary language teaching incorporates attention to pronunciation in ways compatible with **communicative language teaching** and task-based approaches to language teaching and is, therefore, sensitive to learners' real world needs. In the chapter, I introduced some of the fundamental concepts, techniques, and resources in pronunciation teaching. My definition of pronunciation highlights the fact that listeners' perceptions play a critical role. Pronunciation is more than precise enunciations of individual vowel and consonant sounds, but includes broader dimensions of spoken language such as speed of speech, tone, pausing patterns, intonation, and even the use of our whole bodies as complementary tools for getting spoken messages across. The chapter treats some additional topics such as fluency and accuracy, speech intelligibility, segmentals and suprasegmentals, and variation in the sound system of English. Some of the classroom techniques include ways of establishing openness to change, contextualizing minimal pairs, tracking, analyzing written transcripts, and focusing on vowel sounds in context.

Further readings

Celce-Murcia, M., D. Brinton, and J. Goodwin 1996. *Teaching Pronunciation: A Reference for Teachers of English to Speakers of Other Languages*. New York: Cambridge University Press.

> This book is possibly the best teacher resource in the area of pronunciation.

Dalton, C. and B. Seidlhoffer 1994. *Pronunciation*. Oxford: Oxford University Press.

> Designed for either self-study or use in a teacher development course, this book features over 130 projects/tasks to develop awareness and skills in pronunciation teaching.

Laroy, C. 1995. *Pronunciation*. Oxford: Oxford University Press.

> This resource is filled with imaginative ideas and suggested activities for teaching pronunciation.

Murphy, J. M. 1991. Oral Communication in TESOL: Integrating speaking, listening & pronunciation. *TESOL Quarterly,* 25(1):51–75.

John Murphy presents an organizing framework for integrated instruction in this area.

Helpful Web sites

Dave's ESL Café Web Guide for Pronunciation (http://www.eslcafe.com)

This site has a rich source of annotated pronunciation links.

IATEFL Pronunciation SIG (http://www.wlv.ac.uk/~le1969/psig)

Monitored by the special interest group of the International Association of Teachers of English as a Foreign Language, this site has valuable resources about pronunciation (links, articles, bibliographies, and information about a newsletter).

Pronunciation Web Resources (http://www.sunburstmedia.com/PronWeb.html)

Provided by Marsha Chan, this site links to an impressive array of resources.

Supports for Pronunciation Teaching (http://www.gsu.edu/~esljmm/ss/furtherreading.htm)

John Murphy's site is where to go if you want to learn more about this area.

TESOL Speech and Pronunciation Interest Section (http://www.public.iastate.edu/~jlevis/SPRIS)

This site contains information about pronunciation issues, resources, activities, articles, and links to relevant sites.

References

Celce-Murcia, M. 1987. Teaching Pronunciation as Communication. In J. Morley (ed.) *Current Perspectives on Pronunciation.* Washington, DC: TESOL.

Handman, W. (ed.) 1978. *Modern American Scenes for Student Actors.* New York, NY: Bantam Books.

Laroy, C. 1995. *Pronunciation.* Oxford: Oxford University Press.

Morley, J. 1979. *Improving Spoken English.* Ann Arbor, MI: University of Michigan Press.

Morley, J. 1994. Multidimensional Curriculum Design for Speech-Pronunciation Instruction. In J. Morley (ed.) *Pronunciation Pedagogy and Theory: New Views, New Directions*. Alexandria, VA: TESOL.

Richards, J., D. Gordon, and A. Harper 1987. *Listen For It: Teacher's Guide*. New York, NY: Oxford University Press.

Richards, J., J. Platt, and H. Weber 1992. *Longman Dictionary of Applied Linguistics*. London: Longman.

Schulman, M. and E. Mekler 1984. *The Actor's Scenebook*. New York, NY: Bantam Books.

Chapter **Seven**

Vocabulary

I.S.P. Nation, Victoria University of Wellington (New Zealand)

Goals

At the end of this chapter, you should be able to:

✔ **provide** your own definition of the term vocabulary.

✔ **distinguish** the different types of vocabulary (high frequency, academic, technical, low frequency) and describe how a teacher should deal with them.

✔ **describe** the strands of a well-balanced course and the conditions they require to be effective for vocabulary learning.

✔ **help** learners apply a range of effective vocabulary learning techniques and strategies across the four learning strands in a language course (meaning-focused input, deliberate learning, meaning-focused output, and fluency development).

1. What is vocabulary?

Before we do anything else, we need to decide what should be considered as vocabulary in a language course.

Multiword units

Words are clearly vocabulary, but what about groups of words like *absolutely fantastic, at once, in a minute, portable TV, the United States of America*? If learners want to use language fluently and want to sound like native-speakers, they need to be able to put words together quickly in typical combinations (Pawley and Syder, 1983). Research on very large collections of language use like the British National Corpus show that although there are many possible ways of putting words together, language users have preferred ways of doing this (Kennedy, 1992). That is, we typically say *There's no answer* rather than *There isn't an answer, heavy rain* rather than *severe rain*, and *take medicine* rather than *have medicine or drink medicine*.

There are many ways of learning these typical combinations including deliberately learning them as units, deliberately searching for them in texts, learning the patterns they are based on, and picking them up incidentally through large quantities of language input. For people beginning to learn a language, Palmer (1925) noted that "the most fundamental guiding principle [for] those who are anxious to be proficient in foreign conversation ... is this: *Memorize perfectly the largest number of common and useful word-groups!*"

As a way of quickly developing **fluency** and of picking up native-like expressions, groups of words should be learned as units. This learning is made easier in most cases if the meanings of the single words that make up the multiword units are also understood. It is thus useful to see vocabulary as also including multiword units. A useful starting point for learning such units is Crabbe and Nation's survival vocabulary (Crabbe and Nation, 1991).

Word families

Do we count different forms of the same word as different words? Researchers need to count words to answer questions like: How many words do you need to know in order to read this book? How long is this book? How fast do people speak? How many words does a five-year-old native speaker know? How many words can you learn in week? What is a suitable vocabulary learning goal for a first-year English course?

One way of counting words is to count running words or tokens. That is, each word is counted one after the other and even if the same word form occurs again it is counted again. So the previous sentence to this one contains 23 tokens and several of these tokens are the same words – *is, the, counted, word, again* – occurring more than once.

Another way to count words is to count different forms or types. So a page of tokens will consist of a smaller number of types. But this means that words like *goal* and *goals* will be counted as different types. When learners know some of the basic word building patterns of English, particularly plural, past tense, present tense, stem+*ing*, stem+*ed*, possessive, it is more sensible to count word families than to count word types. That is, it is more realistic to count *walk, walks, walked, walking* as one **word family**. There are occasional exceptions to this, like *being* and *beings, hard* and *hardly* where the meanings differ more than that involved in the affixes, but usually counting the word family better represents the receptive learning burden of the words.

| Example |

Word families from the first 1000 most frequently used words of English

Agent	Agree	
agencies	agreed	disagree
agency	agrees	disagreeable
agents	agreeing	disagreed
Ago	agreement	disagreeing
	agreements	disagreement
	disagreements	disagrees

Core meanings

So far we have looked at multiword units and word families. The last issue we will consider in deciding what is counted as vocabulary is meaning. If we look at an entry for a word in a dictionary, we will find several different senses of the word listed. For example, the entry for neutral in the COBUILD dictionary lists the following senses:

> **Example**
>
> Neutral
>
> 1. *a country that does not officially support either side in a war*
> 2. *a position not supporting either side in an argument*
> 3. *not showing emotions or preference*
> 4. *a neutral voice does not show emotions*
> 5. *not causing change because is equal on both sides*
> 6. *a position between the gears of a car*
> 7. *neutral wire—not earth or positive*
> 8. *neutral color*
> 9. *neutral atomic particles neither positive nor negative*
> 10. *neither acid nor alkali*

Reflection

What is similar in the ten senses of *neutral* outlined above? Do you consider them to be different words or just different, closely related uses of the same word?

If we look closely at these senses we can see that they all share a common **core meaning**–something like "not taking a particular side or position." When teaching and learning vocabulary, it is important to draw attention to this core meaning because this reduces the number of items the learner has to cope with, provides access to a wide range of uses, and often contrasts with the first language of the learners. This contrast can be seen as one of the educational values of foreign language learning in that it shows learners that different languages organize the world in different ways.

When we look at the important vocabulary teaching principles, these ideas of multiword units, word families and core meanings will be touched on again. We have seen that there are arguments for teaching related uses, related forms, and multiword units made from known items as part of a larger word family. This is particularly useful for **receptive** learning. For **productive** use, distinctions may need to be made.

2. Background to the teaching of vocabulary

Vocabulary teaching and learning must fit into the broader framework of a language course. One way to make sure that there is a balanced range of learning opportunities is to see a language course as consisting of four strands. They are as follows:

1. learning from meaning-focused **input**—learning through listening and reading
2. deliberate language-focused learning—learning from being taught sounds, vocabulary, grammar, and discourse
3. learning from meaning-focused output—learning by having to produce language in speaking and writing
4. developing **fluency**—becoming quick and confident at listening, speaking, reading and writing

Distinguishing the strands means that there is a balance of deliberate learning and incidental learning, of learning from input and output, of learning through oral and written skills, and of learning and fluency development.

These four strands apply for all aspects of a language course, and possibly most kinds of learning, but here we will only look at vocabulary.

Learning from meaning-focused input

The "learning from meaning-focused input" strand involves learning from listening and reading. For vocabulary learning to occur in this strand, learners need to know 98 percent of the running words already. That means that, at most, there should be only one unknown word in every fifty running words (Hu and Nation, 2000). This one unknown word in fifty is something that can be learned through guessing from context and which does not stop comprehension of the text.

The learning from input strand needs to be present even in the early stages of language learning, and so it is essential that learners have access to simple written and spoken texts. Graded readers are the most important source of these.

Deliberate learning

The deliberate learning strand is sometimes called form-focused instruction, language-focused learning, or language study. It involves paying deliberate attention to language features such as sounds, spelling, vocabulary, grammar, or discourse that are presented out of context. The most obvious deliberate learning technique is learning new vocabulary by memorizing their first language translations.

Like the other strands, no more than 25 percent of the course time should be given to this particular strand. It is an essential strand of a course but it should not overwhelm the other strands.

Learning from meaning-focused output

The "learning from meaning-focused output" strand involves learning through speaking and writing where the learners' main attention is on communicating messages. It may seem a little strange to see the **productive** skills as sources of vocabulary learning, but using vocabulary productively can strengthen learning and can push learners to focus on aspects of vocabulary knowledge that they did not need to attend to when listening and reading (Swain, 1985). For example, when having to say that someone took their medicine, the speaker has to choose the right verb—do people *eat, drink,* or *take medicine?* When listening and reading, no such decision has to be made.

Corson (1997) argues that **academic vocabulary** needs to be learned both receptively and productively because being able to produce it is one way of showing that you are part of a particular **discourse community**.

Fluency development

Vocabulary must not only be known, it must be readily available for use. The fluency development strand of a course aims at helping learners make the best use of what they already know. It is important to see fluency as being related to each of the four skills of listening, speaking, reading, and writing with fluency needing to be developed independently in each of these skills. Fluency development activities should involve only known language items (there should be no unknown vocabulary or grammatical features), should be message-focused, should involve substantial quantities of input and output, and should involve some pressure to perform faster than usual.

Classify these teaching techniques into the four learning strands in a language course given below. Add five more techniques from this chapter and from your experience.

<u>Four learning strands</u>

Meaning-focused input; Deliberate learning; Meaning-focused output; Fluency development

<u>Teaching techniques</u>

1. Intensive reading
2. Learning word parts
3. Speed reading
4. Listening to stories
5. Listening to morning talks

6. Reading easy graded readers
7. Extensive reading
8. Prepared writing
9. Strategy training
10. Communication activities with written input

3. Principles for teaching vocabulary

Learners see vocabulary as being a very important part of language learning and one of the difficulties in planning the vocabulary component of a course is making sure that it does not overwhelm other essential parts of the course. The best way to avoid this is for the teacher and course designer to have a set of guiding principles that can be applied in a variety of teaching and learning situations. These can then be applied in courses where there are parts of the course deliberately set aside for vocabulary development, or in courses where vocabulary is dealt with as it occurs in skill-focused or content-focused lessons.

1. Focus on the most useful vocabulary first.

Some words can be used in a wide variety of circumstances. Others have much more limited use. For example, the word *help* can be used to ask for help, to describe how people work with others, to describe how knowledge, tools, and materials can make people's work easier and so on. The word *advertise* has much more limited usefulness. It is still a useful word to know, but there are many more useful words to learn before this one. Teaching useful vocabulary before less useful vocabulary gives learners the best return for their learning effort.

The most useful vocabulary that every English language learner needs whether they use the language for listening, speaking, reading, or writing, or whether they use the language in formal and informal situations, is the most frequent 1000 word families of English. This vocabulary is so useful that it covers around 75 percent of the running words in academic texts and newspapers, over 80 percent of the running words in novels, and about 85 percent of the running words in conversation. It contains most of the 176 function word families (words like *a, the, of, because, could*), and words like *keep, kind, know, lack,* and *land.* It is possible to say and write a lot using only the first 1000 words of English. The next most useful list is the second 1000 words of English. There are numerous lists of these words.

After this, the most useful vocabulary depends on the goals of the learners. If learners want to do academic study in senior high school or university, then the Academic Word List (Coxhead, 2000) is the most useful vocabulary to learn (http://www.vuw.ac.nz/lals/div1/awl). This is a list of 570 word families that occur frequently in a wide range of academic texts. Here is part of an academic text with the words from the Academic Word List marked in bold type. Note that there are about three Academic Word List words in almost every line.

> ### Example
>
> The second idea used to **justify** a rule based **approach** to **policy,** is the idea of time **consistency** which **implies** that **discretionary policy** has systematic inflation **bias. I attach** less **significance** to this second idea than many of my **colleagues** in the profession do. The reason is that in the time **consistency theories,** the **benefits** of **policy** rules largely arise from how they influence inflation expectations.

As well as Academic Word List words, each subject has its own special technical vocabulary, which needs to be learned while studying that subject. Beyond that, the rest of the vocabulary is **low frequency words.** At the most conservative estimate, English contains 120,000 low frequency words and this largely excludes proper nouns. Learners need to learn low frequency words but, except for special needs, they are best learned after the **high frequency words** are known. Native speakers of English do not know all of the words in the English language.

How much vocabulary do you know?

The words at the beginning of the list below are high frequency and the words at the end of the list are very low frequency. Put a check next to each word for which you know the meaning. This short test will help you to get a feeling for how many words you know. Multiply the number of words you know in this list by 500 to find your vocabulary size.

1. bird	18. monologue	35. plainchant
2. fell	19. tamper	36. astrochemistry
3. improve	20. acanthus	37. nondurables
4. barn	21. blowout	38. carboxyl
5. fatigue	22. crupper	39. eyestalk
6. kettle	23. gloaming	40. curragh
7. combat	24. minnesinger	41. gunlock
8. resent	25. perpetuity	42. dipole
9. redeem	26. riffle	43. rigorism
10. hurrah	27. behindhand	44. localist
11. conversion	28. embolism	45. benchboard
12. fixture	29. angst	46. stirabout
13. accede	30. blowhard	47. hypothallus
14. avocation	31. devolute	48. doombook
15. calyx	32. envoi	49. paradiplomatic
16. conclave	33. golliwog	50. poroplastic
17. hierarchy	34. neonate	

It is estimated that the average native speaker with a university education knows at least 20,000 word families. To cope well in English, a second language learner would need around 5,000 words and preferably 10,000 words. It is most efficient to learn these words from the most useful to the least useful. In this way, at each stage of learning, learners get the best return for their learning effort.

2. Focus on the vocabulary in the most appropriate way.

The first principle looked at what words to teach and learn. This principle looks at how they should be taught and learned. Here we will look at the four most important vocabulary learning strategies of using word parts, guessing from context, using word cards, and using dictionaries. We will see that teachers need to clearly distinguish the way they treat high frequency words from the way they treat low frequency words.

English is a language that has been strongly affected by other languages. The core of the English language is the Germanic words from Anglo-Saxon and Norse which make up most of the function words and well over half of the first 1000 words of English. These are words like *the, a, because, home, cut, instead, iron.* Beyond the first 1000 words, most of the words, around 60 percent, came into English from French (through conquest), Latin (through religion) or Greek (through scholarship). These French, Latin and Greek words are typically made up of prefixes, stems and suffixes: *as/soci/ation, de/fin/ition, col/loc/ate, con/tain, un/in/form/ative.* This means that using word part knowledge is a very useful way of learning low frequency words. The most common word parts (prefixes and suffixes) occur in a very large number of different words.

Because high frequency words cover a large proportion of the running words of a text, they provide a helpful context to allow learners to guess the meaning of the low frequency words. This means that if learners develop skill in reading and, along with that, skill in guessing from context, they will have an effective strategy for coping with the many low frequency words that they meet in their reading.

Using word parts to help remember words, and using guessing from context are two very important strategies for dealing with low frequency words. There are two more very important strategies—using word cards for deliberate learning, and looking up words in dictionaries.

Using word cards involves making small cards and writing the English word on one side and the first language translation on the other. These cards are kept in packs of about fifty and are looked at when the learner has a free moment, while travelling on the subway, waiting for a bus, or during TV commercials. It may seem surprising to recommend using first language translation and deliberate, decontextualized learning. The use of the first language helps because it provides the meaning in a simple, clear, and comprehensible way. Learning from word cards is a very unfashionable technique (among teachers wedded to a communicative approach) but research (Nation, 2001) has shown it to be very effective. In every vocabulary learning experiment where deliberate and incidental learning is compared, deliberate learning always achieves faster and stronger vocabulary learning results. This should not be interpreted as saying that deliberate learning should replace incidental learning, but it does show that deliberate learning should be part of a well-balanced course. Deliberate learning and meaning-focused learning complement each other.

Write thirty words in another language on word cards. Study them. Work to learn them all.

1. Keep a record of how much time and how many repetitions were needed to learn the words. How many repetitions were needed to learn half of the words, three-quarters, all of them?

2. What words were difficult to remember? Why?

3. Describe a trick you used to help remember a particular word. Was it effective?

4. Briefly list three research questions that would be worth exploring with this type of technique.

Learning how to use a dictionary well is another important strategy in which many learners require training and practice.

So far we have looked at ways of helping learners with low frequency words. High frequency words are so important that anything the reader can do to help in learning them is a well-justified use of classroom time. This includes

- directly teaching high frequency words

- getting learners to read and listen to graded readers containing these words

- getting learners to study the words and do exercises based on them

- getting learners to speak and write using the words

From the teacher's point of view, the low frequency words do not deserve teaching time in the same way. In class, time can be spent working on the strategies that help learners deal with low frequency words, but teaching time should not be spent on the words themselves. Low frequency words do not deserve classroom time because of their low frequency. This means that when learners ask about particular low frequency words, the teacher should either deal with the word very quickly or use the opportunity to focus on a strategy.

3. Give attention to the high frequency words across the four strands of a course.

High frequency vocabulary needs to occur in all four strands of a course. It should get deliberate attention through teaching and study and should be met and used in communicating messages in listening, speaking, reading and writing. High frequency vocabulary should also be fluently accessible for receptive and productive use.

4. Encourage learners to reflect on and take responsibility for learning.

So far we have looked at principles that relate to choosing what vocabulary to teach and the conditions needed for learning it. There is an important principle that lies behind choosing and learning and that is that learners need to realize that they must be responsible for their own learning. Taking this responsibility requires (1) knowledge of what to learn and the range of options for learning vocabulary, (2) skill in choosing the best options, and (3) the ability to monitor and evaluate progress with those options.

Learners often find it difficult to take on this responsibility, partly because of the way they have learned in the past. The following quotations are from interviews with language learners about their vocabulary learning while they followed an English proficiency course.

> "I think course is 85 percent learning by myself. Teacher not always teach about English in here. This is different from Hong Kong. I suggest teacher can use three hours concentrated teach vocabulary—just use simple English to explain some word meanings."

A factor affecting what vocabulary learners study is the assessment that is used in a course.

> "I think it is not good way. We are studying for test. Before the test we study hard, very hard. After the test we forget everything."

In order to take responsibility for their own vocabulary learning, learners need to choose words that will be useful for them. Here, an effective language learner describes what words he chooses to study.

> "Mostly I just choose the words that I already know but I have to improve them or make them clear to me. Or I choose the one that are difficult to—me—about how to use them in different situations."

> "I learn words from talking to people, from TV and from radio. If that word is interesting I write on a small book. I always have a pen and notebook. Later I can put them in this list (vocabulary notebook)."

Contrast this with learners who are not taking control of their own learning.

> "I don't have no time to finding the words. Just I open my book and then I just pick up the words."

> "I choose very big academic word, but academic word is not useful. Of course I should know that word, but I think I don't use after this course."

(Moir and Nation, 2002)

Unless learners take control, the course will not be as effective for them. Teachers can help them do this in the following ways:

1. Inform the learners of the different types of vocabulary.
2. Train the learners in the various ways of learning so that they are very familiar with the range of learning options available for them.
3. Provide genuine opportunities for choosing what to learn and how to learn.
4. Provide encouragement and opportunity for learners to reflect on their learning and to evaluate it.

These ways include a mixture of informing, training, and encouraging reflection; or in other words, knowledge, skill, and awareness.

Vocabulary learning is a large and continuing task. Although teachers can provide useful input and support to help learners deal with this, it is ultimately the learners who have to learn and carry on learning.

The four principles we have looked at in this chapter can be applied in a variety of ways and in a variety of types of courses. What is most important is that a principled approach is taken to vocabulary development so that learners get the best return for their learning effort.

4. Classroom techniques and tasks

The techniques in this section are grouped under the four strands described in the background section of this chapter.

Meaning-focused input activities These involve the learners focusing on understanding messages where there is a low density of new vocabulary.

- Teachers can read to learners from graded readers, briefly noting difficult words on the board and giving quick translations or definitions. The reading can be done as a serial with the story unfolding week by week.

Action

1. Choose an interesting story for an ESL/EFL class you are familiar with. You might choose a story from a simplified reader.
2. Prepare to read this story aloud to the class. For the first one or two paragraphs, lightly mark in pencil in each sentence where you will pause and repeat.
3. For the first page, circle the words that students might not understand.

- Doing regular silent extensive reading of graded readers is a vital means of vocabulary development, as well as providing numerous other benefits.
- Learning through meaning-focused input can come from presenting talks to each other, from reading other learners' writing, and from interacting with the teacher. Vocabulary learning through input is increased if a little bit of deliberate attention is given to the vocabulary by noting unfamiliar words, by reflecting on the new vocabulary, by the teacher quickly explaining new words while the learners listen to the story, and by learners quickly previewing a reading to choose a few words to focus on when reading.

Deliberate learning activities These involve direct study or direct teaching.

- Having the meanings of words explained and examples of use provided
- Learning prefixes and suffixes, and cutting up words to see their parts
- Studying vocabulary on bilingual word cards
- Learning and using mnemonic techniques like the **keyword technique** to help remember vocabulary
- Practicing spelling rules
- Doing **cloze** exercises where the missing words in a text are recently met items
- Building word families by adding prefixes and suffixes to a stem
- Learning to use the vocabulary learning strategies of word cards, guessing from context, using word parts, and dictionary use. (For some learners these strategies require deliberate attention to bring them into use.)

Meaning-focused output activities These involve producing spoken or written messages.

An effective way of turning input into output is to base speaking and writing activities on written input. If this input contains a few words that are outside the learners' knowledge, but which are relevant to the topic, then there is a high probability that these words could be used and negotiated in spoken interaction, or picked up for use in the written output of the task. Combining written input with speaking and then writing increases such vocabulary learning opportunities. Although there are several important studies focusing on vocabulary learning from output, more research needs to be done to see how the written input is best designed and how different kinds of tasks affect use and learning.

The following activity focuses on the word *registration*, which occurred in a reading text about a nurse (see Nation and Hamilton-Jenkins, 2000). The learners read the text and then do productive work on some of the vocabulary by doing such tasks.

> ### Example
>
> Group these jobs into those that you think require registration (like nursing) and those that do not.
>
> | | | |
> |---|---|---|
> | teacher | doctor | shop assistant |
> | lawyer | plumber | bus driver |
> | cleaner | engineer | computer programmer |

Fluency activities These involve receiving or producing easy messages with pressure to go faster.

- A very basic listening fluency activity involves the learners pointing to or writing numbers as the teacher quickly says them in an unpredictable order.

- At a slightly more advanced level learners can listen to stories from graded readers which are well within their vocabulary knowledge. That is, where they have 100 percent coverage of the running words.

- Speaking fluency activities involve speaking on very familiar topics with some pressure to speak faster as in a 4/3/2 activity where the learners speak to one listener for four minutes on a topic, then give exactly the same talk to a different listener but in three minutes, and then to a different listener in two minutes.

Reflection

Analyse the 4/3/2 technique mentioned above to show which of the following fluency conditions it puts into practice. Part of it (*in italics*) has been done for you.

1. Easy language (*The learners choose what to talk about and what to say.*)
2. Message-focused communication
3. Pressure to perform quickly
4. Large quantity of language use

- Very elementary reading fluency activities can involve learners responding orally to flashcards of words and phrases.
- Once learners have a vocabulary of around seven or eight hundred words, they can do speed reading training using very easy graded readers or a speed reading course with a controlled vocabulary.
- Speed writing involves writing under time pressure about topics that are very familiar or that have just been read and talked about.
- Reading lots of very easy graded readers for pleasure can develop reading fluency.

5. Vocabulary in the classroom

The purpose of this section is to show you some of the ways the principles and techniques are used in the classroom. It is organized using the principles described in this chapter.

Focus on the most useful vocabulary first For elementary and intermediate learners, teachers should use material that is at a suitable level.

Before using a text with learners, it is useful to see how much of the vocabulary in the text is likely to be new for them. One way of doing this is to see the frequency level of the vocabulary in the text–how much is in the first 1000, the second 1000, the Academic Word List, and how many are not in those lists. This can be done by checking the words in the text against frequency lists. There are computer programs that can do this for you.

Go to one of these addresses on the Internet and type in a word or paste in a short text to see the different kinds of words in your text.

Frequency Level Checkers

http://language.tiu.ac.jp/flc/

http://www.er.uqam.ca/nobel/r21270/textools/web_vp.html

Focus on the vocabulary in the most appropriate way Teachers should give attention to high frequency words and should focus on the strategies for dealing with low frequency words. Notice how the teacher in Extract 1 deals with useful and not so useful vocabulary in the following examples.

Extract 1

A low frequency word

> **S:** *What does* regurgitate *mean?*
>
> **T:** *It means "repeat ideas from the book."*

A high frequency word

> **S:** *What does* punish *mean?*
>
> **T:** *That's a useful word, although I hope it is not needed in this class. See if you can guess its meaning from these sentences.*
> > He was punished for eating in class.
> > She was punished for coming home late.
> > What is the punishment that you hate the most?
> > Tell me some things that you get punished for.

In the first example, the word is dealt with quickly and the lesson moves on. The teacher could have added, "The *re-* at the beginning means *again* so that is where the *repeat* part of the meaning comes from." By doing this the teacher directs attention to the widely used prefix rather than the much less useful word. In the second example, the teacher spends time on the word and gets the learners to think about it. The teacher will also come back to it again in later lessons.

In Extract 2, the same word is being taught in two different ways. Once again, the principle of treating high frequency and low frequency words differently lies behind the teaching. The word *composition* has been met in this context—*It involves using parts of a musical composition in a new work.*

Extract 2

> **S:** *Sir, what does* composition *mean?*
>
> **T1:** *A piece of music, like a song.*

(The explanation given by Teacher 1 suits the meaning of the word in its context. Teacher 2 gives more helpful explanation using word parts.)

> **S:** *Sir, what does* composition *mean?*
>
> **T2:** *Well, what does* com- *mean? With, together. So, a composition is something that is put together in a planned way. For example, a piece of writing, a picture, a piece of music, a committee, or a chemical mixture.*

Teacher 2 connects the meaning of the parts to the meaning of the whole word. It also goes for the **core meaning** of the word. It works well if the learners have already learned the thirty or so most useful prefixes:

non-, un-, anti-, ante-, arch-, bi-, circum-, counter-, en-, ex-, fore-, hyper-, inter-, mid-, mis-, neo-, post-, pro-, semi-, sub-, ab-, ad-, com-, de-, dis-, ex- ("out"), in- ("in"), ob-, per-, pro- ("in front of"), trans-.

Reflection

Open a dictionary and look at some of the words beginning with *com-* (and its variants *co-, col-, con-, cor-*).

How much does the meaning of the prefix help with understanding the meaning of the words that contain them?

In the following extract with a low frequency word, notice how the teacher switches the learners' attention from the word to the guessing strategy. Here is the piece of text containing the unknown word.

> At age 15 he entered the University of Leipzig as a law student and by the age of 20 received a doctorate from the University of Altdorf. Subsequently, Leibniz followed a career in law and international politics.

Extract 3

S: *What does* subsequently *mean?*

T: *What part of speech do you think it is?*

S: *Adverb?*

T: *Why?*

S: *It's got -ly on the end.*

T: *Good. If we took away* subsequently, *what other word could we put there to join the two sentences?*

S: *Then? Next?*

T: *Great. That's the meaning of* subsequently. *The* sequ *part means "to follow."*

Balance attention across the four strands

Learning from input Graded readers may be the major means of learning from input. Graded readers are books written within a controlled vocabulary. Some graded readers are considerably reduced simplifications of well-known texts like *Robinson Crusoe, Lord Jim, Free Willy, The Secret Garden,* and *The Boys from Brazil.* Others are original stories written especially for language learners within a controlled vocabulary. There are hundreds of such books available in numerous series such as Oxford Bookworms, Cambridge English Readers, Penguin Readers, Heinemann Guided Readers, and Longman Classics. These are an extremely valuable resource for teaching and learning English, and teachers should be very familiar with them.

Here is part of a graded reader. Notice how it contains mainly high frequency words and yet it still is an interesting story.

> ### Example
>
> Soon we were on our way to Castle Dracula. The mountains were all around us and the moon was behind black clouds. I could see nothing, but I could still hear the wolves. The horses went faster and faster, and the driver laughed wildly. Suddenly the carriage stopped. I opened the door and got out. At once the carriage drove away and I was alone in front of the dark, silent castle. I stood there, looking up at it, and slowly, the big wooden door opened. A tall man stood in front of me. His hair was white and he was dressed in black from head to foot.
>
> "Come in, Mr Harker," he said. "I am Count Dracula." He held out his hand and I took it. It was as cold as ice!
>
> I went into the castle and the Count carefully locked the door behind me.
>
> (*Dracula* from the Oxford Bookworms Series of Graded Readers Level 2)

The few low frequency words like *castle, wolves,* and *carriage,* which are needed for the story, are repeated many times in the story.

Reflection

Here are criticisms which are made of graded readers. For each criticism think of a possible argument against that criticism. The first one has been done for you.

1. Simplified texts have difficult grammar. *"Only poorly simplified texts have easy words and difficult grammar."*
2. Simplified texts are not like the original.
3. Simplified texts take away the richness of the language.
4. Simplified texts deny learners access to vocabulary.
5. Simplified texts do not give learners the chance to develop guessing and dictionary use skills.

A very important means of vocabulary growth in the meaning-focused input strand is an extensive reading program. An extensive reading program involves learners reading large quantities of graded readers primarily for enjoyment. Ideally, the learners should read one graded reader every one or two weeks and should read at least twenty in a year. As well as being excellent for motivation and developing reading skill, this can be an important source of vocabulary growth. Learners can pick up new vocabulary and establish and enrich partly known vocabulary through such reading. The reading can be done in classroom time or as homework. There is now plenty of research that shows the language learning benefits of such "book floods" (Elley, 1991). Graded readers can also be used for listening, and some graded readers have accompanying tapes.

Learning from output Speaking activities with a vocabulary focus need to be monitored carefully to make sure the target vocabulary is getting attention. Often, only small changes to the design of the activity are needed to keep the focus on vocabulary.

Reflection

The following discussion occurred when learners were doing the task in the example given on page 143. In the text, *registration* as a nurse was described. The learners performed a speaking task which got them to consider what kinds of jobs would require someone to be officially registered. Find two examples from the discussion below which shows how the discussion contributes to the learning of the word.

S12: *Bus driver? I don't think so*

S10: *Bus driver because it is ...*

S9: *If you don't have a license how can you drive a bus, the police will catch me.*

(The others agree)

S11: *I see, so we need **registration.***

S12: *... so bus driver also need **reg ... registration** because of competence so at first I think teacher, doctor, and lawyer is a very specific occupation so um it um at first they have to go to the university and polytech so they need require **registration** so ah in my opinion er I bus driver ... if we want to be bus driver only we have ah licence and then we can ah get as a driver so I don't forget **registration** so I mistaked ah Japanese guess.*

S10: *Maybe it is not **registration**, maybe it is not **registration**, I think*

(Continued on page 149)

> *maybe it is only bus driver license ... maybe **registration** is just like a list where you can find some name like doctor.*

Fluency development Here is part of the four-minute delivery of a 4/3/2 activity and the corresponding part from the two-minute talk. Notice the changes that accompany the increase in fluency. You should notice less hesitations and repetitions, and more complex and accurate language use.

Extract 4

Four-minute delivery

S: Today I will tell you about my experience with er Burmese ethnic group in Thailand. I work th in the village as a school teacher for four years. It is very interesting. They have their own leader. They have their own language. They have their own law. erm So it's like a independent state in Thailand which is illegal. I I teach in ah in that school before it become the normal school like this, it's a patrol police school before and we have about three hundred students in that school. It is primary school. When the children first come to school, they cannot speak Thai at all. They speak their own language and the student in form one the teacher has to speak Mon.

Two-minute delivery

S: Today I will tell you about my experience in Thailand. You know I teach um Burmese ethnic group on the western part of Thailand before I came here. In the village where I teach there are about six thousand people. They have their own leader. They have their own law. They have their own language like an independent state. um Their occupation they they plant ah corn, cotton and sugar cane. I have about three hundred students in the school and the children when they come to school they don't speak Thai. They speak their own language. So every teacher ha has to know the Mon language, especially the teacher who teach in grade one.

Because meaning-focused activities do not give special overt attention to vocabulary, the teacher needs to observe them carefully from a vocabulary perspective. In this way, vocabulary can get attention across all four strands of a course.

The thoughtful application of principles in the classroom will ensure that learners can gain the most from the vocabulary component of the language course.

6. Conclusion

The teacher's role is to focus on the most useful vocabulary, to provide strategy training for the low frequency vocabulary, to ensure that vocabulary learning has a chance to occur in all parts of a course, and to help learners take control of their own vocabulary learning.

It is necessary to have a broad view of what can be considered vocabulary so that multiword units are included. It is also necessary to see that there are shared meanings underlying the range of senses of a word as well as its various family members.

Vocabulary learning cannot be left to itself. It needs to be strengthened by careful planning and well-directed teaching.

Further readings

Nation, I. S. P. 1990. *Teaching and Learning Vocabulary.* Rowley, MA: Newbury House.

This is an easily read, practical text.

Nation, I. S. P. 2001. *Learning Vocabulary in Another Language.* Cambridge: Cambridge University Press.

This book is a current comprehensive survey of research, theory, and practice in the teaching and learning of vocabulary.

Schmitt, N. 2000. *Vocabulary in Language Teaching.* Cambridge: Cambridge University Press.

Very readable, this book is an up-to-date review of vocabulary teaching.

Schmitt, N. and M. McCarthy (eds.) 1997. *Vocabulary: Description, acquisition and pedagogy.* Cambridge: Cambridge University Press.

An excellent collection of review articles, this book covers a wide range of aspects of vocabulary.

Helpful Web sites

**Learning Vocabulary in Another Language
(http://uk.cambridge.org/elt/nation)**

This Web site contains a range of supplementary material for the book including a very large classified list of references about vocabulary.

The Academic Word List (http://www.vuw.ac.nz/lals/div1/awl)

**Kyoto Sangyo University Extensive Reading
(http://www.kyoto-su.ac.jp/information/er)**

**Second Language Vocabulary Resources
(http://www1.harenet.ne.jp/%7Ewaring/vocab/index.html)**

References

Corson, D. J. 1997. The Learning and Use of Academic English Words. *Language Learning,* 47(4):671–718.

Coxhead, A. 2000. A New Academic Word List. *TESOL Quarterly,* 34(2):213–238.

Crabbe, D. and I. S. P. Nation 1991. A Survival Language Learning Syllabus for Foreign Travel. *System,* 19(3):191–201.

Elley, W. B. 1991. Acquiring Literacy in a Second Language: The effect of book-based programs. *Language Learning,* 41(3):375–411.

Hu, M. and I. S. P. Nation 2000. Vocabulary Density and Reading Comprehension. *Reading in a Foreign Language,* 13(1):403–430.

Kennedy, G. 1992. Preferred Ways of Putting Things with Implications for Language Teaching. In J. Svartvik (ed.) *Directions in Corpus Linguistics (Trends in Linguistics: Studies and Monographs,* 65:335–373). Berlin: Mouton de Gruyter.

Moir, J. and I. S. P. Nation 2002. An Investigation of Learners' Success in Personalising Vocabulary Learning. *Prospect,* 17(1).

Nation, I. S. P. 2001. *Learning Vocabulary in Another Language.* Cambridge: Cambridge University Press.

Nation, I. S. P. 2001. *Managing Vocabulary Learning.* RELC Portfolio Series, Number 2. Singapore: RELC.

Nation, I. S. P. and A. Hamilton-Jenkins 2000. Using Communicative Tasks to Teach Vocabulary. *Guidelines,* 22(2):15–19.

Palmer, H. E. 1999. Conversation. In R.C. Smith, *The Writings of Harold E. Palmer: An Overview.* Tokyo: Hon-no-Tomosha.

Pawley, A. and F. H. Syder 1983. Two Puzzles for Linguistic Theory: Nativelike selection and nativelike fluency. In J.C. Richards and R.W. Schmidt (eds.) *Language and Communication.* London: Longman.

Swain, M. 1985. Communicative Competence: Some roles of comprehensible input and comprehensible output in its development. In S.M. Gass and C.G. Madden (eds.) *Input in Second Language Acquisition.* Rowley, MA: Newbury House.

Chapter **Eight**

Grammar

David Nunan, University of Hong Kong (China)

At the end of this chapter, you should be able to:

 provide your own definition of the term grammar.

 explain the following concepts: declarative and procedural knowledge, form and function relationships, inductive and deductive teaching.

demonstrate familiarity with practical classroom techniques including the following: substitution drills, input enhancement, grammar dictation, and the garden path.

Goals

1.   What is grammar?

Grammar is generally thought to be a set of rules specifying the correct ordering of words at the sentence level. The *Longman Dictionary of Applied Linguistics* defines it as "a description of the structure of a language and the way in which units such as words and phrases are combined to produce sentences in the language" (Richards, Platt and Weber, 1985). Sentences are acceptable if they follow the rules set out by the grammar of the language. For example, in English, one rule states that "a subject followed by a verb followed by an object" is *grammatical*. The sequence of words "The bit dog man the" is ungrammatical because it violates this rule, while "The dog bit the man" is grammatical because it obeys the rule. (The sentence "The man bit the dog," is grammatical, but would be considered unacceptable by many people for other reasons.)

Grammarians distinguish between **prescriptive grammars** and **descriptive grammars.** A prescriptive grammar lays down the law, saying what is right and what is wrong. A descriptive grammar, on the other hand, sets out to describe the way that people actually use language. In recent years, the trend has been away from prescriptive and towards descriptive grammars.

Each of the following statements would be judged ungrammatical by prescriptive grammarians. However, they were all produced by native speakers, and would therefore find their way into a descriptive grammar. In a recent study, the vast majority of native speakers and advanced non-native speakers of English judged the statements to be grammatically acceptable.

The gang were plotting a takeover.

Everybody is ready now, aren't they?

Neither Fred nor Harry had to work late, did they?

Someone has deliberately made themselves homeless.

Anyone running a business should involve their spouse.

What the cat did was ate the rat. (Celce-Murcia and Olshtain, 2000)

Reflection

1. Why would each of the sentences above be ruled ungrammatical by a prescriptive grammarian?

2. Why do you think most native speakers and advanced users of the language find them acceptable? Do you find them acceptable?

3. What would you prefer as a learner, a descriptive or a prescriptive grammar? Why? What would you prefer as a teacher?

2. Background to the teaching of grammar

The place of grammar in the language classroom has had a rather checkered history. Thirty years ago, language teaching and grammar teaching were synonymous in most language classrooms. The primary aim of teaching was to ensure that learners mastered the grammar, pronunciation and vocabulary of the language.

The dominant methodology at the time was **audiolingualism,** which, in fact, is still influential today. The principles underlying audiolingualism were derived from **structural linguistics** and behaviorist psychology. The behaviorists believed that learning was a matter of acquiring habits.

A typical audiolingual lesson might look something like this.

1. Present the new language item to be learned, giving a clear demonstration of its meaning through nonverbal means such as by pictures or actions. (Do not give grammatical explanations.)

2. Model the target pattern, using a number of examples.

3. Get the whole class to mimic and memorize the new pattern following the teacher's model.

4. Introduce a substitution drill, first to the whole class, then with the class divided into two, and then with individual responses.

5. Repeat the first four steps, using negative versions of the target structure.

6. Repeat the first four steps, using interrogative (question) versions of the target structure.

7. Check for transfer, using previously unrehearsed cues. Solicit both whole class and individual responses.

Reflection

1. What are two advantages of an audiolingual lesson?
2. Audiolingualism ended up being heavily criticized (although it remains very popular to this day). Why do you think it was criticized, and why do you think it remains popular despite the criticism?

The heart of the audiolingual lesson set out above is the substitution drill. Such drills are a stock-in-trade for most teachers, and remain popular to this day. Unfortunately, in many audiolingual classrooms such drills tended to be rather mechanical. For example, the teacher might say:

"That's a book. Pen!" and the students were expected to reply.

"That's a pen."

These days, teachers and textbook writers try to give a communicative and meaningful dimension to such drills. Here is an example from one of my own textbooks, *Expressions 1* (Heinle/Thomson, 1998).

1. The teacher and students brainstorm titles of movies to fit the categories: *science fiction, comedy, thriller, drama,* and *action film.*

2. Students listen to and then practice the following conversation:

   Alice: *Do you want to see a movie?*

   Rob: *Which one?*

   Alice: *How about* Arrival of the Visitors*?*

   Rob: *Great! I love science fiction. (Or "Oh no, I don't like science fiction.")*

3. Students practice the conversation again, using the film titles generated in Step 1, and giving answers that are true for them.

Make up your own substitution type dialogue following the model above. You can either use the same content, or make up your own.

In the 1970s, two developments were to have a far-reaching effect on language teaching. Firstly, researchers began to look at the order in which learners acquired the grammar of the language. Prior to this, it had been assumed that the learners' first language would have a strong influence on the order in which grammatical items were acquired. It was also assumed that if a teacher taught a given item on a given day (and it was taught well), it would have a strong impact on what was learned. In fact, researchers came up with some surprising results:

- learners from very different language backgrounds (Spanish and Chinese, in the first instance) appeared to acquire grammatical items in the same order;

- this order differed from the order in which items were taught in class;

- the order did not appear to be alterable by instruction;

- knowing a rule was no guarantee that the rule could be used for communication.

(Dulay and Burt 1973, 1974; Krashen, 1981, 1982)

As a result of their investigations, researchers concluded that acquisition orders were determined by the nature of the language to be learned, rather than through a contrast between the first language and the target language. The fact that individual grammar items appeared to be impervious to instruction, along with the fact that many learners could state rules, but then violated those very rules in communication, led to the notion that grammar instruction was of limited value. Stephen Krashen argued that grammar teaching led to conscious learning, whereas what was wanted was subconscious acquisition. He went further in suggesting that grammar instruction was unnecessary for the acquisition of a second language.

More recently, the consensus seems to be that some form of grammar instruction is useful. For example, two researchers recently wrote:

> Our view is that some degree of carefully timed and delivered focus on form is likely to be appropriate in most cases of L2 learning difficulty. ... we believe that leaving learners to discover form-function relationships and the intricacies of a new linguistic system wholly on their own makes little sense. This does not mean, however, that we advocate a constant focus on all forms for all learners all the time. (Doughty and Williams, 1998, p. 11)

The second development that had an important influence on the course of language teaching was a rethinking of the nature of language itself. Rather than being viewed as a set of linguistic systems, it was seen as a tool for communication. This reconceptualization led directly to the development of communicative language teaching.

Two recent related trends in language teaching are *focus on form* (Doughty and Williams, 1998), and *consciousness-raising* (Fotos and Ellis, 1991). Focus on form refers to the practice of explicitly drawing students' attention to linguistic features within the context meaning-focused activities. In other words, communication comes first, and a focus on form comes second. The advantage of this reorientation is that "the learner's attention is drawn precisely to a linguistic feature as necessitated by a communicative demand" (Doughty and Williams, 1998:3). Learners are therefore more likely to see the relationship between language form and communicative function. (See Principle 2, p. 159.)

Consciousness-raising is a type of focus-on-form approach to grammar teaching. According to Larsen-Freeman (2001, p. 39-40), these exercises do not require students to produce the target structures. Instead, students are made aware of the target grammatical item through discovery-oriented tasks. (Examples of consciousness-raising exercises are presented in this chaper in the section Classroom techniques and procedures.)

The current interest in focus on form has grown out of research questioning the idea that as teachers all we need to do is to create opportunities for learners to be immersed in and to communicate in the target language, and that it is unnecessary to focus on form at all. Work carried out in immersion classrooms in Canada and elsewhere has shown that when a focus on form is entirely absent, the learners do not develop an adequate mastery of certain grammatical features. In fact, they appear to end up with a kind of classroom pidgin language.

3. Principles for teaching grammar

1. Integrate both inductive and deductive methods into your teaching.

In the **deductive** classroom, the teacher gives a grammatical explanation or rule followed by a set of exercises designed to clarify the grammatical point and help the learners master the point. In deductive teaching, you work from principles to examples. **Inductive** procedures reverse this process. In inductive teaching, you present the learners with samples of language and, through a process of guided discovery, get them to work out the principle or rule for themselves.

So, which is better, deductive or inductive teaching? The answer is—it depends. It depends on the grammar point being taught, and the learning style of the student. (Some learners appear to learn more effectively through a deductive approach, others appear to do better through an inductive approach.) In my own teaching, I try and combine both approaches. There are times when I will introduce a grammar point deductively and other times when I use an inductive approach. I know which approach most of my students prefer—deduction, I suspect because it requires less mental effort. I prefer induction because I believe that it demands greater mental effort and that this will result in more effective learning in the longer term. The disadvantage of an inductive approach is that it takes more time for learners to come to an understanding of the grammatical point in question than with a deductive approach. However, inductive techniques appear to result in learners retaining more of the language in the long term.

Is the following teaching sequence an example of a deductive or inductive approach? What grammar point is being practiced?

1. Students have pictures illustrating the following actions.
   Students write the number of the activity next to the correct picture.
   1. Take a cooking lesson. 2. Take driving lessons. 3. Study English.
   4. Take singing lessons. 5. Take a swimming class. 6. Study computers.

2. Students listen to and practice the conversation.

   Glenda: What are you doing over the break?
   Valerie: I'm going to take a swimming class.
   Glenda: Oh really? Where?
   Valerie: At the Plaza Fitness Center.
   Glenda: That sounds like fun.

3. Students practice the conversation again using different activities from Number 1.

2. Use tasks that make clear the relationship between grammatical form and communicative function.

Many grammar-based courses are relatively ineffective because they teach grammar as an abstract system, present the language as isolated sentences, and fail to give learners a proper context for the grammar point. Teaching was largely limited to the form of the new grammatical item. For example, when the passive voice was introduced, typically students were given a list of sentences in the active voice ("The boy broke the window." "The dog bit the man." etc.) along with a model of how to form the passive. ("The window was broken.") The task for the students was to turn the active voice sentences into the passive. Such a procedure does not give students any insights into the communicative contexts in which they should use the passive rather than the active voice.

However, the solution proposed by some–do away with teaching grammar altogether–is no solution. The solution is to present the grammar in a context that makes clear the relationship between the grammatical form and the communicative function. For example, when teaching the passive voice, show WHY the passive voice is used–to place the emphasis on the action rather than the doer, to hide the identity of the doer, etc.

3. Focus on the development of procedural rather than declarative knowledge.

In the field of language learning, **declarative knowledge** is knowing language rules. **Procedural knowledge** is being able to use the knowledge for communication.

Most of us who have been teaching for any time at all know learners who can give a more-or-less standard textbook explanation of a grammatical rule or principle, but who violate the rule when using language communicatively. For example, I have students who can tell me that you have to put an s on the end of the verb when making third person singular declarative statements. When making such statements themselves, however, more often than not, they leave off the s. These students have declarative knowledge (they can state or declare the rule), but not procedural knowledge (they can't or don't use the rule when using the language to communicate).

There are also learners who have procedural but not declarative knowledge. In fact, the vast majority of native speakers fall into this category. Unless they have studied grammar formally, few native speakers can state the rule for third person s.

While declarative knowledge can facilitate the development of procedural knowledge, it is not a necessary and sufficient condition for the development of such knowledge. Students need to develop mastery of target language items, not by memorizing rules, but by using the target items in communicative contexts. This learning through use or learning by doing principle is one that has come to us through the approach to education known as experientialism.

Action

Examine one or two ESL/EFL textbooks and find examples of tasks that exploit the students' procedural knowledge. What grammar items are taught through the procedure? What kind of context is provided for each grammar point? Compare your analysis with someone who has examined other grammar points.

4. Classroom techniques and tasks

In this section, we look at some popular grammar teaching techniques. Most of the techniques can be used either for introducing a new grammar point for the first time or for recycling a point that has already been introduced.

There are various ways in which grammar techniques are classified.

Doughty and Williams (1998) distinguish between techniques in which the grammar point is relatively **implicit** and those in which the point is relatively **explicit**. Ur (1996) places techniques on a continuum from those that focus on accuracy to those that focus on fluency. I distinguish between reproductive techniques in which learners basically reproduce models provided by the teacher or the textbook and creative techniques in which learners have the freedom to use a range of structures to express their meanings.

Input enhancement Input refers to the language that is made available to the learner. **Input enhancement** is a technique for getting students to notice the grammar item that the teacher wants to introduce. With this technique, teachers draw students' attention to items that are meant to be noticed by "flagging" them in some way such as through highlighting, underlining, or coloring. Such awareness-raising techniques are at the accuracy end of Ur's accuracy-fluency continuum.

> **Example**
>
> (For third person singular possessive determiner)
>
> Once upon a time there was a king. *He* had a beautiful young daughter. For *her* birthday, the king gave *her* a golden ball that *she* played with every day. The king and *his* daughter lived near a dark forest …. (Doughty and Williams, 1998)

Consciousness-raising Consciousness-raising activities are designed to get learners to notice a particular grammatical feature or principle. However, learners are not required to use or practice the target item.

> **Example**
>
> Study the following examples, and work out the rule for the correct order of direct and indirect objects in English.
>
> We took a gift for the teacher.
>
> We took the teacher a gift.
>
> He recited a poem for his girlfriend.
>
> He recited his girlfriend a poem.

Grammar dictation **Grammar dictation** (or Dictogloss, as it is called by its creator, Ruth Wajnryb) involves learners collaborating in small groups, actively using their language, and reflecting on the way grammar works in context (thus reinforcing form/function relationships). It also encourages students to reflect on their own output.

The technique is a relatively simple one. The teacher dictates a passage containing target language forms at normal speed. Students take notes and then work in small groups to reconstruct the original passage. The following example is taken from Ruth Wajnryb (1990) who devised the technique.

1.6 Garlic, the great healer

TOPIC	Health and medicine
LANGUAGE POINTS	Time expressions Present perfect simple tense Past simple tense Causal connections
PREPARATION	Bring to class a clove of garlic.
WARM-UP	1 In class, ask for a volunteer for a guessing game. 2 Blindfold the volunteer and ask him or her to try and identify the clove of garlic by touch alone. (This stage of the activity should be carried out with the volunteer's back to the class.) 3 If the student is unable to guess, invite others to try, until the garlic has been identified. 4 Then point out to the students that people often have strong attitudes to garlic. Ask your class how they feel about it, and why.
PRE-TEXT VOCABULARY	**to use** (*v*) to put into action for some purpose **to heal** (*v*) to make well again **natural** (*adj*) found in nature, not artificial **safe** (*adj*) free from risk or danger **antibiotic** (*n*) a medicine that kills bacteria **juice** (*n*) the liquid part of a plant **infection** (*n*) the spread of germs
TEXT	1 All through history people have used garlic for healing. 2 People used it in India and China over 5000 years ago. 3 Because it is a natural medicine, it is a very safe antibiotic. 4 During World War I, for example, doctors used garlic juice because it helped stop infection.

Figure 1 *Books for Teachers: Grammar Dictation* (Oxford University Press, 1990)

Garden path This technique could be considered rather cruel. In order to encourage students to process the target structure somewhat more deeply than they might otherwise do, the task is set up to get students to overgeneralize. It thus leads them into error. This is a technique based on inductive learning. Students study examples of the language and come to an hypothesis or generalization. The generalization is too broad. They are given disconfirming evidence and then have to modify their hypothesis.

> ### Example
>
> *T:* Look at these examples for forming superlative adjectives. (Writes on the board. cute → the cutest; grand → the grandest.) Now make superlatives out of "beautiful," "outrageous," "expensive." … OK, now, what have you written? Sonia?
>
> *S:* Beautifulest, outrageousest, expensivest.
>
> *T:* No, for these words, the superlative forms are "the most beautiful," "the most outrageous," and "the most expensive." Now, I want you to get

into groups and figure out the rule. .... Who thinks they have the answer? Jose's group.

S: *It's about how big the word is. If it's a big word, you use 'most'.*

T: *Big. Hmm. How do we measure the size of words?*

S: *The number of syllables.*

T: *The number of syllables. OK. And how many syllables do "beautiful," "outrageous," and "expensive" have?*

S: *Three.*

T: *Three. OK. So, who can state the rule?*

S: *Adjectives with three syllables form the superlative with "most."*

(Note: This is an invented example based on White, 1998. It is not an authentic classroom extract.)

Action

Design a grammar exercise to highlight the distinction between the simple past and the present perfect, or the distinction between "going to" and "will" for future actions. Use one of the techniques discussed in Section 4.

5. Grammar in the classroom

The purpose of this section is to show you some of the ways that the concepts and techniques already discussed are realized in the classroom. In the first two sequences, Teachers A and B were using the same task, as were Teachers C and D. It is interesting to notice the very different ways in which a set of materials can be exploited by different teachers.

Reflection

Study the following teaching sequences (page 164) in which two different teachers (Teacher A and Teacher B) are using the book *Expressions 1*. Then think about these questions.

1. In what ways are the lessons similar? In what ways are they different?

2. What is the purpose of each teaching lesson?

3. Which is the more effective teacher? Why?

Figure 2 *Expressions 1* (Heinle/Thomson, 2001)

In the extracts, *T* stands for teacher and *S* represents a particular student. *Ss* stands for students.

Teacher A	Teacher B
T: OK, now, look at the picture and the words. Can you see the people?	**T:** Right everybody! Remember these words? Siu Ming?
Ss: Yes, yes.	**S:** Yes.
T: So, now we're going to practice the words. Listen to me and repeat. "Erik is tall." "Erik is tall."	**T:** Tan?
	S: Yes.
Ss: Erik is tall.	**T:** OK. I'm going to say a word, and I want you to make a statement. And NOT one you can see on the page, OK? Um … George. Siu Ming?
T: Again.	
Ss: Erik is tall.	
T: Good! Amy.	**S:** George has a mustache.
Ss: Amy is tall.	**T:** (laughs) Well, yes, that's true, but NOT one that you can see on the page. Try again.
T: Good! Glasses. Jun?	
S: Amy is glasses.	**S:** Um … George is middle-aged.
T: Is?	
S: Has.	
(Continued page 165)	

Teacher A	Teacher B
T: *Yes…?*	**T:** *George is middle-aged. Yes, right. Short hair. Tania.*
S: *Amy has glasses.*	**S:** *Kathi has short hair.*
T: *Amy HAS glasses. Yes, right. Everyone.*	**T:** *She does?* (shakes head)
Ss: *Amy HAS glasses.*	**S:** *Oh … Um… Tony has short hair.*
T: *George.*	**T:** *That's good. Tony has short hair. Repeat everybody! Tony has short hair.*
Ss: *George HAS glasses.*	**Ss:** *Tony has short hair.*
	T: *Good. Tony's almost bald!* (laughs)

Commentary Both teachers are getting students to learn key vocabulary that they will need later in the lesson and to practice making statements about appearance using the simple present tense with "be" and "have." Teacher A is using a classical audiolingual substitution drill. Unfortunately, the teacher is only concerned with grammatical accuracy, not with meaning. When a student makes the grammatically correct, but semantically incorrect statement "Amy is tall," (Amy is NOT tall, she's short!) the teacher responds by saying "Good!"

Teacher B achieves the same goals, but within a communicative context. The students have to make statements that are grammatically correct and semantically true. The exercise is also slightly more creative, in that the students have a choice over who to describe and what aspect of their appearance to focus on.

Action

Imagine that you had just observed these teachers. List the questions you wound like to ask them. Compare your questions with another student.

Reflection

Study the following teaching sequences (page 166) in which two different teachers (Teacher C and Teacher D) are using the book *Expressions 1*. Then think about these questions.

1. In what ways are the lessons similar? In what ways are they different?

2. What is the purpose of each teaching lesson?

3. Which is the more effective teacher? Why?

(A) Look at the chart. When do we use *does/doesn't*? When do we use *do/don't*?

Questions and answers with *do/does*

Do you know George?	Yes, I **do**.
Do they know your boss?	No, they **don't**.
Does he have glasses?	Yes, he **does**.
Does she wear earrings?	No, she **doesn't**.
Does he have curly hair?	No, he **doesn't**. He has straight hair.

(B) Match the questions and answers. Then practice them with a partner.

1. Do you know Lisa?
2. Does she have long hair?
3. Do they wear glasses?
4. Does he have curly hair?
5. Do I know him?

a. No, you don't.
b. Yes, they do.
c. No, he doesn't.
d. Yes, I do.
e. No, she doesn't.

(C) Fill in the missing information. Then ask your partner the questions.

1. _____ your parents wear glasses?
2. _____ you know my English teacher?
3. _____ you know my best friend?
4. _____ your best friend have curly hair?
5. _____ your best friend speak English?
6. _____ your sisters wear earrings?

Figure 3 *Expressions 1* (Heinle/Thomson, 2001)

Teacher C	Teacher D
T: *OK, then, I want you to work in your pairs. Kevin, who's your partner? Jackie, is it?*	**T:** *I want you all to look at the grammar box. What … what does it show us? … Anyone? Alice?*
S: *(nods)*	**S:** *About do/does.*
T: *Good. OK, look at the questions and answers in the, um, yellow box. I want you to practice the questions and answers in your pairs. OK? Kevin— Can you and Jackie do the first one for the class?*	**T:** *OK, good. It shows us when we use the verb do/don't, does/doesn't in questions. Look at this table. (Puts the following table on the board.)*
S: *Do … do you know George?*	
S: *Yes, I do.*	
T: *OK. Excellent. … So—off you go.*	
(Ss practice the questions and answers in pairs).	

do/don't	does/doesn't
I, you, we, they George and Kathi	he, she, Erik,

(Continued page 167)

Teacher C

T: *Everyone finished? ... That sounded pretty good. Now, I'm going to ask you some questions, and I want you to answer me, OK? Sharmy, do you know Kevin?*

S: *Yes, I do.*

T: *Of course you do!* (laughs) *Kevin, do you wear earrings?*

S: *No, I don't.*

T: *How about Sharmy, does she wear earrings?*

S: *Yes, she does.*

T: *Yes, she has great earrings, doesn't she? Um, Lillian, do you have curly hair?*

S: *Yes, I am.*

T: *Yes, I ...?*

S: *Does ... sorry ... do.*

T: *Yes, I do. Yes, I do. Good. OK, so ... when do we use* do/don't *and when do we use* does/doesn't?

(Puts the following table on the board.)

do/don't	does/doesn't
I, Sandra, you, we, your best friend	he, Erik and Amy, your boss, they

T: *Some of these words are in the wrong box. Understand? Yes?*

Ss: (nod)

T: *OK, I want you to work with your partner. Copy the table, but put the words in the right box. Then see if you can add two more items to each box.*

Teacher D

T: *Understand?*

Ss: (nod)

T: *OK, now I want you to look at Exercise B—matching the questions and answers. I want you to put a circle around all of the* do *and* don't *words you can find, and underline all of the* does *and* doesn't *words. OK, Fan? Understand?*

S: (nods)

T: *All right. And I want you to notice the pronouns they go with—I, you, he, she —maybe you can highlight them. OK? Right. Then I want you to match the questions with the right answers, and when you've done that, practice the questions and answers with your partner.*

Commentary Teacher C begins by getting the students to practice the target language (yes/no questions with do/does; asking and answering questions about appearance). She then personalizes the exercise by getting students to answer questions about the appearance of their classmates. She then tries an inductive activity designed to focus students on the appropriate pronouns and noun phrases to match with do/don't and does/doesn't. She does this through a *spot-the-mistake* exercise. This is a good exercise to introduce in a review/recycling lesson, but probably unwise if the grammar point is being introduced for the first time.

Teacher D has the same pedagogical objectives as Teacher C. However, she tackles the task somewhat differently. She focuses the students on the grammar point to be studied, presents the grammar box deductively, and then gets students to find examples of the grammar item. Only after students have studied the grammar point does she get them practicing questions and answers using the point.

Again, we see that two different teachers have exploited a set of materials in very different ways.

Action

Imagine that you have just observed these teachers. List the questions you would like to ask them. Compare your questions with another student.

Reflection

Study the textbook excerpt in Figure 4 and the teaching sequence that follows. Then think about these questions.
1. Is Teacher E an effective teacher? Why or why not?
2. What comment would you make about the teacher's approach to grammar?

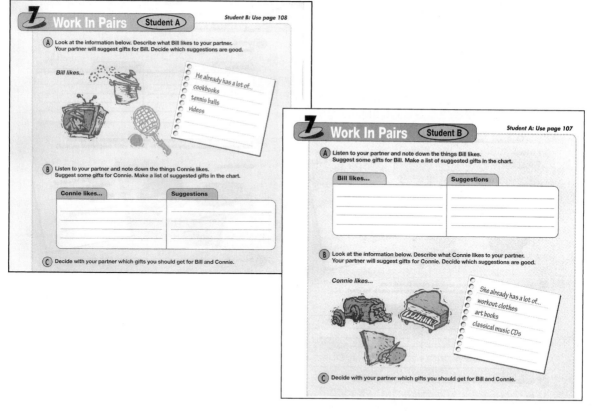

Figure 4 *Expressions 1* (Heinle/Thomson, 2001)

Teacher E

T: *Right, now are you ready to do the info gap task? Yes? We've done lots of these, now, haven't we?*

Ss: *(nod)*

T: *The purpose of this task is to give you more practice in the language we're learning in this unit. What ARE we practicing? Remember? Johnny?*

S: *Talk about what people like.*

T: *Talking about what people like—good. And?*

S: *Talking about gift giving.*

T: *Talking about gift giving. Right. These are our communication goals. And*

what structures do we use to do these things? ... Anyone? ... Yes, Mary?

S: *What do you like? And what do you like doing?*

T: *Great! And we use* like *to talk about things, right? And* like doing *to talk about activities. What about making gift giving suggestions?*

S: *Let's.*

T: *OK, good,* Let's get him a CD, *or* Let's get Tom a golf club. *OK, now WHEN do we give people gifts? WHEN? Yes, Monica?*

S: *Birthday.*

(Continued page 170)

Teacher E

T: Birthdays are good. (Writes *birthdays* on the board.) *Johnny?*

S: New ... new baby.

T: That's a good suggestion. (Writes *new baby* on the board and continues eliciting until there are a number of events on the board.) *OK, now get into your pairs and I want Student A to look at page 107, and Student B to look at page 108. ... (Peers over students' shoulder) Johnny, you're the B student aren't you? You're looking at the wrong page. 108, please. Good. Now, Bill likes the things the A students can see in the picture, but he already has these things. OK? Understand, Monica? Right. So, tell your partner what Bill likes, and your partner will suggest gifts. Write the suggestions in the space, and then decide on the best idea. Oh, Student A—start off by suggesting a reason for buying a gift—look at the board—it's his birthday, he's going away, and so on. Right, off you go.*

(The students complete the task. As they do so, the teacher circulates and monitors. When she hears a mistake, she writes it in a notebook, but doesn't interrupt the students.)

T: OK, I think everybody's finished now.

Are you two finished? Right, good. So, now I want you to do the same thing for Connie. B, tell A what Connie likes. A will make suggestions. Write them down then decide, decide on the best one, OK?

(Again, the teacher circulates and monitors. At one point she is stopped by one pair, listens to their question and says "It's called a subscription—a subscription.")

T: OK, time's up. Let's hear what each pair decided. (Teacher elicits responses from the students and writes them on the board.) *Well, that's great—look at all these interesting gifts. Which of these gifts would YOU like to receive, Johnny? ... Sorry?*

S: The California Fitness Subscription.

T: Yeah, I like that one, too. How about you, Sophie?

(She continues, eliciting students' preferences and writing their names next to the gift.)

T: OK, now, you all did very well, but I noticed a few mistakes creeping in here and there. Look.

(She writes the mistakes from her notebook on the board and gets students to self correct.)

Commentary This teaching sequence is based on an information gap task. The pedagogical objectives are asking about and making suggestions using *Wh-questions* with *do* as well as *like*, *like* +V*ing*. The task illustrates principle two—use tasks that show the relationship between form and function. Unlike the other teaching sequences in this section, the grammar is presented within a context that makes clear to the learners one communicative use for the structure. It also illustrates the way that both declarative knowledge and procedural knowledge can be worked into a pedagogical sequence.

This teacher displays a number of attributes of the effective teacher. She begins by spelling out the purpose of the task, reminding students of the language point and communication goal. She elicits ideas from the students rather than simply telling them, checks to see that students are correctly set up for the task, provides models, monitors the students, acts as an informant for one pair, personalizes the task during the debriefing, and provides corrective feedback at the end of the task.

Action

Select a language function and a grammar point, and design your own information gap activity. For example,

Function: Making a polite request   **Grammar point:** Modal verbs: could, can, may

6.   Conclusion

At the beginning of this chapter, I set out to define grammar and describe the rather unstable place that grammar has occupied on the language teaching stage. At various times it has occupied center stage, while at others it has been relegated to the wings. At one point, it was pushed off the stage completely.

Having provided some background and context, I articulated three key principles to guide the selection, adaptation, or creation of grammar learning opportunities in the classroom. The rest of the chapter exemplified these principles by presenting a range of techniques. In the final part of the chapter, we looked at how the principles have been applied at the level of classroom action.

Further readings

Fotos, S. 2001. Cognitive Approaches to Grammar Instruction. In M. Celce-Murcia (ed.) *Teaching English as a Second or Foreign Language*. Boston, MA: Heinle & Heinle.

Although the first part of the chapter is somewhat theoretical, it contains a very detailed example of a communicative ESL/EFL grammar lesson.

Larsen-Freeman, D. 2001. Grammar. In R. Carter and D. Nunan (eds.) *The Cambridge Guide to Teaching English to Speakers of Other Languages*. Cambridge: Cambridge University Press.

This chapter provides a very clear explanation, with examples of the relationship between grammatical form, meaning, and use.

Ur, P. 1988. *Grammar Practice Activities*. Cambridge: Cambridge University Press.

This book presents many great, practical ideas for introducing specific grammar points.

Helpful Web sites

Virtual English Centre (http://ec.hku.hk/vec/grammar/default.htm)

This site provides links to resources on the Internet for developing grammar teaching materials. It also provides links for students who want to brush up their grammar.

References

Celce-Murcia, M. and E. Olshtain 2000. *Discourse and Context in Language Teaching*. Cambridge: Cambridge University Press.

Doughty, C. and J. Williams (eds.) 1998. *Focus on Form in Classroom Second Language Acquisition*. Cambridge: Cambridge University Press.

Dulay, H. and M. Burt 1973. Should We Teach Children Syntax? *Language Learning*, 23:235–52.

Dulay, H. and M. Burt 1974. Natural Sequences in Child Second Language Acquisition. *Language Learning*, 24:37–53.

Fotos, S. and R. Ellis 1991. Communicating About Grammar: A task-based approach. *TESOL Quarterly*, 25(4):605–628.

Krashen, S. 1981. *Second Language Acquisition and Second Language Learning*. Oxford: Pergamon.

Krashen, S. 1982. *Principles and Practice in Second Language Acquisition*. Oxford: Pergamon.

Larsen-Freeman, D. 2001. Grammar. In R. Carter and D. Nunan (eds.) *The Cambridge Guide to Teaching English to Speakers of Other Languages*. Cambridge: Cambridge University Press.

Richards, J. J. Platt, and H. Weber 1985. *Longman Dictionary of Applied Linguistics*. London: Longman.

Ur, P. 1996. *A Course in Language Teaching: Practice and Theory*. Cambridge: Cambridge University Press.

Chapter **Nine**

Discourse

Michael McCarthy, University of Nottingham (United Kingdom)
Steve Walsh, Queen's University of Belfast (Northern Ireland)

Goals

At the end of this chapter, you should be able to:

✔ **understand** how discourse is different from other core aspects of language.

✔ **see** how discourse analysis changes the way we think of language learning.

✔ **understand** how the way teachers communicate with learners can affect learning.

✔ **design** and edit language teaching dialogues and other spoken materials so that they focus more on discourse and are more natural and realistic.

1. What is discourse?

The study of **discourse** is the study of the relationship between language and its contexts of use. Grammarians study sentences, pieces of language taken out of context. The rules for using the English past tense, for example, can be stated generally, without reference to any particular context or situation. When we study discourse, however, we are interested in why someone chooses a past tense in a particular situation when addressing a particular listener (e.g., *I might say "I wanted to ask you a question."* where the past tense expresses politeness or indirectness). So discourse is concerned with speakers and listeners and normally, with extended stretches of language (e.g., a whole conversation, a story, a phone call) rather than single sentences. Important questions in the study of discourse are:

- What is the relationship between the speakers and how is this reflected in their language?

- What are the goals of the communication (e.g., to tell a story, to teach something, to buy something)?

- How do speakers manage topics and signal to one another their perception of the way the interaction is developing? How do they open and close conversations? How do they make sure they get a turn to speak?

All of these questions are relevant to the language teaching classroom. We can study discourse in written and spoken texts (see McCarthy, 2001, for a summary). However, most discourse analysis is concerned with speaking, and in this chapter we focus on speaking, especially speaking in the classroom, where the talk that takes place between teachers and learners is one of the most important ways that learners can gain access to the language they are trying to learn.

Reflection

1. When you studied foreign languages or your own language at school, did your lessons and coursebooks concentrate on grammar and sentences, or did you look at longer stretches of language (e.g., phone calls, stories, shop interactions)?

2. In what ways do you think language learning would be different if teachers and coursebooks concentrated more on discourse and less on fine grammar points?

3. In typical language lessons you have experienced as a student, how much opportunity did *you* get to talk, rather than listening to the teacher talking?

2. Background to the teaching of discourse

In the past, most language teaching was done through invented sentences or invented dialogues, and real discourse (in the form of real conversations on tape or transcribed) was rarely used in classrooms or materials. This often led to very artificial models of language, which did not resemble real-world talk or the type of language learners are exposed to when they try to use English outside of the classroom. However, two important approaches to the study of spoken discourse in recent years have influenced language teaching and brought a focus on real language into the classroom and teaching materials: exchange structure and conversation analysis (known as CA).

Exchange structure

Exchange structure analysis was originally based on mother-tongue classrooms. Sinclair and Coulthard (1975) recorded teachers and pupils interacting in class and produced a model for understanding classroom discourse. They found that teachers divided their lessons into different phases of activity (called transactions). The transactions were marked at their beginnings and ends by discourse markers such as *okay, so, right, now.* Discourse markers are signals people give one another which reflect how they are monitoring the conversation (e.g., in English we might say *anyway,* or *okay then* when we want to signal that we think the conversation should come to an end). During classroom transactions, Sinclair and Coulthard observed that there were three basic kinds of exchanges of language: (1) question-and-answer sequences (2) pupils responding to teachers' directions, and (3) pupils listening to the teacher giving information. These exchanges consisted of different numbers of moves: the question-answer sequences, for example, consisted of a minimum of three moves, the question (or Initiation), the answer (or Response) and the teacher's feedback (or Follow-up). Here is an example from a second language classroom:

> **Example**
>
> **Teacher:** So, can you read question two, Junya?   *I*
>
> **Junya:** (Reading from book) Where was Sabina when this happened?   *R*
>
> **Teacher:** Right, yes, where was Sabina.   *F*
>   In Unit 10, where was she?   *I*
>
> **Junya:** Er, go out …   *R*
>
> **Teacher:** She went out, yes.   *F*
>
> *(Walsh, 2001)*

The teacher marks the new phase of activity (the transaction) with *so*, then initiates a question (I), the pupil responds (R) and the teacher follows up (F), and then the IRF sequence is repeated. Notice that the teacher's follow-up evaluates the learner's answer (*Right, yes*); such feedback is important to the learner. Classroom talk of this kind takes place every day all around the world. Conversations outside of the classroom also have these same IRF patterns, but speakers do not usually evaluate one another's performances. A typical real-world exchange is:

> **Example**
>
> | **A:** What's the last day of the month? | *I* |
> | **B:** Friday. | *R* |
> | **A:** Friday. | *F* |
> | We'll invoice you on Friday. | *I* |
> | **B:** That would be great. | *R* |
> | **A:** And fax it over to you. | *I* |
> | **B:** Er, well I'll come and get it. | *R* |
> | **A:** Okay. | *F* |
>
> (CANCODE spoken corpus)

In the world outside the classroom, responses and follow-ups are not usually reactions to test-questions (speaker A is not testing speaker B on what day it is, unlike the teacher in the first example who was testing the learners' understanding), but show that the speakers have understood one another and are satisfied with the way the interaction is progressing (*Friday/ that would be great/ okay*).

For language teachers, understanding the discourse of the classroom itself is crucial, for we teach discourse *through* discourse with our learners. This is another way of saying that in many parts of the world, the main exposure to discourse in English that learners will have is in the classroom itself, via the teacher. A number of studies have compared the discourse of the classroom with "real" communication (e.g., Nunan, 1987). But as van Lier says (1988, p. 267), "the classroom is part of the real world, just as much as the airport, the interviewing room, the chemical laboratory, the beach and so on."

What is important to note about classroom discourse is:

- All classroom discourse is goal-oriented.
- The prime responsibility for what is said in the classroom lies with the teacher.
- Teaching goals and language use are inextricably linked.
- Exchange structure analysis is important for two reasons:

1. It enables us to understand interaction in the classroom and its special nature.
2. It enables us to model spoken language in the world outside the classroom, suggesting ways of constructing dialogues for teaching, role-plays for practicing conversation, etc.

Conversation analysis

Conversation analysis (CA) is a way of looking at the detailed, local aspects of interaction and the way participants in a conversation work hard to make it successful. (See Pomerantz and Fehr, 1997.) CA is concerned with turn-taking, i.e., how speakers manage to take turns without interrupting one another, how they select who shall speak next (Sacks et al, 1974), and how they show they are listening (e.g., by using backchannels, small noises and words such as *uhum, yeah, right, mm*). It is also concerned with **adjacency pairs,** how two bits of language fit or do not fit appropriately with each other. For example, a greeting normally prompts a greeting in return, congratulations normally prompt thank-yous, etc. When the two pair-parts do not fit (what CA analysts call a **dispreferred sequence**), speakers have to work hard to repair potential problems. For instance, if I invite you to dinner and you have to decline, do you just say "No!" or do you say something like "I'd love to come, but I'm busy Friday. I'm so sorry." CA is also concerned with openings and closings of conversations (Schegloff and Sacks, 1973) and with topic management (i.e., how speakers launch new topics, change the subject, decide what to talk about, etc.) (Gardner, 1987). A typical CA analysis is very detailed and complex. Things such as pauses, laughter, false starts (indicated by =) and *ers,* unfinished utterances, overlaps (indicated by ^{L}) and points where speakers continue something they started earlier (indicated by +) and backchannels (*yeah*) are all considered important.

> **Example**
>
> (On the telephone, confirming delivery of an order from a company.)
>
> **Speaker A:** *They'll be finished by mid-morning tomorrow.*
>
> **Speaker B:** *Right.*
>
> **Speaker A:** *That means we could pack them up and have them delivered tomorrow afternoon if there's going to be somebody there Saturday.*
>
> **Speaker B:** *Oh right. Oh well, Jim will be pleased about that, George, I'll= I'll let him know all that and I'll get him to ring you before+*
>
> **Speaker A:** ^{L}*If you= if you could.*
>
> **Speaker B:** *+as soon as possible obviously because [Speaker A: Yeah] er you need to know to arrange things.*

Speaker A: *That's right.*

Speaker B: *Right. Leave it with me, George.*

Speaker A: *Okay.*

Speaker B: *Okay?*

Speaker A: *Thanks.*

Speaker B: *Thanks a lot.*

Speaker A: *Bye.*

Speaker B: *Bye.*

CA, like exchange structure, gives us insights for language teaching:

- Teachers and learners have to deal with the special turn-taking circumstances of the classroom (e.g., only teachers normally select the next speaker, it is difficult to interrupt, teachers often do not wait long enough for students to answer, etc.).

- Some adjacency pairs will be easy to learn (e.g., the ritualized ones like greeting-greeting, offer-accept), but dispreferred sequences will require skill and practice (Dörnyei and Thurrell, 1994).

- Talking about different topics in a conversation class is difficult; much depends on motivation, familiarity with the topic, etc. Whose topics should be used, the teacher's, the coursebook topics, or the learners' own?

Teaching and learning as discourse

A way of looking at the talk that takes place in the classroom described by Steve Walsh (2001) helps teachers to evaluate their own discourse with their learners using the Self-Evaluation of Teacher Talk (SETT) procedure. We said above that understanding classroom discourse is vital because it is in the classroom that many learners get their main exposure to the target language.

In the SETT procedure, the teaching of discourse and the discourse teachers and learners engage in come together. Walsh's SETT model is based on different modes, or ways of talking, which have clearly defined teaching goals and distinctive discourse features. As the focus of a lesson changes, the pedagogic goals change, and so do the discourse modes.

Walsh's four modes of classroom discourse are:

1. Managerial mode
2. Materials mode
3. Skills and systems mode
4. Classroom context mode

The modes are observed through looking at turn-taking and topic management (see the section on CA, p. 177), and by looking at the IRF patterns (see Exchange structure section, p. 175) in stretches of classroom discourse. Observing the different modes can help teachers understand more fully the discourse of their own classes. In particular, observing different modes can help teachers understand the need to use teacher talk which is *appropriate*. Rather than trying to minimize teacher talking time (TTT), teachers need to learn how to adjust their use of language to their teaching aims. At times, high levels of teacher talk and tightly controlled turn-taking will be appropriate; at other times, depending on the teacher's goal, learners may be given more freedom to control both the direction of the discourse and its content.

Managerial mode

Managerial mode occurs most often at the beginning of lessons, as illustrated in Extract 1:

Extract 1

Teacher: *Ok, we're going to look today at ways to improve your writing and at ways which can be more effective for you and if you look at the writing which I gave you back you will see that I've marked any little mistakes and eh I've also marked places where I think the writing is good and I haven't corrected your mistakes because the best way in writing is for you to correct your mistakes so what I have done I have put little circles and inside the circles there is something which tells you what kind of mistake it is so Miguel would you like to tell me one of the mistakes that you made?*

- Here we see an extended teacher turn and no learner turns.
- The focus is on the business side of the lesson (how mistakes are corrected, etc.).
- There is repetition, and the teacher handing over the exchange to the learners at the end of the teacher's monologue.
- The teacher uses discourse markers *okay* and *so,* which are essential signals that help the learners to follow the talk.

Materials mode

In this mode, pedagogic goals and teacher-learner discourse flow from the materials being used:

(The teacher is doing a blank-filling exercise with the students.)

Teacher: *ok ... now ... see if you can find the words that are suitable in these phrases* (reading) *in the world cup final of 1994 Brazil XXX Italy 2 3 2 and in a XXX shoot-out ... what words would you put in there?*

Student A: *beat*

Teacher: *what beat Italy 3 2 yeah in?*

Student A: *in a penalty shoot-out*

Teacher: *a what?*

Student A: *in a penalty shoot-out*

Teacher: *in a penalty shoot-out, very good, in a penalty shoot-out ...* (reading) *after 90 minutes THE?*

Students: *the goals goals goals* (mispronounced)

Teacher: *the match was ... what?*

Student B: *match*

Students: *nil nil*

Teacher: *nil nil* (reading) *and it remained the same after 30 minutes OF?*

Student C: *extra time*

Teacher: *extra time, very good, Emerson.*

- Here the learners are completing a blank-filling exercise on sports vocabulary and the teacher directs the students' contributions; the talk is almost entirely determined by the materials.

- The sequence is classic IRF, the most economical way to manage the interaction, where each turn by the teacher is an evaluation of a learner's contribution and an initiation of another exchange.

- The discourse evolves from the material, which determines turn-taking and topic.

Skills and systems mode

In this mode, the teaching goals are related to language practice (phonology, grammar, vocabulary) or language skill (reading, listening, writing, speaking), and the IRF sequence frequently occurs. The management of topic and turn-taking lies with the teacher. Pedagogic goals focus on accuracy rather than fluency, and the teacher's aim is to get learners to manipulate the L2 system.

(For an explanation of the symbols and capitalization used here, see Appendix page 193.)

> **Extract 3**
>
> **Teacher:** he went to what do we call these things the shoes with wheels=
>
> **Student 1:** =ah skates=
>
> **Student 2:** =roller skates=
>
> **Teacher:** =ROLler skates roller skates so [he went]
>
> **Student 1:** [he went] to=
>
> **Student 3:** =roller SKATing=
>
> **Teacher:** =SKATing=
>
> **Student 1:** =he went to=
>
> **Teacher:** =not to just he went [roller skating he went roller skating]
>
> **Student 1:** [roller skating he went roller skating]=

Here, the teacher's goal is to get the learners to use irregular simple past forms (e.g., *went*). In skills and systems mode, the focus is the language system or a skill. Learning is typically achieved through controlled turn-taking and topic selection, determined by the teacher. Learners respond to teacher prompts in an endeavor to produce accurate utterances.

Classroom context mode

In classroom context mode, opportunities for genuine, real-world-type discourse are frequent and the teacher plays a less prominent role, taking a back seat and allowing learners all the space they need. The principal role of the teacher is to listen and support the interaction, which often takes on the appearance of a casual conversation outside the classroom.

In Extract 4, the teacher is working with six advanced adult learners. The teacher's aim is to generate discussion before doing a cloze exercise on the subject of poltergeists.

> **Extract 4**
>
> **Student 1:** =ahh nah the one thing that happens when a person dies my mother used to work with old people and when they died ...the last thing that went out was the hearing about this person =
>
> **Teacher:** =aha
>
> **Student 1:** so I mean even if you are unconscious or on drugs or something I mean it's probably still perhaps can hear what's happened

Student 2: *but it gets=*

Students: *but it gets/there are=*

Student 1: *=I mean you have seen so many operation and so you can imagine and when you are hearing the sounds of what happens I think you can get a pretty clear picture of what's really going on there=*

Student 3: *=yeah=*

Here the turn-taking is almost entirely managed by the learners, with competition for the floor and turn gaining, holding and passing, typical features of natural conversation. Topic shifts are also managed by the learners, with the teacher responding more as an equal partner. Teacher feedback shifts from form-focused to content-focused and error correction is minimal, and there is genuine communication rather than a display or test of knowledge.

Reflection

1. What sorts of problems do you think learners have when they want to take a turn in a conversation in a new language they are learning, especially if they are conversing with native speakers?

2. How were the four SETT modes (pages 179-182) distributed in typical language lessons you experienced in school? Was there too much or too little of any of the four modes?

3. Principles for teaching discourse

1. Help learners achieve discourse skills *through* discourse.

The classroom is where most learning happens for most learners around the world. In the classroom exchanges, turn-taking, topic management, and all the things we can observe in everyday language outside the classroom are present, but in different and special ways. Learn to observe the discourse process in the classroom.

2. Remember that the classroom is not the outside world; it has its own discourse.

Sometimes it will be appropriate to engage in typical teacher-talk (e.g., asking questions to which you already know the answer, evaluating the students' responses), other times it will be advisable to be more natural and genuinely communicative (getting students to exchange real information about themselves and their worlds). Plan lessons to create a balance between language as *display* (i.e., skills and systems mode of discourse) and language as genuine communication (e.g., listening to authentic recordings, allowing relaxed, natural conversation without constant error correction).

3. Wherever possible, make language dialogues and classroom activities as natural as you can.

Listen to people speaking, in English or in any other language, and observe all the time! If possible, make transcripts of real conversations (starting with very simple ones) from tape recordings you have made. You may not wish to use dialogues in class that look as messy as our example of a CA analysis, so editing the script might be the best way. Alternatively, edit coursebook dialogues by adding small items that will make them seem more natural. Make sure any dialogue you use from your textbook has natural patterns of IRF that occur in the real world. Make sure dialogues contain natural features such as contractions (e.g., *I'm* instead of *I am*), tags (You're from Taiwan, *aren't you?*), backchannels (*uhuh, mm*), discourse markers (*right, well*) and so on, and add them where you feel they are unnaturally absent.

4. Use recordings of spoken language.

These can either come from published sources (e.g., Carter and McCarthy, 1997) or from radio/TV/Web casts. Or make your own in natural situations, building activities around them, which will help raise awareness of discourse in different contexts. These extracts need only be brief snapshots of dialogue, rather than whole conversations. Dramas, soap operas, talk-shows, and other types of discourse offer good data where natural, casual conversation is not available. Set up role-plays and simulations in class which will enable everyone to have something to say, and where students can prepare what they are going to say to lessen the stress of having to speak spontaneously.

5. Create conditions in the classroom where real-world discourse is most likely to be encouraged.

Sometimes you will want to move from a focus on grammar, vocabulary, pronunciation, etc. to a more relaxed, natural "conversation class." Make sure the classroom is set up to facilitate this. Is everyone facing *you,* or are they able to look at one another? Where have the topics come from? You? The coursebook? The students? Are the students allowed to be more relaxed, with you taking a back seat temporarily?

6. Make sure your learners are exposed to the language they will need to manage their own discourses, both in and out of class.

Help learners to become aware of how discourse markers such as *right, good, now, you see,* etc. are used. Practice ways of opening and closing conversations in different contexts. Expose your learners to typical ways of responding and following up, which are different from your evaluative responses to their performances (e.g., responding appropriately to good/bad news, expressing interest, frustration, etc.).

7. Observe yourself and your learners in class; remember, in trying to *teach* discourse you yourself and your learners are engaged in a discourse.

Monitoring the discourse of your classroom is central to being a good teacher. Record yourself occasionally, monitor how evenly turn-taking has been distributed among the students. And monitor your own turns: do you give enough *waiting time* for students to answer questions, or do you always jump in and fill awkward silences or immediately correct errors and slips before they have the chance to compose or recast what they want to say? Do you engage in too many long monologues? Use SETT to monitor the different modes that occur in your classes.

1. Record five minutes of English conversation (either in real life, or from a broadcast or Web cast source such as a soap opera or talk-show) and transcribe it in the way the conversational analysis sample (page 177) is transcribed in this chapter.

2. What features described in the sections on exchange structure and conversational analysis (pages 175-178) can you observe in your transcript

(e.g., IRF patterns, topic management, discourse markers, openings/closings, adjacency pairs, etc.)?

3. How could your transcript be used in a class? Consider whether you would need audio/video as well as the printed script, whether you should edit it first, and how, and what the script could be used for.

4. Classroom techniques and tasks

We noted earlier that the IRF pattern was a powerful means by which conversations in and out of the class are organized. Among the problems associated with teaching the IRF structure are the following:

1. In many classes learners only get the opportunity to perform the R (responding mode) and have little opportunity to initiate (I) and even less to follow up (F).

In Extract 5, for example, the teacher is working with a class of preintermediate learners. Her aim is to revise and consolidate sports vocabulary. The discourse structure is classic IR(F); learners have no opportunity to initiate or follow-up and simply respond to the teacher's prompts.

> **Extract 5**
>
> **Teacher:** Ken what is the past of win?
>
> **Student 1:** won/won/won
>
> **Teacher:** won good and the past participle?
>
> **Student 1:** won/won
>
> **Teacher:** won good lose?
>
> **Student 2:** lost [lost]
>
> **Teacher:** [lost] lost beat?=
>
> **Students:** =beat beaten=
>
> **Teacher:** =beaten good lead?=

2. There is not a simple list of expressions one can teach for initiating or for responding or for following up, as appropriate moves will depend on the local context.

3. Teachers control the boundaries, openings, and closings of transactions, so discourse markers are rarely used by learners.

In Extract 6, the teacher is working with a group of upper-intermediate students. The discussion centers around the concept of world peace, and here the teacher is trying to elicit the phrase *military force*. Note how the turn-taking is tightly controlled by the teacher, indicated by frequent interruptions (marked = in the transcript). The teacher, pursuing his pedagogic goal of eliciting vocabulary, tightly controls the turn-taking in order to steer the discourse towards the target language, *military force*. Learners have little opportunity in this context to control either the direction or content of the discourse.

> **Extract 6**
>
> **Teacher:** =what do we call I'm going to try and get the class to tell you what this word is that you're looking for ... er we talk about military (claps hands) ... military what?
>
> **Student 1:** ((1))=
>
> **Teacher:** =like fight=
>
> **Student 2:** =kill=
>
> **Teacher:** =no not [kill]
>
> **Student 2:** [action] action=
>
> **Teacher:** =no ((2)) military?=
>
> **Students:** =power=
>
> **Teacher:** =power think of another word military?
>
> **Students:** ((3))force=
>
> **Teacher:** =so she believes in a FORCE for?=
>
> **Student 3:** =that guides our lives=
>
> **Teacher:** =that guides our lives=

Despite these problems, some teaching materials do focus on the structure of exchanges and offer practice in the different move-types. An example of material focusing on responding moves, is the following example from *Gateways 2* (Oxford University Press, 1998), a coursebook for adults and young adults. The students are invited to think about why Conversation 1 is less successful than Conversation 2. Conversation 2 has more productive responding moves, which answer the other speaker's questions but also expand a little; this is presented to the learners as a strategy which they can both observe and practice in a pair-work activity which follows it:

Conversation Management

Strategies: Keeping the conversation going–answer and add.

Read the two conversations. Notice that in Conversation 1, B kills the conversation each time he or she speaks. How? In Conversation 2, B keeps the conversation going each time. How?

Conversation 1

A: Gee, it's nice to see you, Pat. So, tell me, what are you doing now?

B: I'm working.

A: Oh, where?

B: In the travel department at American Express.

A: That's great! Do you like it?

B: Yeah.

A: Well ... that's good. Are you still taking classes?

B: Yes.

A: Uh ... that's nice. Good luck.

B: Thanks.

Conversation 2

A: Gee, it's nice to see you, Pat. So, tell me, what are you doing now?

B: I'm working in the travel department at American Express.

A: That's great. Do you like it?

B: Oh, yeah. The work is really interesting, and I get to travel.

A: Well, that's terrific. Are you still taking classes?

B: Uh-huh. I'm going for my master's degree in business.

A: Hey, that's great! Good luck.

B: Thanks. Take care.

Figure 1 *Gateways Student Book 2* (Oxford University Press, 1998)

Figure 2 deals with discourse markers, which are taught as vocabulary items, and the term *discourse marker* is explicitly used and explained. A selection of markers is presented, and then there are several exercises and activities to practice them.

Discourse markers in speech

Discourse markers are words and phrases which organize, comment on, or in some way frame what we are saying or writing. An example from spoken language is *well*. For example,

A: So, you live in Boston?

B: Well, *near Boston.*

Well here shows that the speaker is aware he or she is changing the direction of the conversation in some way (not giving the expected "yes" answer). In other words, well is a comment on what is being said. Another example is how teachers use words like *right* and *OK* to organize what is happening in a classroom. For example, "*Right/OK,* let's have a look at exercise 3."

Here are some common markers which organize the different stages of a conversation.

- *Now,* what shall we do next? *So,* would you like to come to the table now, please?
- *Good,* I'll ring you on Thursday, then. *Well then,* what was it you want to talk about?
- *Now then,* I want you to look at this picture. [said by someone in control of the conversation, e.g., a teacher]
- *Fine/Great,* let's leave it at that, then, shall we?

In these minidialogues, the markers in bold *modify* or *comment* on what is being said:

> **A:** It's cold, isn't it?
>
> **B:** Yeah.
>
> **A:** **Mind you,** it is November, so it's not surprising. (an afterthought, used like however)
>
> **A:** It's quite a problem.
>
> **B:** **Listen/Look**, why don't you let me sort it out?
>
> **A:** Would you? Thanks a lot. (introducing a suggestion/point)

Figure 2 *English Vocabulary in Use, Upper Intermediate* (Cambridge University Press, 2001)

In some materials, writers have attempted to incorporate the principles of adjacency pairs into activities without actually using the linguistic terminology, which might be off-putting for students. In the next example from a beginner's course for adults, the focus is on giving "dispreferred" responses, in this case declining invitations, without being too blunt and causing offence. The learners have listened to an audiotape and are now set a task based on the conversations they have heard.

Here are parts of the conversations. Fill the spaces with one of these words or phrases.

listen   a pity   perhaps   probably   sorry   sure

1.

  SATOSHI: *John, this is Satoshi. Can you come to the party next Friday?*

  JOHN: *No, I can't. ....*

  SATOSHI: *Oh, that's ....*

2.

  PETER: *Mayumi! How are you?*

  MAYUMI: *I'm fine. ...., can you come to our party on Friday?*

  PETER: *I'm not .... I'm very busy this week. ....*

  MAYUMI: *Can you come to the party on Friday?*

  Lucy: *I don't really know. ....*

Listen to these conversations again and check your answers.

The expressions provided for the blank-filling task are ones which enable the speaker to soften his/her refusal or uncertainty on being invited. The task is followed up by another exercise in providing the second parts of adjacency pairs. Note that the instructions explicitly ask the student to give reasons why they are refusing; this is very important, since just saying *no* will probably create offence.

Quick Check

A. Answer these invitations.

1. Can you come to the party next weekend? (Say *yes.*)
2. Can you come to the cinema on Monday? (Say *no* and then say why you can't.)
3. Can you come for lunch tomorrow? (Say *not* sure and give a reason.)
4. Can you come to the international conference in Paris? (Say *yes.*)
5. Do you want to go on holiday in August? (Say *no* and give a reason.)

True to Life, p. 94

5. Discourse in the classroom

Teachers play an important role in *shaping* classroom discourse and in maximizing opportunities for learning. Rather than accepting a learner's first response, for example, teachers can construct genuine opportunities for learning. They do this through careful control of their own language and by helping learners to say what they mean. Note that this is not simply a matter of reducing the quantity of teacher talk, but more a case of using teacher talk which is appropriate.

Reflection

1. Can you think of stages in a lesson when it would be considered normal to have high teacher talking time (TTT) and others when low TTT would be desirable?

2. What strategies can teachers use to help learners express themselves? For example, *feeding in* new vocabulary as and when it is needed.

3. Based on your own experience as a language learner, which teacher strategies seem to be effective?

In Extract 7 (p. 191), the teacher is discussing amusing incidents at school with a group of intermediate adult learners. The actual interaction is presented on the left and the teacher's own commentary on the lesson on the right.

Note how the teacher is helping the learner to construct meaning:

• In turn 5, the teacher pushes the learner to extend his contribution by asking for clarification (*So what happened, what made it funny?*).

• In turn 7 (and the commentary), the teacher clarifies a learner's contribution for the whole class.

• In turn 9, the teacher checks for confirmation and feeds in the phrase *closer relationship* for the whole class.

• Throughout, the teacher is aware of the need to shape the learner's contribution in order to help the learner's self-expression and clarify for the rest of the class.

Lesson transcript

1. **T:** what was the funniest thing that happened to you at school (1) Tang?

2. **S1:** funniest thing?

3. **T:** the funniest

4. **S1:** the funniest thing I think out of school was go to picnic

5. **T:** go on a picnic? So what happened what made it funny?

6. **S1:** go to picnic we made playing or talking with the teacher more closely because in the school we have a line you know he the teacher and me the student=

7. **T:** =so you say there was a gap or a wall between the teacher and the students so when you=

8. **S1:** if you go out of the school you went together with more (gestures 'closer' with hands)=

9. **T:** =so you had a closer relationship [outside the school]

10. **L1:** [yeah yeah]

Teacher's commentary

Basically he's explaining that on a picnic there wasn't this gap that there is in a class-room—psychological gap—that's what I'm drawing out of him.

There's a lot of scaffolding being done by me in this monitoring, besides it being managerial, there's a lot of scaffolding because I want to get it flowing, I want to encourage them, keep it moving as it were. I'm clarifying to the class what he's saying because I know in an extended turn—a broken turn—and it's not exactly fluent and it's not articulate—I try to re-interpret for the benefit of the class so that they're all coming with me at the same time and they all understand the point being made by him.

Using Extract 7,

1. paraphrase what you think the learner is saying and if possible, compare with a classmate.

2. comment on the ways in which the teacher clarifies the learner's contribution.

3. what is the value of allowing learners to "struggle" with what they are trying to say?

6. Conclusion

In this chapter, we have examined two approaches to analyzing discourse: the study of exchanges and conversation analysis. Exchange analysis shows us how speakers initiate, respond, and follow up; how they divide their discourse into longer segments (transactions); and how they mark these using discourse markers. Conversation analysts study turn-taking, adjacency pairs, topic management, discourse marking, and other local features of talk.

The language class is unique: we are engaged in a discourse with our learners in order to help them achieve satisfactory discourse in the target language. But if we want directly to teach aspects of discourse, how should we do this–through teaching specific items (such as discourse markers), by practicing appropriate responses and follow-ups in context? Which topics should teachers and learners talk about, and whose topics?

Above all, teachers and learners are always engaged in the discourse of the classroom, and the teacher is in control. Being aware of what you say in the class and how you help your learners say what they want to say is very important. The SETT framework will help you to be aware of what you say as a teacher, how the four classroom modes are appropriate to different goals, and how you can improve your management of the interaction to produce the best results.

Transcription system

The transcription system is adapted from van Lier (1988) and Johnson (1995).

T:	-	*teacher*
L:	-	*learner (not identified)*
L1: L2: etc.	-	*identified learner*
LL:	-	*several learners speaking at once or the whole class*
/ok/ok/ok/	-	*overlapping or simultaneous utterances by more than one learner*
[do you understand?]		
[I see] or	-	*overlap between teacher and learner*
= or +	-	*latching: a turn continues, or one turn follows another without any pause.*
...	-	*pause of one second or less marked by three periods.*
(4 sec) (pause)	-	*silence; length (where specified) given in seconds*
((4 sec))	-	*a stretch of unintelligible speech with the length given in seconds*
Paul, Peter, Mary	-	*capitals are only used for proper nouns*
?	-	*rising intonation, not necessarily a question*
acCUSED	-	*indicates that a syllable or word is given extra stress*

Further readings

Cook, G. 1989. *Discourse.* Oxford: Oxford University Press.

> This book is a good introduction to discourse, pitched for teachers in training and others new to the area.

Drew, P. and J. Heritage (eds.) 1992. *Talk at Work: Interaction in institutional settings.* Cambridge: Cambridge University Press.

> This book gives a good cross section of typical CA investigations and shows CA techniques in operation.

McCarthy, M. 1991. *Discourse Analysis for Language Teachers.* Cambridge: Cambridge University Press.

> McCarthy explores in more detail the concepts found in Cook's introduction.

van Lier, L. 1996. *Interaction in the Language Curriculum: Awareness, Autonomy and Authenticity.* New York, NY: Longman.

> This gives a useful introduction to the ways in which teachers can influence classroom interaction and its effects on language learning.

Useful Web sites

ERIC (Educational Resources Information Centre) (http://www.cal.org/ericcll), links to Digest: Discourse Analysis for Language Teachers (http://www.cal.org/ericcll/digest/0107demo.html)

> ERIC is an invaluable source of information.

Conversation Analysis.Net (http://www.conversation-analysis.net) Ethno/CA News (http://www.pscw.uva.nl/emca)

> Sponsored by newsgroups dedicated to conversation analysis, these are sites that have information about publications, conferences, research in conversation analysis, and membership details.

US Department of State Office of English Language Programs (http://exchanges.state.gov/education/engteaching/onlineca.htm)

> This is an excellent general site for teaching resources. Use their search box to search for "classroom discourse" or "discourse."

References

_____, CANCODE spoken corpus. Cambridge: Cambridge University Press.

Carter, R. A. and M. J. McCarthy 1997 *Exploring Spoken English*. Cambridge: Cambridge University Press.

Dörnyei, Z. and S. Thurrell 1994. Teaching Conversational Skills Intensively: Course Content and Rationale. *ELT Journal,* 48(1):40–49.

Gardner, R. 1987. The Identification and Role of Topic in Spoken Interaction. *Semiotica,* 65(1/2):129–41.

Heritage, J. 1995. Conversational Analysis: Methodological Aspects. In U. Quasthoff (ed.) *Aspects of Oral Communication*. Berlin: Walter de Gruyter.

Johnson, K. E. 1995. *Understanding Communication in Second Language Classrooms*. Cambridge: Cambridge University Press.

Lantolf, J. P. 2000. *Sociocultural Theory and Second Language Learning*. Oxford: Oxford University Press.

McCarthy, M. J. 2001. Discourse. In R.A. Carter and D. Nunan (eds.) *Teaching English to Speakers of Other Languages*. Cambridge: Cambridge University Press.

McCarthy, M. J., D. Slade, and C. Matthiessen (2002) Discourse Analysis. In N. Schmitt. (ed.) *An Introduction to Applied Linguistics*. London: Edward Arnold.

McCarthy, M. J., and F. O'Dell 2001. *English Vocabulary in Use. Upper Intermediate*. New Edition. Cambridge: Cambridge University Press.

Nunan, D. 1987. Communicative Language Teaching: Making it work. *English Language Teaching Journal,* 4(1/2):136–145.

Pomerantz, A. and B. J. Fehr 1997. Conversation Analysis: An approach to the study of social action as sense making practices. In T. A.van Dijk (ed.) *Discourse as Social Interaction*. London: Sage.

Sacks, H., E. A. Schegloff, and G. Jefferson 1974. A simplest systematics for the organisation of turn-taking for conversation. *Language* 50 (4): 696-735.

Schegloff, E. A. and H. Sacks 1973 Opening up closings. *Semiotica 8* (4): 289-327.

Seedhouse, P. 1996. *Learning Talk: A study of the interactional organization of the L2 classroom from a CA institutional discourse perspective*. Unpublished Ph.D thesis, University of York.

Sinclair, J. McH. and R. M. Coulthard 1975. *Towards an Analysis of Discourse*. Oxford: Oxford University Press.

van Lier, L. 1988. *The Classroom and the Language Learner*. London: Longman.

Walsh, S. 2001. *Characterizing Teacher Talk in the Second Language Classroom: A process approach of reflective practice*. Unpublished Ph.D. thesis, Queen's University of Belfast, Northern Ireland.

Supporting the learning process

T his section deals with ways of integrating and supporting the ideas presented in the first two sections of the book. The first chapter looks at a unique application of communicative language teaching called content-based instruction. In this section, you will find a recycling and integration of many of the ideas presented in the preceding section.

Coursebooks are a staple in most classrooms, providing guidance, coherence, and practical ideas. In Chapter 11, you will find ways of using coursebooks to support your teaching. A similar treatment for computer-assisted language teaching is presented in the chapter that follows. The next two chapters also form a pair. Chapter 13 introduces the idea that in addition to focusing on language, the classroom should focus on the learning process. Helping learners identify and develop their own learning styles and strategies is fundamental to the idea of autonomy, which is the theme of the chapter that follows.

The final chapter looks at assessment and evaluation from the perspective of the classroom teacher. As with other chapters in the collection, the chapter provides background and articulates key principles before providing practical examples of assessment and evaluation in action.

Chapter Ten

Content-based instruction

Donna Brinton, University of California, Los Angeles (USA)

At the end of this chapter, you should be able to:

Goals

✔ **define** content-based instruction (CBI).

✔ **differentiate** between common forms of CBI (e.g., theme-based, sheltered, adjunct, sustained-content language teaching).

✔ **understand** how these forms apply to different student populations and instructional settings.

✔ **demonstrate** familiarity with the principles of CBI.

✔ **apply** these principles to your instructional context.

1. What is content-based instruction?

My personal interest in **content-based instruction, CBI,** derives from an experience I had when I was 11 years old. My family moved to Germany for a year and I found myself, with no knowledge of German whatsoever, attending a school in Germany where the medium of instruction was German. I was fortunate that the headmistress of the school designated me as a *Gaststudentin* (guest student). This meant that I was allowed to audit classes but was not required to do all the homework or take tests.

Certain subjects were easier than others. For example, in math I could partially follow what the teacher was presenting by looking at the problems she wrote on the board. History was much more difficult to follow. Approximately three months into the experience, however, something happened. I was sitting in biology class and the teacher had drawn a large circle on the board. She then filled in a smaller darkened circle in the center of this circle, labeling the circles with two unfamiliar words–*Zelle* and *Kernzelle*. This was followed by a series of additional sketches showing concentric outer circles and an inner mass that appeared to first grow, then begin to divide. "Oh," I remember thinking, "she's teaching us about cell division." Since we'd studied cell division in my school in the U.S., I was able to apply my background knowledge. I decided that *Zelle* must mean cell and *Kernzelle* nucleus. Even more amazingly, I realized that if I concentrated, I could figure out almost everything the teacher was saying. Without consciously realizing it, I was beginning to acquire German–not in the traditional way (in a language classroom with a language teacher), but in the subject matter classroom, through **content**. Within a month, I was understanding most of my subject matter classes and within a year I was relatively fluent.

Years later, having been trained as a language teacher, I realized my experience in Germany had a name, CBI. I also learned that my success learning German could be explained by certain theories of second language acquisition.

Before proceeding further, let's examine two important notions, **context** and content. To comprehend the difference between these, try the following. First, picture a teacher's use of the *context* "Los Angeles vs. San Francisco" in a one-hour lesson on writing paragraphs of comparison and contrast. In this lesson, the teacher might first present ways to organize compare/contrast paragraphs (e.g., block style vs. point by point style), then elicit from students the differences between the two cities and brainstorm with them an organizational plan for the paragraph. Next, picture a five-week CBI unit centered on the *content* of urban issues (e.g., crime, traffic, youth culture) in Los Angeles. In this unit, students read articles about urban issues in the city, conduct independent research on one of the subtopics, and discuss and write about their findings. All language instruction (e.g., grammar, vocabulary, writing) is conducted using the content of urban issues as a point of departure. Thus, students might study the grammar of conditional sentences within the context of urban crime ("If police efforts were more community-based, the inhabitants of that community would not perceive the police as enemies.")

In the first example, the teacher uses the context of differences between the two cities to illustrate a single teaching point (comparison/contrast). Whereas in the second example, all language activities in the extended five-week unit revolve around the content of urban issues in Los Angeles. This content-rich environment provides optimal conditions for students to acquire language since (1) language is being continually recycled throughout the unit and (2) students are given multiple opportunities to use the new language they acquire as they read, discuss, and write about the topics.

Reflection

1. Think back to your own experiences in the second language classroom (either as a learner or a teacher). Can you remember any of the contexts used to present language items? What were these?
2. Think of other examples to illustrate the difference between context and content.

What, then, are the characteristic features of CBI? Quite simply, CBI refers to the teaching of language through exposure to content that is interesting and relevant to learners. This content serves several purposes. First, it provides a rich context for the language classroom, allowing the teacher to present and explain specific language features. Additionally, it provides for what Stephen Krashen (1985) calls comprehensible **input**–challenging language that is slightly above the current linguistic level of the students which, according to Krashen, provides the foundation for successful language acquisition.

Let's return to the example of the CBI unit on urban issues mentioned above. In this unit, the content of urban life in Los Angeles has been chosen because of its relevance to the learners' lives and its potential interest level. The course materials, which consist primarily of readings about various aspects of urban life in the city (e.g., violence, traffic, urban settlement patterns), provide a context for the teacher to use when teaching lessons on issues such as citing sources or achieving paragraph unity. It is important in our definition of CBI to note that the selection of content extends over more than one lesson. In fact, CBI units are often several weeks or more in length. As we will see later in the chapter, the use of sustained content over a period of time effectively differentiates this approach from the previous practice of simply selecting a context for the presentation of new language.

Assume that you have been asked to design a CBI unit around the theme of the city or area where you live. Make a list of at least five topics you would include in this unit. Share this list with other members of the class.

2. Background to content-based instruction

Basing language teaching on content is not a new idea. For probably as long as second languages have been taught, materials developers and teachers have sought interesting content to engage learners' interest. However, the approach that has come to be known as CBI first appeared in the mid-1980s with the publication of Bernard Mohan's work, *Language and Content*. Mohan characterizes his work as an exploration into the ways in which the "learning of language and subject matter… [can] be accomplished" (Mohan, 1986, p. iii). Following closely on the heels of Mohan's exploratory work are two other early works on CBI by Cantoni-Harvey (1987) and Crandall (1987)–both of which helped to further launch this movement.

In the work I have done with my colleagues Ann Snow and Mari Wesche (Brinton, Snow, and Wesche, 1989), we identify several "prototype" forms of CBI–namely theme-based language instruction, sheltered content instruction, and adjunct instruction. These forms differ in several important respects: (1) the type of population and setting that they serve; (2) the respective degree of focus on language or content; (3) the selection of content; and (4) the degree of coordination with subject matter courses and instructors.

Reflection

1. Think about a situation where you learned or have taught English.
2. What was the setting (e.g., at school, a private language institute, a university)?
3. Who were the students in the class and why were they learning English?
4. In what way did the setting, the population of students, and their reasons for learning English influence how English was taught?

To better understand these three prototype forms, let's examine the following scenarios:

Scenario 1

Theme-based language instruction: Beginning-level English language learners studying English at the fourth grade level work with the theme of friendship. Since the primary aim of this class is language acquisition, the English teacher uses this theme as a point of departure for instruction in reading, listening, speaking, and writing skills (Brinton, 2001a). The thematic content stretches over several weeks of instruction, providing rich input for lessons that are either language-based (i.e., with a focus on vocabulary, pronunciation, and grammar) or skills-based (i.e., with a focus on listening, speaking, writing, or reading). In this environment, students can successfully acquire language.

Scenario 2

Sheltered content instruction: English language learners enrolled in a sheltered seventh grade science class improve their English language skills while studying about the big bang theory of the origin of the universe (Brinton and Holten, 1997). The science teacher in this class has received special training in working with second language (L2) learners. Because the students are all still acquiring English as a second or additional language, she modifies her presentation style to help the students comprehend the material. The teacher's primary goal is for students to understand the content materials (in this case, about the origin of the universe). But she also spends some time helping students with language-related issues (e.g., academic vocabulary, reading skills) that pertain to the science unit they are studying. The exposure to higher-level language (through the content materials) and the explicit focus on language issues by the teacher set the stage for successful language acquisition.

Reflection

Teachers teaching sheltered classes modify their teaching to facilitate learners' comprehension. Examine the partial list below. Then decide for each type of accommodation which category it belongs to.

Categories: (1) linguistic accommodation
(2) paralinguistic accommodation (use of body language)
(3) instructional routine

Type of accommodation:
- slower rate of speech
- gesturing to emphasize important points
- checking students' background knowledge
- frequent comprehension checking
- simpler sentence grammar
- outlining the day's activities on the board
- shorter sentences
- use of audio-visual aids

Adjunct instruction: University-level ESL students are enrolled in paired or "adjuncted" English and psychology classes (Brinton, Snow, and Wesche, 1989; in press). Two separate instructors teach the classes—an English language instructor and a psychology instructor. Although the two classes meet and are graded separately, the two instructors meet regularly to coordinate their teaching objectives, and the English language instructor uses the psychology materials as content for the English language course. The instructional goals of these two classes differ since the main goal for the psychology class is for students to understand and learn the subject matter; the main goal for the English class, on the other hand, is for students to improve their English language skills. Students are able to achieve this goal through their exposure to challenging, yet comprehensible, input in the psychology class and through the language support and systematic language instruction that they receive in the English class.

These scenarios are real-life examples of the prototype models my colleagues and I described in our 1989 work. To summarize the differences in these models, let's return to the differences noted on page 202.

1. Population/setting—The first difference concerns the types of students and settings to which the models are best suited. Since theme-based instruction is the most generally applicable, it is appropriate at virtually any level of language learning and in a wide variety of settings. Sheltered and adjunct instruction, however, are more restricted in their applicability. Sheltered courses are typically found in middle schools and high schools where large populations of learners are receiving subject matter instruction in a language other than their first language. Finally, adjunct courses are typically found in settings where students are studying language as well as subject matter, such as high schools, colleges, and universities.

2. Lesson focus—The second distinction between the models concerns the focus of the lesson itself. As can be seen from the above scenarios, the instructional focus in CBI may be on language (as in theme-based instruction), on content (as in sheltered instruction), or on both (as in adjunct instruction).

3. Selection of content—The third distinction concerns the type of content that is selected. Because most CBI instruction occurs in schools, colleges, and universities, the content of the language class often overlaps with that of students' subject matter classes. In our ESL courses at my university, for example, we have selected content from a range of required general education courses that students take to graduate from the university.

4. Degree of faculty coordination—A final distinction involves the degree or amount of coordination required between language and content faculty. Adjunct instruction is quite different from the other two models in this respect since it requires the systematic coordination of the language and content instructors. For example, these instructors typically meet before the course (and periodically throughout the course) to discuss curriculum and to coordinate objectives. They may also use this time to discuss the types of assignments they will set for the students. This in not true for sheltered and theme-based instruction, where the instructors do not coordinate in this fashion.

These "prototype" models represent early attempts of practitioners to apply CBI principles to various student populations and instructional settings. As such, they are useful for understanding the flexibility of the CBI approach. However, since that time CBI has been applied in virtually all parts of the world, with the result that numerous additional CBI models continue to evolve.

A recent innovation in CBI is **sustained-content language teaching (SCLT)**. SCLT (Pally, 2000; Murphy and Stoller, 2001) involves a focus on a "single content area, or carrier topic ... [along with] a complementary focus on L2 learning and teaching" (Murphy and Stoller, 2001, p. 3). According to Murphy & Stoller, because the use of sustained content simulates the conditions and demands of the subject matter classroom, it allows language learners to more deeply engage the content, in the process acquiring the academic vocabulary and language skills needed for the mainstream. SCLT does not require coordination of the language teacher with a content-area expert. Instead, the content serves as a point of departure for language instruction. As such, SCLT most closely resembles theme-based instruction, with the difference that theme-based courses typically cover a variety of topics, whereas in SCLT the content is "sustained," and students work with only one topic. In theme-based instruction, according to this distinction, a ten-week course might consist of five different topics (e.g., nuclear energy, cloning, volunteerism, leadership, and life expectancy).

3. Principles for content-based instruction

1. Base instructional decisions on content rather than language criteria.

Two issues that language course planners or materials designers face at the outset of the planning phase are selection (i.e., which items to include) and sequencing (i.e., how to order these items). In the days of the grammar translation approach, it was thought that certain language items (e.g., simple present tense) were more easily acquired than others. Thus, the decision was made to include these easier items in the beginner course and to sequence them at the beginning. Content-based instruction takes a rather radical departure from this approach since it allows the choice of content to dictate or influence the selection and sequencing of language items. In adjunct instruction, for example, the psychology professor's introductory lecture on "What is Psychology?" might be coupled with the English instructor's focus on the language of definition (Brinton, Snow, and Wesche, in press). Similarly, in the sheltered unit about the origins of the universe mentioned above, the focus might be on helping students understand and acquire core academic vocabulary (e.g., "expand" equals "get bigger;" "decrease" equals "get smaller," etc.).

2. Integrate skills.

Rather than isolate skills in skill-specific classes (e.g., "English Grammar," "Writing," "Listening and Speaking"), CBI practitioners use an integrated skills approach to language teaching, covering all four language skills as well as grammar and vocabulary. This reflects what happens in the real world, where interactions involve multiple skills simultaneously. Also, unlike other approaches that dictate a specific skill sequence within each lesson (i.e., starting with listening, then reading, then writing, etc.), there is no set sequence of skills to be taught in CBI. Instead, a lesson may begin with any skill or, alternatively, with a focus on grammar or vocabulary. As we have seen in principle one, it is the content itself that influences the decisions about selection and sequencing.

Action

Examine the teaching sequences (Figure 1) for the UCLA introductory units on local winds (atmospheric science unit) and kinship (anthropology unit) (from Brinton, et al., 1997). Are these sequences the same or different? What explanation can you find for the sequencing? Share your ideas with other classmates.

Introduction: Local Winds	Introduction: Images of Family Life
Strategy: Cubing	**Grammar:** Using modals to express possibility
Vocabulary: Expressing power through verbs	**Vocabulary:** Kinship terms
Literature: A Year in Provence	**Reading:** The Way We Are
Grammar: Participial phrases	**Vocabulary:** Figurative language

Reading: *Relish the Rhône* **Grammar:** *Verb tense in description, narration and explanation* **Video lecture:** *Wind direction* **Strategy:** *Comprehending unstressed words* **Reading:** Demon's Gates and Devil's Doors **Grammar:** *Expressing contrast through subordination* **Strategy:** *Sensory description in storytelling*	**Reading:** Why Men Need Family Values **Grammar:** *Referring to sources* **Strategy:** *Reacting to readings* **Video lecture:** *Post-marital residence* **Vocabulary:** *Key terms*

Figure 1 Teaching sequences: Units on local winds and kinship

3. Involve students actively in all phases of the learning process.

Because it falls under the more general rubric of **communicative language teaching** (CLT), the CBI classroom is learner rather than teacher centered (Littlewood, 1981). In such classrooms, students learn through doing and are actively engaged in the learning process; they do not depend on the teacher to direct all learning or to be the source of all information. Central to CBI is the belief that learning occurs not only through exposure to the teacher's input, but also through peer input and interactions. Accordingly, students assume active, social roles in the classroom that involve interactive learning, negotiation, information gathering, and the co-construction of meaning (Lee and VanPatten, 1995). Richards and Rodgers (1985) and Nunan (1989) characterize some possible roles played by students in the communicatively-oriented classroom as follows: recipient/listener; planner, interactor and negotiator, tutor of other learners; and evaluator/monitor of his/her own progress. All these roles are ones assumed by learners in the CBI classroom. In keeping with the multiple roles assumed by learners, the CBI teacher also assumes multiple roles. She may serve as the primary resource for students, particularly where issues of language or culture are concerned. But she also serves as the organizer of tasks, the controller or facilitator of student-centered activities, the prompter of student responses, and the assessor (both formal and informal) of student efforts.

4. Choose content for its relevance to students' lives, interests, and/or academic goals.

The choice of content in CBI courses ultimately depends on the student and the instructional setting. In many school contexts, content-based language instruction closely parallels school subjects. Thus, in a middle school context, topics may be drawn from social science, history, and/or life science areas that students are studying in their subject matter classes. Similarly, in the college or university setting, students may enroll in linked or adjunct language and content classes, with dual instructors covering the same content from a different perspective and with differing instructional objectives. In other settings, topics may be drawn from students' occupational needs or be determined by general interest inventories. In fact, this principle is often criticized as a potential weakness of CBI since determining what is of relevance or interest to students is notoriously difficult for both teachers and materials or curriculum developers. However, because the introduction to content in CBI stretches over an extended period of instructional time, teachers have ample opportunity to engage students' interest and to capitalize on students' prior knowledge about a given topic. This mandate for the teacher to sell the students on the content that has been selected is an important underpinning of CBI teacher training.

Action

Decide on a setting (either the one in which you are currently teaching or one in which you hope to teach in the future). With this setting in mind, locate interesting and relevant authentic content. Share this content with class members and discuss your reasons for selecting it.

5. Select authentic texts and tasks.

A key component of CBI is authenticity—both of the texts used in the classroom and the tasks that learners are asked to perform. To better understand this principle, we need to examine the meaning of authenticity. Hutchinson and Waters define **authentic texts** as those that are "not originally constructed for language teaching purposes" (1987, p. 159). Thus, an extract from a content area textbook, a cartoon, the lyrics to a popular song, or a short story would all qualify as authentic texts. However, as Hutchinson and Waters note, bringing an authentic text into the classroom alters its original purpose, which was not to teach language, but rather to inform (in the case of the textbook), entertain (in the case of the cartoon), or perhaps both (in the case of the song or the short story). In other words, the use of an authentic text in a language classroom implies that it has been removed from its original context and that its purpose in the language classroom is quite a different one indeed.

This objection also holds true for task authenticity. Our purpose in interacting with texts in the real world varies greatly according to the content itself, as well as to the circumstances. In the case of a textbook passage, we may read for global understanding and/or specific details; in the case of a popular song, we may listen purely for enjoyment or seek to understand the meaning of the lyrics. Similarly, with a political cartoon or newspaper editorial we may read to understand the political point of view being expressed and/or to determine the cartoonist's or author's bias. In CBI, since the objective is to aim for authenticity of task, the task(s) associated with a given text should mirror those that would take place in the real world.

Discuss the real-world purposes that an individual might have for using the content you selected in the previous Action box (page 208) and brainstorm several appropriate tasks that learners could do using this content. Share these with group members or the class as a whole.

6. Draw overt attention to language features.

The purpose of CBI is to expose learners to authentic input with the goal of their being able to use language for communicative purposes. Texts form the primary input source in the CBI classroom, with additional input provided by the teacher (through classroom language) and peers (in pair or group work). All of these provide comprehensible input. However, CBI departs from some other approaches to language teaching in its belief that comprehensible input alone will not lead to successful language acquisition (Brinton and Holten, 2001). Instead, it makes use of awareness-raising tasks to draw attention to specific language features found in the authentic texts.

4. Classroom techniques and tasks

The techniques and tasks used in the CBI classroom are familiar ones to anyone who practices CLT. These techniques and tasks reflect the principles of CBI since they involve the active participation of learners in the exchange of content or theme-related information. The following is a partial list of techniques and activities commonly found in CBI classrooms.

Pair and group work are a hallmark of the communicative classroom. In CBI, they entail the discussion or exchange of information related to the content unit. In pair or group work, the teacher first presents the task, then divides students and sets a time limit for completion of the task. While students work, she circulates to answer questions and makes sure that students are "on task" (i.e., completing the task according to the instructions given). Pair and group work culminate in a reporting stage, with students from each group sharing their ideas or solutions with the rest of the class.

Information gap is a form of pair work in which the participants are each given different pieces of information. Using only language (i.e., without looking at their partner's information), they must communicate to fill in the missing gaps in information.

Jigsaw is another variation of information gap. Students are first divided into "expert" groups, with each group given a different piece of information. Once the students in each group have become familiar with their piece of the jigsaw, they are regrouped. Each new group consists of at least one student from each of the previous expert groups. Students then share their expertise to complete the task and report their findings to the rest of the class.

Graphic organizers involve the use of visuals that assist in organizing information. They can consist of diagrams, tables, clusters, etc. The teacher may use these graphic organizers to present information or guide student brainstorming. Alternatively, learners may be asked to read or listen for key information and enter this information in the graphic organizer.

Discussion and debate involve opportunities for students to express their own opinions about topics, in this case related to the theme of the CBI unit.

Role-play entails having students act out a situation. Each participant is given information about the role and the situation. Role-play can involve two or more students. In CBI, the role-play would be connected to the overall unit theme or topic.

Survey tasks ask students to conduct a poll of people (either inside or outside the classroom) to determine opinions on a selected topic. These opinions are reported back to others, usually in the form of a chart or table.

Process writing is a technique commonly found in CLT. It involves having students write multiple drafts of papers. Each draft receives either comments from the teacher or from a peer. Based on these comments, the student writer revises the draft and resubmits it to the teacher for evaluation. Often, students do two or three drafts of each paper they submit.

Problem solving involves students working in pairs or groups to arrive at a solution to a given problem. In CBI, the context of the problem relates to the theme students have been studying in the content unit.

Sequencing involves students rearranging events or pieces of information into their logical order. This type of task is especially useful in the teaching of reading and listening.

Ranking involves students determining an order of listed items based on their perceived importance. Ranking is often done in pairs or groups, with group members being asked to reach consensus on the ordering. A designated reporter then shares the ranking that has been determined with the class as a whole, often providing a rationale for this ranking.

Values clarification involves students taking a stand (agreeing or disagreeing) on controversial statements related to a chosen topic. Usually done in pairs or groups, it often involves asking students to come to consensus and then report on their decision and their discussion to the rest of the class members.

Reflection

Examine the list of CBI techniques and tasks (pages 209-211). Which ones have you experienced in your own second or foreign language learning? Which of these techniques and tasks have you enjoyed most? Why?

5. Content-based instruction in the classroom

To illustrate CBI in action, let's look at selected classroom extracts from one of the scenarios mentioned earlier—the use of friendship as the content in an integrated language unit for intermediate-level learners in the middle school setting (Brinton, 2001a). This entire theme unit is designed to span several weeks of instruction. (See Appendix page 220 for an overview of the complete unit.) The extracts illustrate the integrated skills focus of CBI as well as the other underlying principles discussed above.

In the classroom extracts, *T* stands for teacher and *S* represents a particular student. *Ss* stands for students.

Background: This interaction takes place at the outset of the CBI unit. The teacher has begun the unit by writing some key words related to the theme on the blackboard (e.g., buddy, friend, acquaintance, pal, schoolmate, class-mate) and asking students to decide whether these words have general or specific meanings and whether they are used in formal or informal contexts. She next displays several definitions on the overhead projector:

T: Who can read aloud the first definition?

S: (raises hand)

T: Okay, Winnie.

S: "Friend—person, not a relation, whom one knows and likes well."

T: Great. So how many pieces of the definition are there?

S: Three.

T: Anybody else?

S: Four.

T: Right. What are they? (enumerates with fingers as students identify person, not a relation, knows, and likes well.) *Is it a good definition? What do you think?*

Ss: Yeah …

T: Any problems that you can see? Does it leave out anybody you think belongs?

Ss: (murmured responses, e.g., *my sister, my dog…*)

T: Yeah, it says "not a relation" so we can't include your sister or your cousin. And it also says a person so we can't include your dog or your cat. Let's look at another definition. Who can read number two? Hyun-sook?

S: "Friend—person whom one likes but is not related."

T: Thanks. Okay, what do you think? Is this the same as the other definition?

S: Yeah.

T: Is it missing anything? Take another look at the first definition …

S: Knows.

T: Right. Is that important?

S: No, not really.

T: I agree. If you like somebody well, we can assume you know them, right? Okay, let's look at the third definition. Any volunteers? Yuri, go ahead …

S: *"Friend—someone whom you like very much and enjoy spending time with."*

T: *Anything different about this definition?*

Ss: *Enjoy spending time with.*

T: *Right. Is that important? Are your friends people you enjoy spending time with?*

Ss: (mumbled responses and gestures of affirmation)

T: *Mmhmmm … we usually enjoy spending time with our friends. If we don't, they aren't very good friends! Anything else different about this definition?*

S: *It says* somebody, *not a person. Maybe it can be a dog or a cat?*

T: *That's interesting. What do the rest of you think? Do you agree with Raoul that this definition includes pets?*

S: *Isn't* somebody *a person?*

T: *Yes, usually. So this definition probably doesn't include pets either.*

T: *What about the last definition? Jinna? Can you read it for us?*

S: *"Friend—person whom one likes and trusts."*

T: *What about this one? Is there anything different here?*

Ss: *Trusts.*

T: *Is* trusts *important?*

Ss: *Yeah.*

T: *I agree. I think it's really important. But the other definitions didn't mention it at all, did they? Okay, so get in your groups and take out one piece of paper per group. I want each group to choose somebody to write. In the space at the end of the page, I want your group to write its own definition of* friend. *You can use the dictionary definitions we just looked at to help you create this definition. Is everybody clear what I want you to do?*

Ss: *Yes.*

T: *Okay, you have five minutes.*

Commentary The teacher begins this lesson by reviewing vocabulary associated with the word "friend." She elicits words and their meanings from students and introduces several definitions of friend from learner dictionaries. She then elicits reactions from students, prompting or guiding them in the discussion activity. This segment of the lesson is controlled by the teacher. However, the atmosphere is interactive and students are free to give their personal opinions. The activity sets the stage for the next, student-centered activity in which students create a group definition of friendship.

Reflection

Read Extract 2 (pages 214-216).
1. What is the language focus of this activity?
2. Which principles of CBI do you see reflected?
3. How well would this topic work in the setting that you teach in/hope to teach in?

| **Extract 2** | **Grammar review** |

Background: Prior to this activity, students have completed a group work task involving magazine pictures. Each group was given a magazine picture of a child and asked to (1) give the child an appropriate name and (2) from a list, select five adjectives (e.g., *funny, generous, dependable, helpful,* and *thoughtful*) that describe the child's personal characteristics. The magazine pictures along with the names and characteristics are posted on the blackboard for all to see. Figure 2 shows the blackboard layout.

Jenny	Tommy	Ling	Sam	Tara
outgoing	rowdy	shy	smart	funny
smart	funny	sweet	helpful	energetic
caring	loud	outgoing	nice	warm
nice	lazy	energetic	loyal	smart
helpful	loyal	warm	shy	caring

Figure 2 Blackboard layout

T: That's great! So now we have all the pictures on the blackboard. Do you think these kids are friends?

Ss: Yeah.

S: Not everybody.

T: Right, they probably aren't all friends. Do you think Jenny and Tara are friends?

Ss: Yeah.

T: Why?

Ss: Because they're the same.

T: Exactly. What about Tommy and Ling?

Ss: Probably not.

T: Right, their characteristics are pretty different. I don't think they're friends. So what do you think the relationship between all the kids is? Sara?

S: They go to school.

T: What's the word we learned?

Ss: Classmate.

T: Right, they're classmates. Okay, so let's take a look at the personal characteristics you've listed. What about Jenny? Who can read me the characteristics listed for Jenny? Martha?

S: "Outgoing, smart, caring, nice, helpful ..."

T: Good. Tell me again ... Jenny is ...

S: Jenny is outgoing, smart, caring, nice, and helpful.

T: Right. Somebody else ... tell me about Tara ... Okay, Winnie?

S: Tara is funny, energetic, warm, smart, and caring.

T: Excellent. Everybody, take a look at the board. Can you find two people who are outgoing?

Ss: Jenny and Ling.

T: Right. So tell me about Jenny and Ling. Raoul?

S: Jenny is outgoing and Ling is outgoing.

T: Can we say it another way? Remember what we practiced yesterday? Try again, Raoul.

S: Jenny is outgoing and Ling is so.

T: ... and Ling is? Grace?

S: Jenny is outgoing and Ling is too.

T: Great. (Writes following pattern on board: *X is ___ and Y is TOO.*) *Everybody, repeat, Jenny is outgoing and Ling is too.*

Ss: Jenny is outgoing and Ling is too.

T: ... and Ling is too.

Ss: ... and Ling is too.

T: Try the whole sentence again, everybody ...

Ss: Jenny is outgoing and Ling is too.

T: Now find two people who are shy. Who can tell me about them? Okay, Yuri ...

S: Ling is shy and Sam is too.

T: Perfect. Everybody (motions students to chorally repeat)

Ss: Ling is shy and Sam is too.

T: (Points on the board to Tommy and Tara) *Tell me about Tommy and Tara* (motions students to chorally repeat)

Ss: Tommy is funny and Tara is too.

T: We learned another way to say it. Can anybody remember? Hyun-Sook?

S: Tommy is funny and so is Tara.

T: (Writes following pattern on board: *X is ___ and SO is Y.*) *Everybody* (motions students to chorally repeat), *Tommy is funny and so is Tara.*

Ss: Tommy is funny and so is Tara.

T: (Points on the board to Sam and Jenny, motioning students to chorally repeat.)

Ss: Sam is helpful and so is Jenny.

T: Okay, get in your groups again and write five sentences using these (points to blackboard) *patterns. Everybody ready?*

Ss: Yeah.

T: Let's go.

Commentary In this grammar review activity, the teacher prompts student responses by pointing out similar characteristics and asking students to construct sentences (either individually or chorally) using the patterns "X is ___ and Y is too/X is ___ and so is Y" which have been previously practiced. Students are active participants. The teacher is careful to recycle language from previous lessons (e.g., the grammar patterns being practiced) and from previous tasks (e.g., vocabulary presented in the introduction to the unit). Because the focus of this activity is on accuracy, the teacher uses peer- and self-correction techniques to focus students' attention on the correct form of the utterance.

Reflection

In CBI, the teacher should draw overt attention to language. How do you see this principle applied in Extract 2? Which components of language is the teacher focusing on?

Extract 3 **Values clarification**

In this activity, which immediately follows the activity in Extract 2, students first respond individually to the values clarification questions. They then join their groups to discuss their answers and reach a consensus. During this time, the teacher walks around to answer questions and help resolve differences of opinion. Once all groups appear to have agreed on their answers, the teacher conducts a tally and asks students to rationalize their answers. Figure 3 shows the student handout.

Values clarification: Look at the statements. Put a check mark (✓) next to your opinion: strongly agree (SA), agree (A), disagree (D), or strongly disagree (SD). Be prepared to explain your opinion.

Statements	SA	A	D	SD
Friends don't keep secrets from each other.	—	—	—	—
Friends have the same beliefs.	—	—	—	—
Friends like to do the same things.	—	—	—	—
A friend always helps another friend in trouble.	—	—	—	—
A friend will lie to help you.	—	—	—	—

Figure 3 Values clarification handout

T: *Okay. Everybody about finished? Raise your hands if you are finished. Good.* (Writes SA, A, D, and SD across the top of the board and to the left underneath, lists the numbers 1-5). *Let's start with a show of hands. What did you think about number one? Who can read the statement out loud? Sylvia?*

S: *Friends don't keep secrets from each other.*

T: *Good. How many people strongly agreed? Everybody? Wow, that's amazing.* (Tallies response.) *What about number two? Yuri, can you read it?*

S: *Friends have the same beliefs.*

T: *Strongly agree? Two groups, okay. Agree? Nobody, hmmm. Disagree? Raoul's group. Strongly disagree? Two, okay.* (Tallies response.) *Number three? Jinna, read the statement please.*

S: *Friends like to do the same things.*

T: *Right. Who strongly agrees? Everybody again? That's interesting ...* (Tallies response.) *Number four? Martha?*

S: *A friend always helps another friend in trouble.*

T: *Okay, how many people strongly agree? Nobody? Agree? Still nobody? Disagree? Wow, four groups! That's a lot. And strongly disagree? Yuri's group. Okay.* (Tallies response.) *And the last statement, Kim?*

S: *A friend will lie to help you.*

T: *That's pretty interesting. A friend will lie to help you. How many of you strongly agreed? Raoul's group? What about agree? Martha's and Sylvia's groups. Disagree? Winnie's group. And strongly disagree? Yuri's group.* (Tallies response). *So we have a lot of disagreement about number five.*

Ss: *Yeah.*

T: *So, I want to hear from someone who strongly agrees with statement number five. That was Raoul's group, right? Who can tell me why your group strongly agreed? Tracy?*

S: *Maybe you are in trouble. You stole something. And your friend lies and says you didn't do it. That's a good friend.*

T: *Okay, so in your group's opinion even if you do something bad a friend should lie to protect you.*

Ss: *(*Murmured responses, e.g., *no and that's bad ...)*

Commentary Values clarification tasks are relatively common in communicatively-oriented classrooms. Here, the task is tied to the theme of friendship, with the statements crafted in such a manner as to reflect themes in the texts that students will encounter later in the unit. As a student-centered discussion activity, it provides a forum for students to voice their personal opinions about controversial topics. Because students are then asked to reach consensus in their groups, it also provides a forum for students to debate and persuade others of their opinions. Finally, it provides an opportunity for students to rationalize their opinions.

Reflection

1. As discussed in Section 3 (pages 205-211), CBI aims for both text and task authenticity. Under what circumstances might we engage in values clarification in the real world?
2. Do you see the task in Extract 3 as an authentic task?

6. Conclusion

This chapter has presented a brief overview of CBI along with a discussion of some of its more commonly practiced models (theme-based, sheltered, adjunct, and SCLT). It has situated CBI within the broader paradigm of CLT, articulated the underlying principles of CBI, and shown how these principles mesh with those of the communicatively-oriented classroom.

The classroom extracts illustrate the underlying principles in action. They provide a clearer picture of how content and language provide complementary aspects of the curriculum and how the input-rich environment of the CBI classroom can lead to successful language acquisition.

Cycle 1	Cycle 2	Cycle 3
(1) Dictionary definitions: Students examine dictionary definitions of the word "friend." They discuss the differences in the definitions and then, in groups, write their own definition.	**(8) Values clarification:** In groups, students discuss controversial statements about friendship (e.g., "A friend will lie to help you") and arrive at consensus. They share their group opinion with class members.	**(15) Poster activity:** In groups, students make posters about the things they do with their friends. They then explain their poster to their classmates.
(2) Scrambled sayings: Students are presented with scrambled sayings about friendship. They unscramble the definitions and discuss their meaning (e.g., "Birds of a feather flock together" vs. "Opposites attract").	**(9) Listening cloze:** Students listen to the song "You've Got a Friend" by Carole King (1999) and complete a listening cloze. The teacher then guides them in a discussion of the song's message.	**(16) Prereading:** Students examine the pictures of four teenagers (Kenyon, Randy, Daryl, and Robin) in their bedrooms (Salinger, 1995). They discuss the clues to the teenagers' personalities that are evident in the pictures.
(3) Pronunciation: Students review the placement of the tongue for /r/ and /l/ and practice the correct articulation of these two sounds using the sayings about friendship in (2) above.	**(10) Definition activity:** Students revisit their definitions of "friend" from cycle 1. They make changes based on the definition of "friend" in the Carole King song. Alternatively, they can write Carole King's definition of "friend."	**(17) Intensive reading:** In an excerpt from In my Room – Teenagers in their Bedrooms (Salinger, 1995), students locate the views of friendship as expressed by the four American teenagers.
(4) Collocations: Students are given sets of verbs, nouns, and adjectives and asked to combine them to form frequently-used collocations (e.g., "a close friend," "a lifelong friend," "to make a friend," "to lose a friend").	**(11) Reading I:** Students receive a scrambled picture sequence from Art Spiegelman's (1991) cartoon novel Maus (Spiegelman, 1991). They work in groups to sequence the events of a story in which the young boy Art is abandoned by his friends and seeks solace from his father, a Nazi concentration camp survivor. Art and his father discuss the concept of friendship.	**(18) Graphic organizer:** In groups, students complete a graphic organizer using information from the reading (e.g., "Who used to argue?" "Who is more mature now?" "Who has new friends?").
(5) Vocabulary building: The teacher presents adjectives that describe personal characteristics (e.g., "thoughtful," "generous," "outgoing," "dependable"). Students then practice pronouncing the words, focusing on word stress patterns.	**(12) Reading II:** Guided by the teacher, students answer literal comprehension questions (e.g., "How old is Art?" "What does he like to do for fun?") about the passage.	**(19) Grammar consciousness raising:** Students reread the "teenager" excerpts looking for instances of past tense and present perfect verbs. They then review the difference in the usage of these tenses with the teacher.
(6) Magazine picture elicitation: Students are grouped. Each group receives a magazine picture of a child and is asked to (1) give the child a name and (2) brainstorm five personal characteristics for the child. The pictures are then posted on the board and the information is written underneath it.	**(13) Reading III:** In pairs or groups, students discuss the answers to interpretive questions (e.g., "Are Art's friends true friends? Why or why not?" "What does Art's father mean when he says 'If you lock them together in a room with no food for a week then you could see what it is, friends'?").	**(20) Writing:** Students are given a picture prompt (two friends having a conversation); they are asked to write the conversation between the friends. Alternatively, they can be asked to write a conversation between Kenyon and Randy, the teenage roommates from the reading.
(7) Grammar review: Using the characteristics students have generated in the magazine picture activity, the teacher reviews previously-studied patterns (e.g., "Both Mike and Angie are energetic." "Leila is studious and so is Tommy.") Using the information on the blackboard as an elicitation table, the teacher drills this information. Students then practice writing sentences using the patterns.	**(14) Jazz chant:** As a whole class activity, students practice apologizing to a friend using the jazz chant "Excuse Me. That's OK. Never Mind. No Problem" (Graham, 1986). They then discuss ways in which Art's friends might apologize for having abandoned him.	**(21) Role-play:** With a partner, students select from two possible role-play scenarios ("Kenyon and Randy need to economize" vs. "Daryl and her boyfriend decide to spend more time with their same-sex friends"). They practice the role-play and then perform it for the class and receive feedback.

Further readings

Brinton, D. M. and P. Master (eds.) 1997. *New ways in content-based instruction.* Alexandria, VA: (TESOL).

> This volume, part of TESOL's *New Ways* series of teacher resource texts, contains a rich collection of ideas and ready-made lesson plans for those interested in implementing CBI in a variety of settings.

Brinton, D. M., M. A. Snow and M. B. Wesche In press. *Content-based second language instruction* (new ed.) Ann Arbor, MI: University of Michigan Press.

> This new edition of the authors' 1989 text describes in detail the three prototype models of CBI discussed in this chapter. It also addresses the issues of implementation, materials development and adaptation, and evaluation in CBI. New to this edition are an updated bibliography of work in the field and a glossary of terminology.

Murphy, J. M. and F. L. Stoller (eds.) 2001, Summer/Autumn. Sustained-Content Language Teaching: An emerging definition. Special issue of *TESOL Journal,* 10(2/3).

> This issue of the *TESOL Journal* is dedicated to examining sustained-content language teaching (SCLT). In the preface, the guest editors provide a definition of SCLT. Six feature articles provide examples of SCLT in action. Also included are reviews and an overview of Web sites for SCLT

Snow, M. A. and D. M. Brinton (eds.) 1997. *The Content-Based Classroom: Perspectives on Integrating Language and Content.* White Plains, NY: Longman.

> This edited volume provides an overview of updated practices in CBI. Included are a focus on the theoretical underpinnings of CBI, curriculum and materials design, teacher preparation, assessment, research, alternative models, and differences between CBI and other current teaching approaches.

Helpful Web sites

The content-based language teaching through technology (CoBaLTT) initiative (http://carla.acad.umn.edu/COBALTT.html)

> This site, part of the University of Minnesota's Center for Advanced Research on Language Acquisition (CARLA) project, is designed to help teachers implement CBI through technology. It includes an extended rationale for CBI, chat rooms for teachers who wish to discuss issues with other CBI practitioners, and a search engine for CBI lessons and units in a variety of languages.

Ohio ESL (http://www.ohiou.edu/esl/teacher/content.html#materials)

This site, hosted by Ohio University, provides a definition and rationale for CBI along with links to numerous rich resources on the topic. These include short articles, sample CBI lessons, and listserv and chat opportunities.

Language and civil society: A forum electronic journal (http://exchanges.state.gov/forum/journal)

This electronic journal consists of several content-based volumes on the following topics: civic education, business ethics, environmental education, and peace education. The accompanying activities, which include short background readings, discussion activities, and suggested World Wide Web links for further research, are aimed at enhancing students' communicative abilities in English.

References

Brinton, D. M. 2001a. Content-Based Instruction: Principles in Action. Workshop presented at the 2001 ARTESOL Conference. Cordoba, Argentina.

Brinton, D. M. 2001b. A Theme-Based Literature Course: Focus on the City of Angels. In J. Murphy & P. Byrd (eds.) *Understanding the courses we teach: Local perspectives on English language teaching* pp. 281–308. Ann Arbor, MI: University of Michigan Press.

Brinton, D. M., J. Frodesen, C. Holten, L. Jensen, and L. Repath-Martos 1997. *Insights 2: A Content-Based Approach to Academic Preparation.* White Plains, NY: Addison Wesley Longman.

Brinton, D. M. and C. Holten 1997. Into, Through, and Beyond: A framework to develop content-based material. *Forum, 35*(4), 10–23.

Brinton, D. M. and C. Holten 2001. Does the emperor have no clothes? A re-examination of grammar in content-based instruction. In J. Flowerdew & M. Peacock (eds.) *Research Perspectives on English for Academic Purposes.* pp. 239-251. Cambridge: Cambridge University Press.

Brinton, D. M., L. Jensen, L. Repath-Martos, J. Frodesen, and C. Holten 1997. *Insights 1: A Content-Based Approach to Academic Preparation.* White Plains, NY: Addison Wesley Longman.

Brinton, D. M. and P. Master (eds.) 1997. *New Ways in Content-Based Instruction.* Alexandria, VA: (TESOL).

Brinton, D. M., M. A. Snow and M. B. Wesche 1989. *Content-Based Second Language Instruction.* New York, NY: Newbury House.

Brinton, D. M., M. A. Snow and M. B. Wesche In press. *Content-Based Second Language Instruction.* Ann Arbor, MI: University of Michigan Press.

Cantoni-Harvey, G. 1987. *Content-Area Language Instruction: Approaches and Strategies.* Reading, MA: Addison-Wesley.

Crandall, J. (Ed.). (1987). *ESL through Content-Area Instruction: Mathematics, science, social studies.* Englewood Cliffs, NJ: Prentice Hall Regents.

Fotos, S. 1993. Consciousness Raising and Noticing through Focus on Form: Grammar Task Performance versus Formal Instruction. *Applied Linguistics, 14,* 385–407.

Graham, C. 1986. *Small talk.* Oxford: Oxford University Press.

Hutchinson, T. and A. Waters 1987. *English for Specific Purposes: A Learning-Centered Approach.* Cambridge: Cambridge University Press.

King, C. 1999. You've got a friend. Tapestry [CD]. Culver City, CA: Sony.

Krashen, S. D. 1985. *The Input Hypothesis: Issues and implications.* London: Longman.

Lee, J. F. and B. VanPatten 1995. *Making Communicative Language Teaching Happen.* New York, NY: McGraw Hill.

Littlejohn, A. and D. Hicks 1997. *Cambridge English for Schools.* Cambridge: Cambridge University Press.

Littlewood, W. 1981. *Communicative Language Teaching: An introduction.* Cambridge: Cambridge University Press.

Mendelsohn, D. 2001. Canadian language and culture: A course for nine academic credits. In J. Murphy and P. Byrd (eds.) *Understanding the Courses We Teach: Local Perspectives on English Language Teaching* pp. 309–327. Ann Arbor, MI: University of Michigan Press.

Mohan, B. A. 1986. *Language and Content.* Reading, MA: Addison-Wesley.

Murphy, J. M. and F. L. Stoller (eds.) 2001, Summer/Autumn. Sustained-Content Language Teaching: An Emerging Definition. Special issue of *TESOL Journal, 10* (2/3).

Nelson, G. and J. Burns 2000. In M. Pally (Ed.), *Sustained Content Teaching in Academic ESL/EFL,* pp. 132–157. Boston, MA: Houghton Mifflin.

Nunan, D. 1989. *Designing Tasks for the Communicative Classroom.* Cambridge: Cambridge University Press.

Pally, M. (ed.) 2000. *Sustained-Content Teaching in Academic ESL/EFL.* Boston, MA: Houghton Mifflin.

Richards, J. C. and T. Rodgers 1985. Method: Approach, design, and procedure. In J. C. Richards (ed.), *The Context of Language Teaching,* pp. 16–31. Cambridge: Cambridge University Press.

Rutherford, W. E. and M. Sharwood Smith (eds.) 1988. *Grammar and Second Language Teaching: A Book of Readings.* New York: Newbury House.

Salinger, A. 1995. *In My Room: Teenagers in Their Bedrooms.* San Francisco, CA: Chronicle Books.

Snow, M. A. 2001. Content-Based and Immersion Models for Second and Foreign Language Teaching. In M. Celce-Murcia (ed.), *Teaching English as a Second or Foreign Language* (Third Edition, pp. 303–318). Boston, MA: Heinle & Heinle.

Spiegelman, A. 1991. *Maus.* New York, NY: Pantheon Books.

Wenden, A. L. and J. Rubin 1987. *Learner Strategies in Language Learning.* Englewood Cliffs, NJ: Prentice-Hall.

Wesche, M. B. 1993. Discipline-based approaches to language study: Research issues and outcomes. In M. Krueger & F. Ryan (eds.) *Language and Content: Discipline- and Content-Based Approaches to Language Study,* pp. 57–82. Lexington, MA: D. C. Heath.

Chapter Eleven

Coursebooks

Kathleen Graves, School for International Training (USA)

At the end of this chapter, you should be able to:

Goals

 **analyze** how a coursebook is organized and what it emphasizes.

 **devise** ways to adapt or supplement an activity for a specific group of learners using techniques such as personalization and format shifting or by introducing supplementary material.

 **explain** how you would prepare learners to do an activity, how you would monitor them, and how you would follow up the activity.

1. What is a coursebook?

Coursebooks are prepackaged, published books used by the students and teacher as the primary basis for a language course. Coursebooks range from those that are broadly focused on developing all language skills to those that focus on a specific skill such as writing, or specific area such as hotel management. In addition to the student book, coursebook packages may include audio-cassettes or CDs, videos, workbooks, CD-ROMs, test packages and Internet materials. They almost always include a teacher's guide. In this chapter, we will focus on the student book, since it is the one component most likely to be used by all the students in the classroom. Examples will be taken from integrated skills coursebooks that are intended primarily for learners in countries where English is not a national language.

A coursebook is a learning tool shared by teachers and learners that can be used in systematic and flexible ways. In order to use a coursebook systematically and flexibly, it is important to understand how it is put together and how it can be adapted to meet the needs of your particular learners. The coursebook provides a plan for learning, a visible outline of what is to be learned in the classroom, as well as a bank of resource material and ideas (Acklam, 1994). What happens in the classroom fills out and transforms the outline into learning experiences for the students.

2. Background to the design and use of coursebooks

Most people who have studied a foreign language have used a coursebook at some point in their studies. The way coursebooks look and what they contain go hand and hand with the prevailing ideas at the time they were published about how languages are best taught and learned. Up until the mid-twentieth century, language books were used mainly in academic settings in order to understand the written texts of the target language. This approach, which is still common in academic settings today, is called the **grammar translation** approach. Coursebooks contain long reading passages, with vocabulary glossaries and grammar notes in the students' mother tongue. Students are tested on their ability to translate texts with lexical and grammatical accuracy. In the 1960s and 1970s, the focus shifted from grammar translation and its emphasis on written texts to **audiolingualism,** which focused on the spoken language. (See the chapters on methodology and grammar, this volume.) Audiolingualism was an outgrowth of **behaviorist** theories that learning is habit formation, the result of response to stimuli. Language coursebooks used dialogues, pattern practice, and substitution drills in which the teacher provided a stimulus such as a sentence beginning with *they* and a cue *she,* and the learners provided a response sentence, changing the subject from they to she. **Structural linguistics,** which views language as a system, reducible to a finite set of grammatical structures, also had a strong influence on language texts. For example, *English 900,* a series first published in 1964, contained 900 sentences. By mastering the sentences, one was supposed to have mastered the language.

In the 1970s and 80s, there was a shift toward the **notional-functional approach,** championed by the Council of Europe (e.g., Van Ek and Alexander, 1975). Language was understood to be used for purposes, or functions, such as expressing opinions, and to talk or write about both abstract and concrete topics, or notions, such as time and weather. Communication took precedence over grammar. Coursebooks began to emphasize functional language as well as pair work and group work activities in which learners used the language to communicate with each other.

The development of English for Academic Purposes (EAP) and of English for Specific Purposes (ESP) also influenced the kinds of materials that were published. EAP coursebooks focus on the development of one or two skills, such as writing or reading for academic purposes. ESP coursebooks focus on the development of specific workplace skills such as public health administration. EAP and ESP coursebooks use authentic material such as newspaper articles and other source materials. The use of authentic or quasi-authentic materials is also common in current coursebooks in order to simulate the use of language in real contexts.

Other approaches to teaching languages have questioned the effectiveness of coursebooks. The introduction of **task-based language teaching** in the 1980s challenged the very use of coursebooks. In task-based approaches, language is learned through negotiation with other learners in problem-solving or task-management situations that focus on meaning, rather than form, not through learning prespecified grammar, functions or notions. Tasks can range from discussing the effectiveness of an advertisement and reporting on the discussion to designing an original advertisement. Because coursebooks specify language to be learned, they were seen as incompatible with this approach. However, many current coursebooks now include tasks or projects to stimulate interaction and negotiation among learners.

Other critics have charged that, because a coursebook specifies what is to be taught and learned, it becomes an operating manual that the teacher and students follow unquestioningly. It leaves little room for decision-making and adapting to the needs of the particular group. (See, for example, Swan, 1992.) Proponents of using coursebooks have argued that they provide a needed structure for interaction in the classroom and that learners see the textbook as a guide that helps them organize their learning and provides security (Hutchinson and Torres, 1994). One purpose of this chapter is to help teachers understand how to take advantage of what a coursebook has to offer and not feel dominated by it.

Reflection

Think back on your own experience learning with a coursebook. Did you notice any differences in the coursebooks you used? Did you find the coursebooks a help or a hindrance? Why?

3. Principles for using a coursebook

1. Understand how the coursebook is organized.

A coursebook provides a visible outline for what is to be learned in the classroom. Coursebooks are often described metaphorically as maps (O'Neil, 1993). Maps provide a guide to the territory to be covered. The actual classroom teaching and learning can be viewed as a journey through the territory. The first principle for using a coursebook is to become familiar with the territory so that you can plan the journey.

Most coursebooks are organized around key features of language. These features include topics and associated vocabulary (e.g. food or transportation), grammar structures (e.g. verb tenses or how to form questions), and social and cultural interaction skills (e.g. how to order in a restaurant or how to politely refuse something). Coursebooks also emphasize two or more of the four skills of speaking, listening, reading, and writing.

The first step is to explore the coursebook to see how it is organized. Often the table of contents (sometimes called scope and sequence) provides a chart that shows how the authors have mapped out the territory within each unit and across units. Knowing how the book is organized can help you to make decisions about how to adapt it to your particular group of students. Each unit or chapter of a coursebook is a microcosm of the book as a whole, so one way to get to know a coursebook is by examining a unit.

Reflection

Look at the Table of Contents extracts on page 229 from three different intermediate level coursebooks. What features of language are they organized around? What are the similarities and differences in the ways they are organized? What do you think accounts for the differences?

Unit Title	Functions	Grammar	Listening and Pronunciation	Reading and Writing	Learning Strategies and Skills
Life Stories	• Talk about past actions • Talk about frequency of actions • Talk about lifestyles • Talk about habits and routines	Simple past tense: Questions, short answers Was born/married Irregular past tense of verbs Used to Had to Reported speech: verb *say*	Listen: listen to a biography to put events in chronological order Pronunciation: use to	Read a biography Write an autobiography Write a biography (Project)	Look for time order cues in biographical material List events in chronological order as a writing strategy

Figure 1 *Super Goal 3* (McGraw-Hill, 2002)

Alike yet different

Speaking *The roles of men and women*

Listening *Short oral report—weekend cooks*

Grammar *Review of contrasting tenses: simple present vs. present progressive; present simple past vs. present perfect*

Reading *Contrast/comparison—How different are men and women?*

Conversation *Sharing news and stating an opinion strategies*

Grammar More adjective clauses: Fran works with a sister that specializes in interior decorating.

Writing *Personal reports*

Figure 2 *CrossCurrents 1* (Pearson Education Limited, 1992)

Topics	Functions	Grammar	Listening/Pronunciation	Writing/Reading	Interchange Activity
Unusual and Exceptional jobs	Giving opinions about jobs; describing and comparing jobs	Gerund phrases as subject and object; comparisons with *er/more/less* than and as ... as	Listening to descriptions of jobs; Sentence stress	Writing about career advantages and disadvantages "Strategies for Keeping Your Job" Reading advice about behavior in the workplace	The best and the worst Finding out about classmates' summer or part-time jobs

Figure 3 *New Interchange 3: English for International Communication* (Cambridge University Press, 1998)

Usually, the different language features or components of a coursebook chapter or unit are linked together around a topic or topics. What is the focus of each of the units profiled on page 229? How are the components of each unit linked?

2. Adapt the material.

Coursebooks are not written for a specific group of people. Since they are meant to be used by different or successive groups of learners, they can't be. They're written for a generalized target group (e.g., for children or adults, for use in English speaking countries or in other countries, for beginner, intermediate or advanced levels, and so on). No book can meet all the needs and interests of each group of learners that uses it. For this reason, a coursebook *must be adapted* to your particular group of learners. Acklam (1994, p. 12) suggests the following acronym for adapting a coursebook: "SARS."

S = Select
What parts of the coursebook do you definitely want to keep?

A = Adapt
What parts of the coursebook do you basically want to keep, but need to change in some way to make them more suitable for your students, and in tune with your teaching style?

R = Reject
What parts of the coursebook do you definitely want to leave out?

S = Supplement
What else do you need to bring to the coursebook to fulfill the requirements of the overall syllabus you are working to, and to respond to the needs of your particular students?

Figure 4 SARS (Select, Adapt, Reject, Supplement)

Remember, a coursebook is not an inflexible document, it is a learning tool that is used by learners and teachers. Your decisions about what to "select, adapt, reject and supplement" depend on who your learners are (age, interests, purposes for studying and language level), what the institution emphasizes, the resources available to you, how much time you have, and what you feel is important. If there is too much X, then do less of X. If there is no Y, then add Y, if Z is unnecessary for your students, then skip Z. For example, Sato (2002) found that Japanese high school students and teachers initially had difficulty using coursebooks that emphasized speaking since they were accustomed to coursebooks that emphasized reading with a focus on translation and grammar. They were able to use the coursebooks more effectively when the teachers designed oral performance assessments to be done at the end of each unit. The addition of the tests gave the learners a goal and thus made them more willing to do the speaking activities in the coursebook. In the section on techniques we will look at ways to adapt and supplement a coursebook.

3. Prepare the learners.

In an on-line research project a colleague and I conducted with a group of teachers from four different countries, we found that coursebook activities usually fail not because they're too boring or too complicated, but because the learners haven't been adequately prepared to do them. Put another way, any coursebook activity can be successful as long as learners know what to do and have the ability to do it. (If they don't have the ability to do the activity, the coursebook may be at too high a level.) Preparing the learners means two things. First, it means orienting them to the content and purpose of the activity, that is, making sure they know *what* the activity is about and *why* they are doing it. Second, it means making sure they understand the steps of the activity, *how* to do it. However, simply telling the learners the *what, how,* and *why* of an activity doesn't prepare them. They need to demonstrate either verbally or in action that they have understood.

Preparing the learner really means preparing yourself. What is the context for the activity? The images that accompany an activity are often helpful in providing a context. How can you make the context clear and interesting to the learners? What is the point of the activity? Is the focus to learn grammar? Is it to practice speaking? Is it to learn vocabulary? The title of the activity often provides clues to the purpose. What are the steps involved in carrying out the activity? How can you ensure that the learners know what to do? How long will the activity take?

Action

Figure 5 is a page from a textbook aimed at young adults/adults at the intermediate level. There are two activities on the page. Describe how you would prepare the learners to do each activity so that

a) they know *what* the activity is about (How would you orient them to the content?);

b) *why* they are doing it (How would you make sure they understand the purpose?);

c) and *how* to do it (How would you break down the steps?).

Decide on a time limit to give the students for each activity.

---

1   Talk it over

Complete the sentences using some of the words in the list.

Women are more _____ than men.
Men are more _____ than women.

competitive	cautious	logical	possessive	emotional	aggressive
considerate	intuitive	industrious	generous	relaxed	sensitive

**Compare your sentences and opinions with a classmate.
Which statements do you agree with?**

2   Talk about... Cartoons

**Look at these cartoons.
Describe what is
happening in each one.
What generalizations do
they show about men,
women, and children?**

"He doesn't know anything except facts."

"Well, if I called the wrong number, why did you answer the phone?"

"Alice can be a little *girl* Commando in your game, Donald."

Figure 5 *CrossCurrents 1* (Pearson Education Limited, 1992)

4. Monitor and follow up.

Any activity actually has three parts: preparation, implementation, and follow-up. While the students are doing an activity, you have an important role: to monitor what and how well they are doing. The easiest way to monitor is to walk around the classroom and observe what they are doing, (in a neutral, not a judgmental way). As you circulate, you can answer questions, keep track of language problems, offer helpful corrections (if they don't inhibit fluency), and make sure they are doing what they are supposed to be doing. Monitoring also helps you to see if the time limit you set was appropriate and whether it will need to be shortened or extended. Often teachers concentrate on the students in the front rows and remain at the front once an activity is underway. Consequently, the students at the back give up on the activity and the learning opportunity is lost.

It helps to develop signals to let students know when to stop. In small classes, this can be done via language such as "OK, time to stop." In large classes, clapping your hands or ringing a bell are more effective than using your voice, unless you have a resonant voice! Once an activity is done, it is important to follow up so that students can demonstrate what they have learned or ask questions about it. For example, if students have practiced a dialogue in pairs, then a few pairs can demonstrate the dialogue to the group. If groups of three have just discussed what they like to read and why, then a few students can report to the class on what they learned about their partners' preferences. Alternatively, the teacher can survey the class. For example, "How many of you like to read ___?"

5. Build a repertoire.

In addition to being organized around key features of language, a coursebook generally has consistent types of activities in each unit or chapter such as pair and group tasks, **role-plays, information gaps,** listening tasks, and vocabulary games. It helps to build up your own repertoire of ways to do each type of activity. For example, most listening activities include some kind of task. One way to approach a listening activity (after the appropriate introduction to what it's about) is for students to listen through once to get the general idea; listen a second time and do the task in the book such as answer questions or fill in a diagram; and then listen a third time and check their answers. If you follow this format consistently, you provide some predictability for the students–they learn familiar ways to approach an activity. It also helps to have ways to vary an activity once students are familiar with the basic format. For example, students can try to do the task before the first listening as a way to create anticipation for what they will hear.

Building a repertoire also means having techniques for supplementing what is in the textbook. Part of my own repertoire includes putting things on cards or strips of paper that students can manipulate. For example, one way to teach vocabulary is to have students write the vocabulary words on cards and then group them in some way. Another way is to put parts of sentences on cards so that students can put them in order and learn the grammar. I sometimes write prompts on cards for speaking and writing activities. I also have students write comprehension questions to reading passages on cards and quiz each other.

The teacher's guide that accompanies the coursebook is an excellent resource for learning about ways to teach and vary activities. When Alison Rice and I were writing the introduction to the teacher's guide for *East West Basics* (Oxford University Press, 1994), we included nine different ways to prepare for a dialogue and ten different ways to practice it. Teacher's guides also give step-by-step suggestions for how to teach each activity in the student book.

4. Classroom techniques and tasks

In this section, we look at techniques and tasks for implementing the five principles outlined in the previous section. The first two techniques are designed to help you understand how the coursebook is organized.

Survey or map the territory When familiarizing yourself with the table of contents, trying to take in the entire contents of the book can be overwhelming. Start small, with a group of units or just one unit. Some books have review units, so a natural chunk is the group of units leading up to the review unit. If you own the book, make notes as you go through it about what you like, what you don't like, what you want to emphasize, supplement, and reject.

Another way to survey the territory is to make a map of it. This means creating a nonlinear visual representation of the contents of the book or unit. By taking apart the pieces and rearranging them in a visual way, you become familiar with what is in the book. These kinds of "mind maps" or "word webs" can be done at any level: book, unit, or activity. (See Andersen, Chapter 4, this volume.)

Group prioritizing There is often more material in a coursebook than you can cover in the amount of time available. Richard Acklam suggests the following activity (1994, p. 13). "Give out the books on the first day [of class], and, for homework, ask students to decide which topics/grammar areas in the book they are most interested in/concerned about. The next day the students vote on the most relevant parts of the book for them, and this immediately helps the teacher to select appropriately."

One advantage of this technique is that the assignment gives the students a reason for looking through the coursebook. It gives them ownership of the "tool" and helps them understand it is flexible. It also opens dialogue among them and the teacher. One disadvantage is that some learners may feel intimidated or inadequate to the task. Or they may feel that making these decisions is the teacher's job. One way to adapt this task would be to have them do the same kind of prioritizing, but only for one unit.

The next three techniques will help you adapt the material to your particular group of learners.

Personalizing Personalizing means asking for or giving personal or culturally familiar information related to the material in the coursebook. This technique draws on the learners' experiences and opinions and so makes the material more real and accessible to the students. I remember observing a high school French teacher teach telephone numbers using the examples in the textbook. The students were bored and inattentive. By simply asking them to use their own telephone numbers, she would have made the material more relevant and motivating. In addition to making material more relevant, personalizing also allows for personal and cultural comparisons. Learning how to order food from a menu is a common coursebook activity. Learners can be asked to compare the way menus are organized in their culture(s), what items cost, and what food items are included.

Personalizing can be done in preparing for an activity, during an activity, or following up an activity. Take the example of ordering from a menu. The menu in the coursebook is unlikely to be one students have actually used. In preparation for the activity, the teacher can ask students to make a list or sketch of what they expect to find in a menu. They can then compare their lists to the menu in the book and discuss how they are similar and different. To personalize during the activity, the learners can discuss foods on the menu that they've tried, and ones they've never tried, and whether they would want to order them or not. As a follow-up, the teacher can ask the learners to talk about the kinds of restaurants they go to and what they usually order. Alternatively, they can prepare menus with only their favorite foods.

Reflection

Why is personalizing important? What are some considerations when planning ways to personalize the material and activities in a coursebook?

Format shift **Format shift** means switching to a different skill or grouping than the one proposed in the book.

- Switching to a different skill: A reading text about places to vacation in Australia can be used as a model for writing about places to vacation in the students' own country. The same text can be used for pair dictation or for pronunciation practice. In one sense, format shift is about supplementing through skill integration: when appropriate, giving students opportunities to speak, listen, read, and write about each activity.

- Switching to a different grouping: a pair question and answer activity about the ideal roommate can become a mixer in which the whole group gets up and walks around and asks different people the same question. An individual writing activity about the pros and cons of school uniforms can be turned into a small group brainstorm and group essay.

Use props, visuals, or realia Props, visuals and realia stimulate visual and cultural interest in a lesson. Realia are objects or texts that are used by people in their everyday lives. Props are theatrical aids to represent a role or situation. Visuals are pictures, drawings, photos or images. (These three categories very often blend.) Realia for a lesson about phone numbers might include a phone book or an advertisement with phone numbers. Realia for a unit about places to vacation might include tourist brochures. Props for a lesson on phone numbers might include a toy telephone, and for a lesson on places to vacation, a beach towel and ski goggles. One of my colleagues uses a plastic bow as a humorous prop to demonstrate a dialogue between a woman and a man. He places the bow in his hair when speaking the woman's part and at his throat when speaking the man's part. Visuals for a lesson on vacations might include pictures of different vacations spots.

Props, visuals and realia can be used both to prepare students for and to supplement or extend an activity. The teacher should not be the only source of these supplementary materials. Students can be asked to bring in materials related to the topics, such as pictures of their ideal vacation spot or photos from their last vacation.

Action

The two activities in Figure 5 (page 232) are aimed at intermediate adult/young adult learners. Think of a group of learners that fits that description.

Describe:

- how you would personalize the activities so that they are relevant to the learners and highlight potential cultural differences.

- different ways of grouping learners to do them (individual, pair, small group, whole class).

- props, visuals, or realia you or the learners could bring in to supplement them.

The next two techniques are designed to help you prepare the learners to do the activities.

Visual instructions Visual instructions is a fancy way of saying "demonstrate what to do." This technique is based on the notion that showing is much more effective than telling. For example, to introduce a pair activity, you can write an example of the pair exchange on the board and then use your hands to represent the two speakers as you demonstrate the exchange. (Some teachers use puppets, others change positions.) You can then ask two students to stand up and model the exchange. If you are introducing a group activity in which students are to survey each other in groups (e.g., about what they like to read and why), you can demonstrate the activity by asking one student the questions first and then having the student ask you the same questions.

Elicitation Elicitation means asking the students to provide information or examples based on what they know. In preparing for an activity that reviews the present perfect tense, you can ask for several examples from the students. However, elicitation doesn't mean putting learners on the spot. It only works when you try to elicit what they are likely to know. Because it emphasizes the learners' experience and knowledge, elicitation helps to take the focus off of the text as the source of authority and helps learners become more self-reliant, an important skill in learning a language. Elicitation works hand in hand with personalization. To prepare for an activity about reading preferences you can first ask the students "What are things we read?" and list their responses on the board. It is also a way to get differences of opinion, or examples that are different from those provided in the coursebook. Students can be asked whether a picture that shows a family living in a large house is the way most people live. Elicitation is also useful when following up an activity.

Reflection

For the Action box on page 232, you made a list of ways to prepare students for the activities in Figure 5. How would you modify them to include visual instructions or elicitation?

The next two techniques are designed to help you monitor and follow up what the students do.

Mistake log One way to monitor what and how well the students are doing is to keep a mistake log. Make a note of the activity and the class and as you circulate, write down the mistakes you hear the students making. Mistakes can be grammatical, lexical (vocabulary), or cultural. The mistake log can then be used in a number of ways. You can use it immediately after the activity and elicit correction from the students. For example, in an activity for practicing polite ways to ask for something, the teacher noticed that many of the students were not using the word *please*, which was included in the examples in the book. After the activity, she wrote two contrasting examples on the board "Could you bring me a glass of water?" and "Could you bring me a glass of water, please?" She asked the students to discuss the difference and why one was more polite than the other.

If there are recurrent mistakes, for example incorrect use of tenses, you can prepare a separate lesson and use examples from the log. The log will also show you and your students in which areas they are improving because the mistakes occur less frequently.

Group survey One way to follow up an activity is to do a group survey of the results. Surveys answer the questions how many, how often, how much, how long, and so on. For example, after an activity in which students have asked for and given information about their families, the teacher writes three headings on the board: only child, one brother or sister, more than one brother or sister, and then surveys the class to find out how many fit in which category. In a group survey after an activity on reading preferences, the teacher writes each type of reading on the board, asks for a show of hands for each, and writes the number after each category. She then asks the group why the categories with the most and least numbers are the most and least popular.

Activity chart Building a repertoire requires setting up some kind of system for keeping track of what has been successful so that you can use the techniques again. One way to do that is to make a chart with the relevant four skills of speaking, listening, reading, and writing (depending on which you teach), as well as other focal areas such as grammar, culture, or vocabulary.

Action

Chapters 2, 3, 7 and 8 in *Practical English Language Teaching* provide descriptions of excellent activities that can be used in the classroom. Refer to the appropriate chapter in order to complete the activity chart. Write one or two activities from each chapter.

Focus area ➡	Listening	Speaking	Vocabulary	Grammar
Activity	• •	• •	• •	• •

5. Using a coursebook in the classroom

The purpose of this section is to show you some of the ways language teachers use the concepts and techniques already discussed. The first example shows how a teacher prepares to teach the first two activities in a unit. The second example shows how a teacher adapts an activity in a unit. The last example shows how a teacher prepares her students to do an activity, how she monitors, and how she follows up the activity.

Teacher A teaches at a language institute in Morocco. The learners are men and women, mainly in their twenties, and at an intermediate level of English. In preparation for teaching the activities in Figure 6, Teacher A has made notes about how she wants to teach the activities on that page.

Look at the textbook excerpt in Figure 6. Notice how the teacher has annotated the page with her comments.

1   Talk it over

Complete the sentences using some of the words in the list.

Women are more _____ than men. ⎱ *expand w/phrases and vocab.*
Men are more _____ than women. ⎰ *make a list on the board*

| competitive | cautious | logical | possessive | emotional | aggressive |
| considerate | intuitive | industrious | generous | relaxed | sensitive |

Compare your sentences and opinions with a classmate.
Which statements do you agree with?

→ *brainstorm more*

2   Talk about... Cartoons

Look at these cartoons. Describe what is happening in each one. What generalizations do they show about men, women, and children?

→ *What stereotypes? What roles?*

Bring in other cartoons for balance.

"He doesn't know anything except facts."

"Well, if I called the wrong number, why did you answer the phone?"

How do these reflect Moroccan culture? American? Why?

"Alice can be a little *girl* Commando in your game, Donald."

Figure 6 *CrossCurrents 1* (Pearson Education Limited, 1992)

Commentary Before the students even open the book, Teacher A plans two preparatory activities (discuss terms and brainstorm) to orient students to the theme of the unit and to generate useful vocabulary based on their own experience. The first activity in the book *Talk it Over* aims to provide the vocabulary and grammar needed to compare men and women as a basis for expressing personal opinions. The activity already has personalization built in since students are expressing their own opinions. However, as it is a forced choice, the students may feel they have to express opinions they don't hold. The teacher plans to add an additional grammar structure *As...as* so that the students can talk about similarities in addition to differences. She plans to review the vocabulary, however it is unclear from the notes how she will make sure they understand new vocabulary. If some students don't know certain vocabulary words, she could elicit explanations or examples from the students who do.

The second activity in the book *Talk about...Cartoons* asks students to describe the cartoons and the way they generalize male and female traits and roles. The teacher questions the viewpoint of the textbook. She feels the stereotypes are too traditional, so she plans to bring in additional visual material to show a variety of perspectives.

Action

Think of a particular group of learners. Consider their age, gender, level of English, and interests and purposes for learning English. Choose a page from a coursebook. Write on the page what you would keep, what you would adapt, what you would reject and what you would supplement.

Reflection

Look at Teacher A's notes in Figure 6. What are ways that she plans to supplement the material? How does she plan to adapt the activities and why? How will she prepare the students? How will she personalize the material?

Teacher B teaches at a language institute in Brazil. His students are adults at an intermediate level. He is teaching Activity 2 in Figure 7. In this activity, they are applying the rule they learned in Activity 1.

PRACTICE

1. Read the sentences in the box and answer the
   questions below.

> **DESCRIBING:** *Relative clauses*
>
> a. In *Ghost*, Patrick Swayze stars as a ghost **who returns to help his girlfriend.**
> b. In *The African Queen*, Katharine Hepburn stars as a woman **who travels downriver in Africa.**
> c. *E.T.* is about an alien **who comes to Earth and becomes friends with a young boy.**
> d. A film buff is someone **that knows a lot about movies.**
> e. What do you call a movie **that makes you laugh?**
> f. A musical is a movie **that has singing and dancing.**
> g. I like movies **that have a lot of action.**

   - Circle the word ⟨who⟩ in the sentences. Underline the word <u>that</u>. When do we use *who*?
     When do we use *that*?
   - Look at sentences "f." and "g." One sentence uses *have*, the other uses *has*. Why?

   Answers on page 100

2. *Pairs.* Make a guess. What do you think these films
   are about? Choose from the list on the right.

   a. In *Roman Holiday*, Audrey Hepburn stars as a princess — • that eats swimmers.
   b. *Trouble in Paradise* is about two thieves — • that wants to be a dog.
   c. *Babe* is about a pig — • who runs away from home.
   d. *Twister* is about two scientists — • that has special powers.
   e. *Jaws* is about a huge shark — • who study dangerous tornados.
   f. In *The Mask*, Jim Carrey finds a mask — • who fall in and out of love.

Figure 7 *Transitions 1* (Oxford University Press, 1998)

The activity takes about fifteen minutes.

The sentences that are in the book have been transferred on to cards.

Teacher B divides the class into two groups of six students and hands out a set of cards to each group. He tells them to match the cards. Six movies are described on the cards; there are twelve cards in each set. Examples: *Trouble in Paradise* is about two thieves…(card 1A)…who fall in and out of love (card 1B); *Babe* is about a pig…(card 3A)…that wants to be a dog (card 6B). Students sit on the floor to work. They spread out the cards on the floor but are confused about what to do. The teacher gives them an example by matching one pair of sentences himself. Once students have understood what the teacher is asking them to do, they get down to work. Students interact loudly with each other as they move the cards around and try to match them correctly. They make an effort to use English to communicate and do so successfully. The teacher stands by the students as he watches them working, but does not intervene in their negotiation. Students are on task throughout the activity and are able to match the sentences correctly in the end. Once they have finished matching the cards, the teacher plays the tape for them to check their answers. (The tape has the correct answers.) The teacher checks to see if they have any questions. There aren't any, so he moves on to the next activity.

Commentary Teacher B adapted Activity 2 by doing two format switches. The first switch was from reading and drawing lines to speaking and matching cards. Instead of having the learners connect the two sentence halves by drawing a line in the book, he transferred the sentence halves onto cards. The second switch was from pair to group work. Instead of having them work in pairs, as suggested in the book, he asked them to work in groups of six. The teacher assumed that telling the students what to do was enough preparation for the activity. It didn't work. Once he had demonstrated what to do, they understood.

Reflection

Why do you think Teacher B adapted the activity this way? What are the advantages of doing the activity the way the teacher has done it rather than the way it is suggested in the book? What are the disadvantages?

I see two important advantages to the way Teacher B has done it—group involvement and kinesthetic manipulation. One possible disadvantage is that students may not want to work on the floor or that there may not be space to spread the cards out on the floor.

Teacher C, in Extract 1 page 243, teaches in a private language school in Hong Kong. Her students are young adults. In the following example, we see how she teaches an information gap activity shown in Figure 8. In this kind of activity, Student A has information that Student B doesn't have and vice versa. The activity requires the students to use the target language in order to find out the missing information. Teacher C prepares the learners to do the activity, monitors them as they do, it and follows up with examples.

Along the side of Extract 1 (page 243), draw lines where the three phases of the activity (preparing, doing, follow-up) begin and end.

Then note where you find the following:

- Orienting the learners to the purpose of the activity
- Orienting the learners to how to do the activity (making sure they know what to do)
- Elicitation from learners
- Providing a context for the activity
- Monitoring the activity
- Personalizing

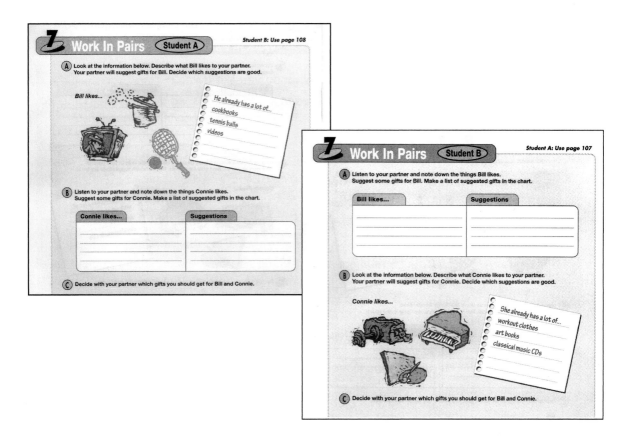

Figure 8 *Expressions 1* (Heinle/Thomson, 2001)

In the classroom extracts, *T* stands for teacher and *S* represents a particular student. *Ss* stands for students.

<blockquote>

Extract 1

T: *Right, now are you ready to do the info gap task? Yes? We've done lots of these, now, haven't we?*

Ss: *(Nod)*

T: *The purpose of this task is to give you more practice in the language we're learning in this unit. What ARE we practicing? Remember? Johnny?*

S: *Talk about what people like.*

T: *Talking about what people like—good. And?*

S: *Talking about gift giving.*

</blockquote>

T: *Talking about gift giving. Right. These are our communication goals. And what structures do we use to do these things? … Anyone? … Yes, Mary?*

S: What do you like? *And* What do you like doing?

T: *Great! And we use* "like" *to talk about things, right? And* "like doing" *to talk about activities. What about making gift giving suggestions?*

S: Let's.

T: *OK, good,* Let's get him a CD, *or* Let's get Tom a golf club. *OK, now* WHEN *do we give people gifts?* WHEN? *Yes, Monica?*

S: Birthday.

T: *Birthdays are good.* (Writes *birthdays* on the board) *Johnny?*

S: *New … new baby.*

T: *That's a good suggestion.* (Writes *new baby* on the board and continues eliciting until there are a number of events on the board.) *OK, now get into your pairs and I want Student A to look at page 107, and Student B to look at page 108.* (Peers over students' shoulder) *Johnny, you're the B student aren't you? You're looking at the wrong page. 108, please. Good. Now, Bill likes the things the A students can see in the picture, but he already has these things. OK? Understand, Monica? Right. So, tell your partner what Bill likes, and your partner will suggest gifts. Write the suggestions in the space, and then decide on the best idea. Oh, Student A—start off by suggesting a reason for buying a gift—look at the board—it's his birthday, he's going away and so on. Right, off you go.*

(The students complete the task. As they do so, the teacher circulates and monitors. When she hears a mistake, she writes it in a notebook, but does not interrupt the students.)

T: *OK, I think everybody's finished now. Are you two finished? Right, good. So, now I want you to do the same thing for Connie. B, tell A what Connie likes. A will make suggestions. Write them down then decide, decide on the best one, OK?*

(Again, the teacher circulates and monitors. At one point she is stopped by one pair, listens to their question and says "It's called a subscription—a subscription.")

T: *OK, time's up. Let's hear what each pair decided.* (Teacher elicits responses from the students and writes them on the board.) *Well, that's great—look at all these interesting gifts. Which of these gifts would* YOU *like to receive, Johnny? … Sorry?*

S: *The California Fitness Subscription.*

T: Yeah, I like that one, too. How about you, Sophie? (She continues, eliciting students' preferences, and writing their names next to the gift.) *OK, now, you all did very well, but I noticed a few mistakes creeping in here and there. Look.*

(She writes the mistakes from her notebook on the board and gets students to self-correct.)

Commentary Teacher C provides an excellent example of how to introduce and maintain control of an activity so that students are free to concentrate on the task and practice the target language. When she elicits examples, she makes sure to call on a variety of students. She is nonjudgmental in the way she makes sure that students are "on task" and in the way she introduces error correction at the end. She provides a human touch in her responses by not only asking for students' personal preferences, but in commenting on what they have chosen and on what she herself would choose.

6.   Conclusion

In this chapter, I outlined some of the ways in which coursebooks have changed through the years, as well as some of the disadvantages and advantages of using coursebooks. I then explained five principles for using a coursebook, followed by techniques that show how to put the principles into practice: how a coursebook is organized, ways to prepare for, monitor, and follow up an activity, ways to adapt and supplement what is in a coursebook, as well as how to build a repertoire of one's own. In the last part of the chapter, we looked at how three teachers prepare to teach using a coursebook.

Further readings

Graves, K. 2000. *Designing Language Courses: A Guide for Teachers*. Boston, MA: Heinle & Heinle.

Chapter 9, "Adapting a textbook," goes into more detail about ways to adapt a coursebook at the syllabus, unit, or activity level with step-by-step examples from teachers. It also discusses the "hidden curriculum" of coursebooks.

Rinvolucri, M. 2002. *Humanising Your Coursebook: Activities to bring your classroom to life*. London: First Person Publishing.

This book describes 95 activities for using a coursebook with sections on warm-up activities, grammar, vocabulary, reading, writing, listening, speaking, and assessment.

Woodward, T. 2001. A Central Tool: The Coursebook, p. 145–160 in *Planning Lessons and Courses.* Cambridge: Cambridge University Press

> This section includes ideas for orienting yourself and the students to the coursebook as a whole as well as thoughtful ways to adapt it.

Helpful Web sites

Many coursebooks now have their own Web sites to provide additional activities.

Here are Web addresses for a few of the major ESL/ELT publishers.

Cambridge University Press (http://publishing.cambridge.org/elt)

Heinle/Thomson Publishing (http://www.heinle.com)

McGraw-Hill/Contemporary (http://mhcontemporary.com)

Oxford University Press (http://www.oup.co.uk)

References

Acklam, R. 1994. The Role of the Coursebook. *Practical English Teaching,* 14/3, 12–14.

Hutchinson, T. and E. Torres 1994. Textbook as Agent of Change. *ELT Journal* 43/4, 315–328.

O'Neil, R. 1993. Are Textbooks Symptoms of a Disease? *Practical English Teaching,* 14/1, 12–14.

Sato, Y. 2002. "Teacher and Student Learning in the Workplace." Paper presented at the annual conference of the Japan Association for Language Teaching, Shizuoka, Japan.

Swan, M. 1992. The Textbook: Bridge or Wall? *Applied Linguistics and Language Teaching,* 2/1: 32–35.

Van Ek, J. A. and L. G. Alexander 1975. *Threshold Level English.* Oxford: Pergamon Press.

Chapter **Twelve**

Computers in the language classroom

Ken Beatty, City University of Hong Kong (China)

Goals

At the end of this chapter, you should be able to:

✔ **explain** the following concepts: CALL, schema, behaviorism, and constructivism.

✔ **explain** how CALL can be used as whole class and small group activities.

✔ **explain** ways to maximize learning opportunities for CALL materials, including poor materials.

✔ **evaluate** language learning software.

1. What is CALL?

Computer-assisted language learning (**CALL**) is closely related to many other disciplines *and* the computer. As a tool to aid teaching and learning, CALL is often subsumed within them. For example, CALL has become increasingly integrated into research on and the practice of the general skills of reading, writing, speaking, and listening as well as into discrete fields, such as autonomy, corpus linguistics, and testing. The difficulty of defining CALL is apparent in this selection of related terms and acronyms:

- Computer-aided instruction (CAI)
- Computer assisted learning (CAL)
- Computer assisted language instruction (CALI)
- Computer-assisted language teaching (or testing) (CALT)
- Computer adaptive teaching (or testing) (CAT)
- Computer-based training (CBT)
- Computer-mediated communication (CMC)
- Computer-mediated instruction (CMI)
- Intelligent computer assisted language learning (ICALL).

Some of these terms are synonymous with CALL, while some shift focus to narrower concerns. But, given the breadth of what may go on in CALL, a general and useful working definition is: *any process in which a learner uses a computer and, as a result, improves his or her language.*

Under this definition, CALL covers a broad range of activities. This is reflected in the diverse topics one is likely to read in CALL journals: materials design, explanations of computer technologies, pedagogical theories about working at the computer, and the computer as a mode of instruction, to name a few. CALL materials include those specifically created to teach language, as well as computer-based materials adapted for teaching language (for example, English language newspaper Web sites or computer games with heavy English content).

CALL continues to grow in many directions. Understanding its scope is further complicated by constant advancements in hardware and software and an increase in computer literacy among both teachers and learners. Three decades ago, CALL would have been constrained to on-screen written exercises with simple graphics. Currently, CALL interactions are likely to include sound, animation, video and communication over local area networks (LANs), email and Internet chat lines. It would not be rash to predict that CALL will soon feature learner immersion in full virtual reality.

CALL is popular both in and out of the classroom. Classrooms may feature a single computer, a class set or even a situation in which portable laptop computers are issued to each learner who carries them from class to class along with, or instead of, books.

In the classroom, CALL activities may be used both as a reward and a remedial aid. Some classes are CALL language labs, building on the functions of traditional listening labs. But because of CALL's difficulty in accommodating listening and speaking, it is almost always used as a supplement to traditional classroom teaching and learning. Outside the classroom, many commercial applications promote themselves as complete methods for learning a language or part of a language, particularly in programs aimed at business travelers. But there is no empirical evidence of anyone ever learning to speak a new language simply by using a computer.

Reflection

1. Why have so many related terms grown up around CALL?
2. What are some implications of CALL not being clearly defined?

2. Background to teaching with CALL

CALL in the language classroom is, in some cases, evolving as quickly as computer technology itself evolves. In other cases, CALL in the language classroom is relatively unchanged from the behaviorist directives of the 1950s. For example, the most traditional and still most common form of CALL programs are behaviorist computer-based **gap-fill drills,** in which learners answer questions or fill in information in **cloze** exercises, where key or random words have been replaced with spaces. This approach is closely associated with B. F. Skinner (1954, 1957, 1968), whose approach emphasized rote learning, along with the techniques of mimicry and memorization through repetitive drills. Learners are rewarded by small positive responses, often including the right to move to a new level of drill.

Skinner's behaviorist theories found practical application in **programmed instruction** or **programmed learning**. A behaviorist model suggests learners can be taught a wide variety of subjects if presented with information in small steps, each step requiring appropriate responses (i.e., correct answers to questions) before offering more difficult or more advanced steps. Such an idea seems machine-like and, in fact, Thorndike put forward the idea of an automated mechanical book in 1912, and such a machine was constructed as early as 1926. It featured multiple-choice questions on a rotating drum and four keys for selecting answers. The machine collected the responses and even distributed a candy when all the correct choices were made (Merrill, et al., 1996).

Skinner (1968) suggested the machine was ahead of its time, but supported the idea of machine instruction as a way of increasing learner autonomy to avoid an essential problem, the pace of instruction in a group of learners whose comprehension and learning rates are at different levels:

> Even in a small classroom the teacher usually knows that he is going too slowly for some students and too fast for others. Those who could go faster are penalized, and those who should go slower are poorly taught and unnecessarily punished by criticism and failure. Machine instruction would permit each student to proceed at his own rate (p. 30).

The potential benefits for learners proceeding at their own rate crosses the boundaries of different models of instruction, and the arrival of the computer presented an ideal technology for programmed instruction. Programs could be **linear**, with all learners following the same path or **branching** with learners facing more difficult questions if their answers were correct or undertaking remedial training and/or questions if their answers were wrong.

Many the above features of programmed instruction are still common in CALL today, but Stevens (1992) notes it fell from popularity in language learning because it tended to focus on details and surface forms of the language at the expense of real-world communication.

Despite these criticisms, programmed instruction continues to be pervasive in CALL, sometimes combined with other, less behaviorist features. The reason for its enduring appeal may simply be that programmed instruction is an easy–if not ideal–thing for the computer to do. Today, a popular use of such programs is in teaching learners how to pass standardized tests.

A typical computer-based gap-fill drill lesson might look something like this.

Example

1. Learners enter the program and are asked for personal information, such as a name, that personalizes some of the coming content.

2. Learners select from a menu of options what they would like to learn. Choices might include presentation of language items in different formats, such as a story, a video of a conversation, a flowchart, or table.

3. A new language item or set of items to be learned are presented, giving a contextual demonstration of its meaning. This on-screen modeling

may be done through associations with pictures, sounds, animation, and/or video. Further explanations may be available through pull-down menus, timed prompts, or hyperlinks (text or images which are linked, by a mouse click, to further information).

4. Learners are given a choice of repeating the presentation of information, seeing the information presented in another form, or proceeding to a test.

5. The test offers some kind of immediate feedback. The feedback may be as simple as a score or may offer detailed critiques of the correct and incorrect answers provided by the learners.

6. Based on the learners success, they are either directed back to the same presentation of information or a variation of it.

7. Steps 3 through 6 are repeated until the learners achieve success. Then they are either moved along to a parallel set of language items or to a more difficult level. Alternatively, if the learners choose to exit the program, the program may keep a record of their attempts for future (and/or teacher) reference.

Reflection

1. What are the advantages and benefits of behaviorist approaches and programmed learning?

2. Programmed learning is popular, yet criticized. Why do you think it is criticized, and why do you think it remains popular despite criticism?

Beyond **behaviorism,** psychologist F.C. Bartlett first proposed the idea of **schema** theory in 1932. Nunan (1993) defines schema theory as, "A theory of language processing which suggests that discourse is interpreted with reference to the background knowledge of the reader or listener" (p. 124). Nunan also notes, "... schema theory suggests that the knowledge we carry around in our heads is organized into interrelated patterns. These are constructed from all our previous experiences and they enable us to make predictions about future experience" (p. 71). Anderson (1988) helps to define a schema approach to teaching and learning by suggesting it is one in which knowledge is:

> ... not merely a collection of facts. Although we may be able to memorize isolated facts for a short while ... meaningful learning demands that we internalize information; we break it down, digest it and locate it in our pre-existing highly complex web of interconnected knowledge and ideas, building fresh links and restructuring old ones (p. 197).

Schema theory is the foundation of **constructivism**. In a constructivist approach, a software program draws on the expertise of the learner and builds on it, offering multiple paths of inquiry and different ways of looking at the same problem or challenge. A typical constructivist program involves the learner in a kind of a quest, in which the teaching and learning objectives are achieved almost as a peripheral consequence of completing some other task.

For example, *Who is Oscar Lake?*, a CD-ROM-based game, is an example of a constructivist language learning program. It is a mystery game in which the language learner has been framed for the theft of a diamond and must go to a foreign city (featuring the target language) and use clues and interviews to try to trace the thief. The pace of the game is controlled by the learner, and different choices change the plot line. In the program, learners learn language as a peripheral activity to solving the mystery. On-line dictionaries and translations with sound are available if needed.

3. Principles for teaching CALL

1. Evaluate the appropriateness of the software program or computer-based resource (e.g., game or Web site):

Expertise Learners who determine what they know and do not know about a task are more likely to engage in productive work. Does the program pretest learners to evaluate what portions of the program will be of most use to them? Teachers can help in this process by identifying each learner's strengths and weaknesses and supplying appropriate software. Is the program at a challenging level for your learners?

Motivation Learners are usually faced with extrinsic motivation and manufacture intrinsic motivation when it suits them. Teachers and learners need to create motivation through establishing goals and understanding how CALL activities can help achieve them.

Program objectives Is it clear what the program aims to accomplish in terms of learning? Are these objectives realistic?

Target audience Many CALL materials may be aimed at specific audiences such as business people or primary students. Is the program pitched at students in your class?

Cognitive overhead How difficult is it to learn how to use the program?

Cost Is the program worth it? Is it better to get a few stand-alone copies rather than an expensive site-license?

Pedagogical approach Is the program behaviorist or constructivist? Does the program teach, or does it merely test?

Authenticity Does the program make use of authentic materials and situations? Do these materials relate to the experiences of the learners?

Feedback How does the program offer feedback?

Role of the learner/teacher What is expected of the learner? What is expected of the teacher?

Self-study/classroom Is the program intended for self-study or classroom use?

Technological appropriateness Does the program require extra hardware or software to make it work efficiently?

In groups, discuss CALL programs you have used or seen in the classroom. Evaluate them in terms of the above criteria. What other criteria might you apply to CALL programs?

2. Create an environment in which CALL is supported.

Arrange the CALL classroom to maximize interaction Many early CALL classrooms were integrated into traditional listening labs with dividers between learners to ensure privacy and discourage cheating during examinations. This type of isolation of learners, especially in a row-on-row situation, discourages interactions and opportunities for scaffolded learning. CALL classrooms should be organized so that learners have opportunities to share computer screens and discuss their common progress.

Ensure easy access to CALL Engaging in CALL should be as painless as taking a book out of a library or using any other common academic resource. Too often computing time is restricted, access to software tightly controlled, and budgets for very visible hardware are not matched with funds for software, upgrades, and repairs.

3. Monitor learner participation in CALL programs and encourage autonomy.

Determine roles When learners work together at the computer, they often select roles for themselves. Depending on the presentation of the software, learners may see the computer as a form of television providing passive entertainment in which they do not need to engage, or they may see it as a teacher, or even a kind of fellow learner.

Encourage responsibility There is seldom enough time or resources for comprehensively learning a language in a classroom, so learners using CALL should be encouraged to take responsibility for their own learning. This means making the best use of computing facilities when they have access to them and finding ways to follow up on what they have learned when they are away from the computer.

4. Encourage the use of CALL programs as a starting point for collaboration and learner interaction.

Encourage collaboration Have learners use the computer as an area for brainstorming. This is made more effective as the learners simultaneously search for information to aid in discussions. As learners interact, they help each other learn at a level appropriate to their language abilities. Collaboration can also take place on the Internet, through e-mail penpal or keypal arrangements.

Imagine, or role-play, two learners using a CALL program for the first time. What kinds of discussions are they likely to have? How might these discussions help their general language awareness and development? How might these discussions help their computer literacy?

4. Classroom techniques and tasks

In this section, we look at common CALL techniques and programs. The techniques can be easily adapted to various languages, ability, and skill levels.

There are several taxonomies to classify CALL techniques. Software reviews often provide examples. One taxonomy, offered by Chandler (1984), is based on how much control there is between the program and the learner:

- Tutorial/hospital model: user as patient
- Games/funfair model: user as emulator
- Simulation games/drama model: user as role-player
- Experimental simulations/laboratory model: user as tester
- Content-free tools resource/center model: user as artist or researcher
- Programming languages/workshop model: user as inventor

In practice, however, programs are likely to stretch across a range of these models. For example, the main part of a CALL program may use a tutorial model, but testing may be done in a game or simulation format.

Below are five examples of simple CALL techniques and programs.

Internet treasure hunt An Internet treasure hunt asks learners to find a number of pieces of information. The teacher organizes the tasks so that learners will learn various strategies, such as paraphrasing. The teacher may also want the learners to encounter peripheral information to encourage general learning. The searches might be of a general nature, such as asking adult learners to find Web sites where they can learn about language related to their occupations, or knowledge domains, such as language related to sports.

The following example lesson might be suitable for a group of ESL learners who are reinforcing their knowledge of the simple past. They might also be studying early American history in another class and the ESL teacher might be using the following as a support activity.

> ### Example
>
> **Teacher:** *For this lesson, I want you to find ten facts about Christopher Columbus. You may find many Web sites mention places named after him, but the facts you need to find are the ones I have written on the board: Where and when was he born? How old was he was when he died? What did he do? (and so on). Think of synonyms when you're searching for your answers. I would also like each student to find out one different fact about him, so you will need to check with each other.*

The task encourages learners to think in terms of keywords beyond the question, for example, birth and birthday as well as born. The request for unique information encourages learner interaction.

Concordancing Concordancing is a process of looking at relationships among words. Even without a concordancing program, a teacher can still ask learners to look up words and strings of words on the Internet to find natural contexts.

Learners can get a better understanding of how the words are used appropriately. It is a self-study technique that the learner can take away from the classroom. Visit Grammar Safari at http://www.iei.uiuc.edu/web.pages/grammarsafari.html.

> ### Example
>
> Look at today's newspaper and find a phrase you don't understand. Use a search engine such as www.google.com to look for occurrences of the phrase (for example, *tongue in cheek*). Collect ten definitions or examples and review the meaning with other students.

E-mail penpals E-mail penpals can be arranged by the learners themselves or as part of a class-to-class exchange. It would be ideal for language learners to correspond with native speakers of the target language, but in practice, native speakers sometimes find it a less than satisfactory exchange and break off contact. Learners may also find it frustrating to be confronted with unfamiliar slang, expressions, and obscure cultural references. A preferable situation is to engage learners of the target language from different native language groups, for example, Portuguese and Norwegian students both studying and corresponding in Japanese. In a class-to-class situation, a series of assignments or prompts might be offered. (For a summary, see Warschauer, Shetzer & Meloni, 1999.)

Chatlines Chatlines are a variation on *penpals* and are commonly referred to as IM (i.e., instant messages) discussions. Such discussions have the advantage of occurring close to real time. Learners can build a conversation, but it may suffer if one or more of the learners has poor typing skills. One of the advantages to both the learner and the teacher is that transcripts of the discussion may be preserved and studied.

Thesaurus The thesaurus function in most versions of popular word-processing software programs is something that can be exploited by teachers and learners to encourage vocabulary expansion. A simple exercise is to have learners complete a piece of narrative or descriptive writing, then go through it, changing all of the adjectives and adverbs by highlighting them and using the thesaurus function to find replacements. Unknown words can be discussed and learned, and known words can be compared for subtle differences to their synonyms.

Companion Web sites In addition to the usual ancillaries such as workbooks, testing packages and teachers' manuals, many commercial textbook series have companion Web sites. These sites vary in quality, but most have something interesting to offer. The beauty of these sites is that they are usually not password protected, and can therefore be accessed regardless of whether or not you are using the printed textbook. (Of course, as they were designed to supplement the textbook series they go with, their effectiveness is limited if you attempt to use them as 'stand alone' resources.)

For example, the textbook series *Expressions* (Heinle/Thomson, 2001) by David Nunan has a site at http://expressions.heinle.com. Each unit in the series has supporting material on the Web, as well as an "exploration section." This section contains a Web-based project that requires the learner to apply the language they have been learning in the unit. One interesting feature of this site is that if the student enters the teacher's e-mail address, the site will, when the student submits his or her work, generate a diagnostic report on the student's answers.

Language learning sites In the last few years a number of commercial language learning sites have appeared on the Internet. Two of the best known of these are Englishtown and GlobalEnglish. These sites are intended as comprehensive language learning solutions. In other words, students should be able to learn English by engaging with the content provided (at a price) through the Internet without necessarily attending a face-to-face class. Many online language learning providers, however, recognize the fact that students need direct interaction with teachers to learn a new language. As such, they promote **blended learning** solutions in which students meet regularly in chartrooms with instructors. The *blend*, then, combines students working on their own on Web-based activities with live sessions with a teacher and other students.

Web-based programs have a number of potential advantages over regular classroom instruction. In the first place, the computer is a "patient tutor." The student can repeat exercises as often as necessary to gain mastery, something that is not always feasible in a face-to-face classroom. Students can also gain instant, individualized feedback on their performance, often with a diagnostic report on where additional practice is needed. Finally, they have the advantage of providing the learner with a "private space" for practicing their English, something which is valued by shy or inhibited students.

Action

Visit the GlobalEnglish Web site at www.globalenglish.com and complete one of the assignments that are offered free of charge. How did the experience compare with other forms of self-study? Based on your experience of completing the assignment, what would you see as the advantages and disadvantages of this mode of learning?

5. CALL in the classroom

The purpose of this section is to show how CALL concepts and techniques can be realized at the level of classroom action. The following two fictional extracts feature distinct approaches to CALL. The first features a CALL classroom with Internet access in which Spanish is being taught; there is no commercial CALL software being used in this lesson other than what can be found free on-line. In the second extract, a teacher in a CALL classroom is making use of a commercial program, Transparent Language *Learn Chinese Now,* to teach Mandarin. In reality, there is little reason why one would choose one approach over the other. Instead, teachers are likely to integrate the two over the course of a single lesson or set of lessons.

Reflection

Study the following two extracts.

1. In what ways are the extracts similar? In what ways are they different?
2. What is the purpose of each lesson?
3. Which activities would be most effective? Why?

In Extract 1, held midsemester, the teacher has welcomed her students (age 15) to her beginner Spanish class and done a few spot-checks on comprehension of the last day's lesson. She now introduces today's topic to her eighteen students. Although some of the discussion would take place in the target language (Spanish), it is presented in English here for the convenience of the reader.

Extract 1

Teacher: *The topic of today's lesson is* mercado. *(She writes the word on the board; it means* marketplace.*) Who knows what* mercado *means? (Six hands shoot up and the teacher makes a mental note of the students for a later task.)*

Teacher: *Okay, let's hear it. Tom?*

Tom: *Isn't it about selling something?*

Teacher: *Perhaps. What do you think, Janet?*

Janet: *I went to a* supermercado *in Mexico last summer, so I think it's a kind of grocery superstore where you buy different kinds of food.*

Teacher: *Mmm. Brett, you have an idea?*

Brett: *Well, if* supermercado *is* superstore, *then* mercado *must just be a store.*

Teacher: *Good logic. Anyone else have something to add? Yes, Amy?*

Amy: *I think* mercado *is a place to sell things, I'm not sure if it's just for groceries.*

Teacher: *Okay, we're going in the right direction, but I'm not hearing that everyone agrees or has a perfect idea of what* mercado *means. This is what we want to do today: we want to build a **knowledge domain** around* mercado*. Who remembers what a knowledge domain is? Yes, Janet?*

Janet: *It's all the words and phrases about an idea.*

Teacher: *Sounds good. Anything else? Yes, Ming?*

Ming: *Pictures about the idea and some activities, too.*

Teacher: *Good. The six people who put up their hands at the start, yes, that's you, Tom, Janet, Brett, Amy, George and Ming, pick two other people each and form teams. This is what I want you to do: use the Internet to collect examples of the word* mercado*. When you are looking, you may also find some digital images of a* mercado *as well. Save these in a separate document and we will see if we can use them later. When you've got your teams, I want you to write me a **learning contract** for how you're going to approach the topic. I expect you to be able to teach the other students about some aspect of* mercado *using information you have found on the Internet. But first you need to learn what a* mercado *is. You've got five minutes. I'll come around to each group.*

(Five minutes pass in which the teacher circulates among the groups. The teacher finds that the students have discovered that *mercado* means marketplace. Armed with this information, the students propose to attack the topic from different directions. The teacher ensures there is no repetition among the proposals and sets the groups to work. Each group has written a "contract" that says what they will complete by the end of the week for presentation in the following week. If they cannot complete it in class, they know that it will be assigned as homework. As the groups work, the teacher addresses the class again.)

Teacher: *I'll just interrupt you for a moment to fill you in on what each team is doing. As always, if you can find a way to help each other, it's worth extra points. Now, Tom's team has decided to use translation software at http://babelfish.altavista.com to make up a mini-dictionary of words related to* mercado*. You're focusing on both English and Spanish, aren't you, Tom?*

Tom: *Yes, that's right. And we'll print out a copy for each student.*

Teacher: *Good, save a copy of the file for me. We'll add it to our other* *mini-dictionaries. Janet's group is also making a dictionary, but they're taking key words and finding a picture (www.corbis.com) for each one, is that right Janet?*

Janet: *Yes, and we'll work with Tom's group to use some of the same words.*

Teacher: *Will you modify the pictures?*

Janet: *Yes. We're using simple photo-editing software to add arrows and key words in the pictures. Uh, we'd also like to borrow the digital camera later.*

Teacher: *Great. You might decide you want to work together as one larger group and make one dictionary with translations and pictures. I've written* mercado *on the board. As your group finds other key words and phrases, use the markers to add words and phrases in a spider chart. That way we all can share. Brett, you're doing something with pictures too?*

Brett: *Yes, sort of ... our group is making a crossword puzzle of lots of words related to* mercado. *We can do it by making a table in our word-processing program. We'll use some clip art at http://dgl.microsoft.com/mgo1en/eula.asp for clues, but we'll use some English words for clues as well.*

Teacher: *Good. Work with the other groups. And don't forget to write an answer key. Amy? Your group is doing something with concordancing?*

Amy: *We're doing a search for* mercado *and writing down all the sentences where it is used. We want to see what words go with it.*

Teacher: *And how will you make it available to the other students?*

Amy: *We'll make a handout and include the addresses of the Web sites, too.*

Teacher: *Don't forget to look for places where* mercado *is used in English pages; use a Boolean search. I want you to think about why a Spanish word would be popular in English. Ming, you're writing a cloze exercise in a word-processing program?*

Ming: *Yes. We'll write one in English and one in Spanish. We'll work with Amy's group and use some of the same sentences.*

Teacher: *Great. And George? Your group is doing something with sound?*

George: *We want you to help us pronounce some of the words and phrases. We'll record them and make a simple Web page with the sentences and the sounds.*

Teacher: *Okay, talk to the other groups and get an idea of the important words and phrases. I like the Web page idea and once the other groups are finished, we might add everything to a single Web page. Now, let's get going.*

(The teacher lets the teams begin and circulates among them, marking progress, offering suggestions and encouraging cooperation. In some groups, she assigns roles, making certain students responsible for liaising with other groups and others responsible for recording progress. She prompts students to use as much Spanish as possible in their discussions. At the end of the lesson, students report on any problems they are having and other team members offer advice. The teacher asks the students, What did you learn today? Then she takes some answers and ends the class with words of praise. After class she makes notes on how she might make use of the student resources in future lessons.)

Commentary The teacher uses a constructivist approach and has created a situation that builds upon the knowledge of the students both in their language knowledge–defining *mercado*–and proposing an approach that makes the students responsible for extending their schema around the word. The teacher also allows students to build on their computer knowledge, allowing them to choose the ways in which they might approach the task of activating the term *mercado* and its peripheral vocabulary and ideas.

The idea of learning contracts, agreements of what the students plan to accomplish, shifts responsibility to the students and frees the teacher from constant supervision so she can devote her time to pedagogical issues. Her offer of extra points for cooperation ensures that students take over part of the teaching duties, sharing what they have found. The teacher shifts her focus as a dispenser of knowledge to a facilitator helping her students work as autonomous learners, and supporting Hutchings, et. al. (1992) suggestion that, "Those who prepare the course material may learn much more than those who receive it" (p. 171).

Action

Imagine you are teaching the same type of lesson as in Extract 1 but on a different topic and, perhaps, in a different language. What challenges do you think you and your students would face? Write your own classroom extract.

In Extract 2, held midsemester, the teacher has welcomed his students (age 15) to his beginner Chinese class and collected their homework. He administers a brief quiz and allows students to self-check to ensure comprehension. Based on the quiz, he decides to review the previous day's work but allows six of the better students to explore a newly-purchased Chinese software program, Transparent Language *Learn Chinese Now*. He asks these students to start the program, find an area that interests them and be prepared to report back to the class what they have learned. There is no paper manual, but he gives the students the carton and explains that he will help them once he has had time to get the rest of the class working.

Reflection

Read Extract 2, then think about these questions.

1. In what ways are Extracts 1 and 2 similar? In what ways are they different?
2. What is the purpose of each lesson?
3. Which is the richer student experience?
4. Should the teacher in Extract 2 have previewed the software before asking the students to use it? Why or why not?

Extract 2

(As the students wait for the computer to warm up, they make small talk and discuss what they are expected to do.)

Juanita: Okay, so let's look at this box. What does it say?

Harris: It's got some pictures on the back, some screen captures about what it looks like. Do you see something you'd like to do?

Juanita: Well, we should just divide up and look at different sections. I'll take the one for this picture on the back, some people are talking and it has the conversation in Pinyin (Chinese Romanization).

Peter: How about inside the box? There's pictures of the Chinese characters, that's what interests me. I'll work with Anna.

Erin: There are some games. Don and I will look at those.

Juanita: Okay then. Let's do it.

(The students start up the program and begin finding their way and working with it. After ten minutes, their teacher takes a break from the rest of his class and stops by to speak with each pair.)

Teacher: How's it going here?

Juanita: Fine. We're working on this section with the conversations.

Teacher: Are you learning anything?

Juanita: Well, it's okay. Some stuff is familiar but …

Teacher: But?

Juanita: Well, you've already taught us a lot of the Chinese characters, but this section doesn't use characters.

Teacher: Is that confusing?

Juanita: Well, I don't know if we'll ever see Pinyin when we go to China.

Teacher: You'd be surprised. It's used quite a bit for street signs and labels.

Harris: The other problem is that they break up the words into syllables.

Teacher: What do you mean?

Harris: Well, you see here? Peng you. That should be one word. Do they write it like that in China?

Teacher: Uh, no, they don't.

Harris: And see, here, they say you means friend. Doesn't pengyou mean friend?

Teacher: Well, yes, but if you saw you written as a single character, you'd expect it to mean friend. Also, friend, as a radical affixed to another character might suggest a friend aspect. But no, to answer your question, I'm not sure this is the best way to learn.

Juanita: So you think it's a garbage program?

Teacher: Too soon to say. You need to look at it and find what's good and bad about it. Listen, can I ask you to write a short review of this feature? It would be helpful to explain your points to other students.

Harris: Sure.

Juanita: Will do.

(The teacher moves on to the second pair.)

Teacher: Peter, how are you doing?

Peter: Well … Anna and I are looking at the Chinese character section.

Teacher: And how does it work?

Anna: You click on each character and it says the sound. The sounds are quite similar, so it helps to be able to hear them together.

Peter: Yes. And there are different colors for different kinds of sounds.

Teacher: Is that helpful?

Peter: Sure.

Teacher: Okay, turn away from the screen. What is blue used for?

Peter: Uh …

Teacher: Well, have another look. Any problems?

Anna: I thought there would be something here for us to practice writing the characters, but there isn't.

Teacher: No? Nowhere in the program?

Peter: Nope. We looked.

Teacher: Well, try to get what you can out of it. Also, I'll give you some index cards and try writing down the characters for flashcards. I'll give you a few minutes at the end of the hour to test the class on the sounds. Questions?

(The teacher moves on to the third pair.)

Teacher: *Okay, what have you two been up to?*

Erin: *Games. We've got the games.*

Don: *We tried the crossword program, which is a little difficult, but then we went on to the ...*

Teacher: *Sorry, what was difficult about the crossword program?*

Don: *Well, we didn't know much of the vocabulary.*

Erin: *And we weren't really sure what the picture clues meant. We had to spend some time figuring out the pictures and then maybe getting a prompt for a free letter.*

Teacher: *Mmm. Do you think it's something you might get better at if you tried it a few times?*

Erin: *Maybe. But I think the words change every time you play. You also get your score at the end to see how well you've done.*

Teacher: *What about the other game?*

Erin: *It's better. It's a cloze exercise. We also tried the sound recording.*

Teacher: *Oh, how was that?*

Erin: *Quite good. It's probably the best thing on the program.*

Teacher: *Mmm. I'd like you to make a couple of notes about the program for the other students. Could you do that for me?*

Don: *What should we write?*

Teacher: *Some of the same things you told me. Add instructions on how to get started in the games and recording sections.*

Commentary The teacher uses a behaviorist program to occupy a group of the better students; he might just as easily have used it as a remedial program but, as it was new, he wanted some of his better students to help find out more about its strengths and weaknesses. Like the teacher in Extract 1, he allows the learners autonomy to structure their tasks as they best see fit. Hopefully, the students act responsibly in the knowledge that they are being rewarded for their performance and will be challenged by the teacher later in the lesson.

Early in the lesson, the teacher finds time to visit the six students and make sure that they are on track. He finds some problems with the program and will perhaps modify his future purchases of software on the basis of the students' feedback. In general, there have been few opportunities for the students to activate their language, but he challenges them to think of ways in which they might get more out of the program. He also finds ways to make the students responsible for sharing their views with other students.

Select a software program and design your own teaching sequence. Now imagine yourself teaching the sequence. How do you think it will go? Write your own classroom extract.

6. Conclusion

This chapter began by defining CALL in loose terms, acknowledging that it is a quickly evolving discipline. CALL practitioners, researchers, and developers face a daunting task of keeping up with developments in the field. This chapter has pointed out some of the ways of presenting CALL in the classroom through simple techniques, but there are also always new software programs for improving language learning. What is important is to evaluate these programs to ensure that they offer pedagogically appropriate materials for your students. That said, even poor materials can present opportunities for learning if handled appropriately.

Further readings

Beatty, K. (forthcoming 2003). *Applied Linguistics in Action: CALL*. London: Pearson.

This book offers a historical overview of computer-assisted language learning and explores the current and future developments.

Chapelle, C. 2001. *Computer applications in second language acquisition: Foundations for teaching, testing, and research.* Cambridge: Cambridge University Press.

This book focuses on the use of the computer for teaching language with particular attention paid to how students acquire information.

Klein, B., M. Hunt, and R. Lee 1999. *The Essential Workbook for Library and Internet Research.* New York, NY: McGraw Hill Higher Education.

This workbook provides step-by-step instructions for teachers and advanced learners on getting the most out of Internet resources.

Fox, J. 1991. *Learning Languages with Computers: A history of computer assisted language learning from 1960–1990 in relation to education, linguistics and applied linguistics.* Unpublished Doctorate thesis, University of East Anglia.

This is a good overview of the history and basic ideas in CALL.

Helpful Web sites

**Open University Language Studies' web directory
(http://www.open.ac.uk/education-and-languages/links/languages.cfm)**

This Web site offers a general collection of language resources for both students and teachers.

**I Love Languages (formerly Human Language Resource Page)
(http://www.ilovelanguages.com)**

This Web site offers a general collection of language resources in many languages.

Evaluating a CALL Initiative (http://edvista.com/claire/eval.html)

This Web site offers several resources for evaluating programs, CALL and Web sites.

Global English Corporation (http://www.globalenglish.com)

Global English offers fee-based English courses for adults and children.

References

_____. 1996. *Who Is Oscar Lake?* New York: Language Publications Interactive.

_____. 2001. *Learn Chinese Now, Deluxe Edition (Version 8)*. Merrimack, NH: Transparent Language.

Anderson, T. G. 1988. *Beyond Einstein. Interactive Multimedia.* S. Ambron & K. Hooper, (eds.) Redmond, WA: Microsoft Press.

Chandler, D. 1984. *Young Learners and the Microcomputer.* Milton Keynes: Open University Press.

Hutchings, G. A., W. Hall, et al. 1992. Authoring and evaluation of hypermedia for education. *Computers Education,* 18(1–3): 171–177.

Merrill, P. F., et al. 1996. *Computers in Education.* Boston, MA: Allyn and Bacon.

Nunan, D. 1993. *Introducing Discourse Analysis.* London: Penguin.

Skinner, B. F. The science of learning and the art of teaching. *Harvard Educational Review,* 24(2), 86–97.

Skinner, B. F. 1957. *Verbal Learning.* New York, NY: Appleton-Century-Crofts.

Skinner, B. F. 1968. *The Technology of Teaching.* New York, NY: Appleton-Century-Crofts.

Stevens, V. Concordancing with Language Learners: Why? When? What? *CAELL Journal,* Summer 1995, 6(2): 2–10.

Warschauer, M., H. Shetzer, and C. Meloni 1999. *Internet for English Teaching.* Alexandria, VA: TESOL Publications.

Chapter **Thirteen**

Learning styles and strategies

Mary Ann Christison, University of Utah (USA)

Goals

At the end of this chapter, you should be able to:

✔ **provide** a definition of a learning style and learning strategy.

✔ **clarify** the difference between learning styles and strategies.

✔ **explain** why learning styles and strategies are important considerations in second language teaching.

✔ **identify** some major learning styles and learning strategies.

✔ **identify** learning styles and strategies in your own lesson plans.

✔ **identify** five important features of your own learning style profile.

1. What are learning styles and strategies?

As an English language teacher you may recognize your students learn differently, but you may not have the necessary skills for dealing with different **learning styles** and **strategies** in the classroom. The purpose of this chapter is to help you learn more about learning styles and strategies so you can help your English language students learn most efficiently.

The terms *learning styles* and *learning strategies* can be confusing. Some English language teachers think they are the same thing, but they are not. Learning styles and strategies are linked to one another, but they are not the same thing.

Learning styles refers to " ... an individual's natural habitual, and preferred ways of absorbing, processing, and retaining new information and skills." (Kinsella, 1995, p. 171). These styles seem to persist regardless of the content you are trying to master (e.g., learning to fly an airplane vs. learning another language) or the method of instruction you are given (e.g., straight lecture vs. problem-solving, small group work). Whether you know it or not you also have preferred ways of absorbing, processing, and retaining new information and skills.

Learning strategies are different from learning styles. Learning strategies refer to "... characteristics we want to stimulate in students to enable them to become more proficient language learners." (Oxford, 1990, p. ix). In this case, we are not talking about preferred ways of doing things, but rather looking at the characteristics of tasks that second language learners must do and purposely teaching students the behaviors that will help them be successful learners. Strategies must first be identified as important to a given task, and then, they are purposely taught. For example, a common task teachers use is to ask students to make a written summary of information acquired from listening to or reading text. The task is to say or write the main idea. This is a cognitive strategy known as summarizing.

Reflection

Do you think knowing about learning styles and strategies is important for second language teachers? Why or why not?

Using the definitions above and without further reading in this chapter, give an example of a learning style and a learning strategy from your own experiences as a student and/or teacher.

2. Background on learning styles and strategies

The major research base for much of the current work on learning styles began in the first quarter of the twentieth century with the work of noted psychologists Carl Jung (1976) and Jean Piaget (1968). In recent years, English language teachers have become very interested in learning styles. In the last decade we have seen works specifically devoted to learning styles and English language teaching appear on the market–Reid (1995, 1997), Kinsella (1995), Oxford (1990), and Oxford and Anderson (1995). This chapter will cover the most common and significant learning styles. As educators, we hear the most about the perceptual learning styles–visual, auditory, kinesthetic, and tactile; however, perceptual learning styles are only one piece of a much larger learning-style picture. It is important to see the different learning styles as connected because learners will have more than one learning style. In addition, different tasks may be approached in different ways, making more than one learning style significant for a given task.

Learning styles are both individually and culturally motivated (Kachru, 1988; Nelson, 1995). Within a given culture and on a larger scale, we can see certain learning style preferences among individuals surfacing. This is not to say that everyone within the culture has the same preferences, but, rather, that culture does play a role in the development of our preferences. This can lead to conflicts in a second language classroom that is made up of students from different language backgrounds when the teacher does not understand the relationship between the students' learning styles and his/her own (Cohen, 1969; Oxford, Ehrman & Lavine, 1991).

Strategies are specific means that learners use to learn or improve their language. There are many different kinds of learning strategies, depending on the context and tasks. Because the scope of this chapter is limited, I will only introduce strategies for learning in a classroom environment. (See Oxford 1990; Silver and Hanson, 1996a, Silver and Hanson, 1996b). These classroom learning strategies are broken down into three areas: **cognitive**, **metacognitive**, and **socio-affective**.

The labels used for describing learning styles and strategies vary greatly. The taxonomies in this chapter work well for English language teachers. They are neither too complex nor too simple, and they identify features of learning styles and strategies that are critical for second language learners. Neither the taxonomy for learning styles nor the taxonomy for learning strategies is meant to be exhaustive. They simply present ways of thinking about learning styles and strategies that are easy and manageable. We will also explore the types of behaviors that students with different learning styles might exhibit in the second language classroom. The ultimate goal in applying these taxonomies to instructional planning and design is to create English language teaching environments that assist different students in learning English efficiently and effectively.

In considering how to apply learning styles in the L2 classroom, I have found it useful to look at three broad categories of learning styles (see Figure 1)—cognitive, sensory, and personality.

Learning Style Taxonomy for the L2 Classroom

Type 1: Cognitive Styles	Type 2: Sensory Styles	Type 3: Personality Styles
Field Dependent—learns best when information is presented in context. They are often more fluent language learners **Field Independent**—learns most effectively step-by-step and with sequential instruction. They are often more accurate language learners	**Perceptual:** **Visual**—learns best when there is visual reinforcement such as charts, pictures, graphs, etc. **Auditory**—learns more effectively by listening to information **Tactile**—learns more effectively when there is an opportunity to use manipulative resources **Kinesthetic**—learns more effectively when there is movement associated with learning	**Tolerance of Ambiguity:** refers to how comfortable a learner is with uncertainty; some students do well in situations where there are several possible answers; others prefer one correct answer
Analytic—works more effectively alone and at his/her own pace **Global**—works more effectively in groups	**Environmental:** **Physical**—sensitive to learning environment, such as light, temperature, furniture **Sociological**—sensitive to relationships within the learning environment	**Right and Left Hemisphere Dominance** **Left-brain** dominant learners tend to be more visual, analytical, reflective, and self-reliant **Right-brain** dominant learners tend to be more auditory, global, impulsive, and interactive
Reflective—learns more effectively when they have time to consider new information before responding **Impulsive**—learns more effectively when they can respond to new information immediately; as language learners, they are risk takers		

Figure 1 Learning style taxonomy for the L2 classroom

Look at the description of each learning style. Make a list of the styles that best describe you. Share your results with a partner.

Each student in your classroom will have cognitive, sensory, and personality type learning styles. In order to use the information presented in Figure 1 most effectively, you must gain a working knowledge of the general categories of learning styles so you can (1) recognize different styles in yourself and your learners, and (2) create lesson plans and classroom activities that address these varied styles.

There are many different ways to categorize learning strategies (Oxford, 1990). Given the emphasis in the past decade on helping learners develop critical thinking skills and cognitive academic language proficiency (CALP) (Cummins, 1996), I have chosen to review some general learning strategies. In the cognitive academic language learning approach (CALLA), Chamot and O'Malley (1994) identified some general learning strategies that contribute to second language student success in academic and classroom environments. While the focus in the CALLA model is on children learning a second language, the general learning strategies are important for all language learners in formal classroom environments. General learning strategies fall into three areas–metacognitive (i.e., strategies to help students think about their own learning), cognitive, and socio-affective.

General learning strategies for second language learners in academic contexts (adapted from Chamot and O'Malley, 1994 and Oxford, 1990)

Learning strategy	Definition of strategy
Metacognitive strategies	
Planning	Previewing main ideas Making plans to accomplish a task Paying attention to key information Seeking out and arranging for conditions to promote successful learning
Monitoring	Self-checking ones comprehension
Evaluating *(Continued page 272)*	Developing the ability to determine how well one has accomplished the task

Cognitive strategies	
Summarizing	Saying or writing the main idea
Induction	Figuring out the rules from samples of language
Imagery	Being able to visualize a picture and use it to learn new information
Auditory representation	Mentally replaying a word, phrase, or piece of information
Making inferences	Using information in the text to guess the meaning
Using resources	Developing the ability to use reference materials
Grouping	Classifying words, terminology, quantities, or concepts
Note-taking	Writing down key words and concepts in verbal, graphic, or numerical form
Elaboration of prior knowledge	Relating new to known information and making personal associations
Social/Affective strategies	
Cooperating	Learning how to work with peers—completing a task, pooling information, solving a problem, and obtaining feedback
Clarifying	Learning how to ask questions to get additional explanation or verification from the teacher or someone else who might know the answer
Self-talk	Reducing anxiety by talking positively to oneself

Figure 2 Learning strategies for L2 learners

3. Principles for teaching learning styles and strategies

1. Vary activities and materials.

Learning style profiles are different for everyone. No two classes of students will be exactly the same. The class of students you have for one session may have very different learning styles from students you have in the next session. Students will also have different needs relative to learning strategies depending on their collective goals and objectives. When I started working with learning styles in the early 1980s, I thought that I needed to determine the learning styles of the students in each class, and then create lesson plans and select activities and tasks to match their learning styles. What I discovered was that the profiles and needs of each class were different. If I had continued with my initial way of thinking, I would have been constantly creating new materials, activities and tasks, changing formats, and refocusing my lessons. A simpler and more logical approach for addressing learning and strategies eventually surfaced. Once I began to understand the different styles and strategies presented in Figures 1 and 2, I began to think of learning styles and strategies in a more global sense. Rather than create tasks and activities for a specific group of students, I began varying the activities and tasks to address a broad range of learning styles and learning strategy needs. Over a period of time, many different styles and strategies would be addressed.

2. Make all learning styles value neutral.

The students in your classes will all have different learning styles. Some styles will work better than others in different learning situations, but no one learning style is better than another one. As an English language teacher, it is important that you understand the learning styles of the students in your classes and value all styles equally. One way that you can show that you value all learning styles is to make certain that you vary your lesson plans so that they include activities that address the different styles. When you, as the teacher, embrace diversity in learning, you set an excellent example for your students to do the same thing.

3. Audit your teaching.

If you are a practicing teacher, conduct an audit of your teaching for two or three weeks. Focus on either styles or strategies, and on one or two specific styles or strategies at a time. Before you begin making changes in your approach to teaching relative to learning styles and strategies, you should always make certain that you have a very clear understanding of what it is that you routinely do. Once you understand what you routinely do, you will be able to make changes in your teaching in order to broaden or change your approach to both learning styles and strategies in your classrooms. For example, if you always have your students work alone, you may want to change your practice and have them work in small groups occasionally. If you always ask questions that have one possible correct answer, you may want to change your practice and ask open-ended questions that can be answered in several different ways. If you are not yet a practicing teacher, you may want to observe an experienced teacher to understand how both learning styles and strategies can be used in the second language classroom.

4. Encourage students to stretch their learning styles.

Rather than think of each learning style as very separate and unique, I have found it useful to think of learning styles on a continuum. By thinking of learning styles on a continuum, I can see more clearly what styles students are using in the classroom and can get a clearer picture of how to help them stretch their learning styles–particularly for students at the extremes of the continuum. For example, the cognitive learning style of impulsive/reflective can be seen on a continuum with the impulsive learning style at one end and the reflective at the other end. When you see students who prefer using the impulsive learning style (e.g., completing work quickly and immediately in class), you can acknowledge the strengths of the global style (e.g., These are generally the students who do get their work finished and in on time!). Then, try to assign some tasks in which the impulsive learning style may not serve them well (i.e., when students must work on a multistep project on their own that requires careful consideration at each step). By recognizing students' learning style strengths and then giving them opportunities to stretch themselves, you help them develop a better understanding of how they learn best. By pointing out that the learning style in question may not always serve them well, you can help them see the limitations in their current ways of learning. By suggesting other behaviors at the opposite end of the continuum, you help them stretch their learning style capabilities.

5. Find ways to link both learning styles and strategies.

Learning styles and strategies are closely related; therefore, it is important to find ways to link these two concepts in course curricula. Learning styles stem from the learners themselves–their preferred ways of perceiving and processing information. Learning strategies stem from the tasks–ways of perceiving and processing information that are important to completing a task successfully. Sometimes learning styles and strategies match up beautifully for students, but at other times, they do not. When preparing lesson plans, it is important to look closely at each task and activity that students are required to complete and ask yourself two questions:

- What learning styles will be most useful in completing these tasks?
- What learning strategies will my students need in order to complete these tasks successfully?

Once you have answers to these questions, you can make adjustments in the planning and presentation of course materials in order to provide an optimal learning environment for your language learners.

Reflection

What specific things might you do to help learners stretch their learning styles?

4. Classroom techniques and tasks

There are many advantages to using learning styles and strategies in lesson planning and curriculum development. The English language classroom certainly becomes a more varied and interesting environment when learning styles and strategies become an integral part of learning. Students learn content and language, and they learn more about themselves and how they learn. Using learning styles and strategies gives teachers a more holistic view of learning and spawns creativity in the development and use of techniques for learning. Here are two techniques for using learning styles and strategies. I have chosen these techniques because I believe they have the broadest appeal.

Creating inventories Language learners enjoy knowing more about themselves and how they learn if they also perceive themselves to be learning English at the same time. Inventories are an excellent way of helping learners develop their language skills and learn more about their individual process of learning. There are a number of useful learning style inventories already on the market (Oxford, 1990b; Reid 1995; Kinsella, 1995; Dunn,

Dunn, and Price, 1975, 1979, 1989) that can provide you and your students with useful and quite reliable information about learning styles and strategies. I also believe there is great value in homemade inventories because they can be useful in providing springboards for important discussion in the classroom both on the results obtained from the inventories and on the process of creating the inventories. The following inventory was created with my students in order to talk about the perceptual learning styles. The perceptual learning styles are visual, auditory, tactile, and kinesthetic.

My students identified the content for the inventory in a brainstorming session. Collectively they brainstormed some typical activities (e.g., driving a car or talking to a teacher about a problem), preferences (e.g., for movies, CDs, sports) and beliefs about self (e.g., personal appearance, disciplining children). I created the inventory by carefully thinking about each item in relationship to perceptual learning styles. I selected the behaviors that were representative of auditory, visual, and kinesthetic learning styles and created the multiple-choice questions below. Students not only participated in useful language activity during the brainstorming session, but also had a chance to take the inventory individually and then discuss the results with a partner or in a small group.

Example **Perceptual style inventory for language learners**

Directions: Work alone. Answer the questions. Choose the one answer that best describes you. When you have finished, summarize your answers. What is your strongest learning style? Do you have more than one? Then, with a partner and share your answers. Where are your answers different? Similar?

1. A person can tell what you are feeling by
   a) the way your face looks
   b) the way your voice sounds
   c) the way you stand, move, and hold your body
2. If I need to talk to someone about something very important, I prefer to
   a) meet face-to-face
   b) talk on the telephone
   c) talk while I am doing something else
3. When I am driving or riding in a car for long distances, I frequently
   a) check the rearview and side mirrors and watch out for other cars.
   b) turn on the radio or listen to a cassette or CD
   c) move about in my seat trying to get comfortable and make frequent stops
4. When I am angry at someone, I
   a) give them the silent treatment
   b) tell others immediately
   c) clench my fist and storm off

5. When I attend a meeting, I
    a) prepare notes, agendas, overheads, etc. in advance
    b) enjoy discussing and hearing others ideas
    c) doodle and daydream
6. When it comes to the clothes I wear, I pay most attention to
    a) comfort and how I feel
    b) how I look
    c) compliments and what others say
7. The best form of discipline is
    a) to take away something of value
    b) to discuss the problem
    c) to refuse to speak or interact
8. When I have a little free time, I like to
    a) participate in some sport or physical activity
    b) watch TV or movies
    c) listen to the radio or my favorite music
9. I try to keep up with what's going on in the world by
    a) scanning the newspaper or catching a few minutes of the evening news while I'm doing other things
    b) reading the newspaper or news magazine
    c) listening to the radio or watching the evening news
10. I think the most effective way to reward someone (including me) is
    a) a pat on the back, a handshake, or a hug (whichever is appropriate)
    b) oral praise in front of peers
    c) letters, notes, and stickers with positive comments

Answer key

Total the points for each a), b), and c) checks. Numbers 1 -5 a) visual, b) auditory, c) kinesthetic; Numbers 6-10 a) kinesthetic, b) auditory, c) visual. If you have more points in any one area, that area will be your dominate learning style. It is quite common to have equal points in two areas. This means that you have a bi-modal profile.

Interactive search and find Interactive search and find works much in the same way as creating inventories in terms of student involvement. The major difference is that creating inventories focuses only on learning styles and Interactive search and find focuses on learning strategies and learning styles.

Again, my students identified the content for the Interactive search and find in a brainstorming session. Collectively they brainstormed some different strategies they use for learning (e.g., using resources, summarizing, etc.) and different ways in which they prefer to learn (e.g., setting their own goals, learning in a step-by-step fashion, etc.). I selected the content for the Interactive search and find based on student input. Again, students not only participate in useful language activity during the brainstorming session, but also have a chance to participate in the Interactive search and find with their peers.

Interactive search and find

Directions: You will need to get up and out of your seats and talk with your classmates. Find someone for whom the following statements are true. Get signatures from your classmates. They should sign their names in the blank spaces under the statements. Try to get as many different signatures as you can.

Find someone who . . .   **Name**

1. learns new information more effectively step-by-step.   _____
2. knows how to use an English/English dictionary.   _____
3. knows how to find information on the Internet.   _____
4. learns best when interacting with other people.   _____
5. can read a passage and pick out the main ideas.   _____
6. knows how to use an encyclopedia.   _____
7. is good at taking notes.   _____
8. notices temperature, sound, and light in the classroom. _____
9. likes to take risks in learning.   _____
10. knows how to cooperate in a group.   _____
11. is good at using information to guess meaning.   _____
12. asks questions to get additional information.   _____
13. learns best when interacting with other people.   _____
14. is a fluent language learner.   _____
15. learns more effectively through hearing language.   _____
16. learns more effectively through hands-on material.   _____

Inventories and Interactive search and find are just two examples of useful and creative techniques that result from learning style and strategy taxonomies and frameworks.

Work with a partner. Look at the Perceptual style inventory for language learners (on page 276) and identify the different learning styles in each of the questions without looking at the answer key. Work with a partner. Look at *Interactive search and find* and identify the different learning styles and strategies in each

5. Learning styles and strategies in the classroom

In the previous section, we focused on techniques and tasks that teachers created with their students. In this section, I would like to show you how to apply the ideas presented in this chapter to already existing commercial materials. For purposes of this example, I have selected two lessons. The first lesson is from *Parachutes Book 1*. The topic is pets and animals. *Parachutes* is a series for very young children. This lesson will be used to illustrate the application of learning styles. The second lesson is from *Quest: Reading and Writing in the Academic World, Book 2*. The topic of this lesson is "The Ancient World: Egypt." *Quest* is a series that prepares adult students for college level work. This lesson will be used to illustrate the application of learning strategies.

Learning styles The lesson in *Parachutes Book 1* (Figure 3) focuses on pets and animals. In this lesson, young language learners are given an opportunity to develop all of their perceptual learning styles–visual, auditory, tactile, and kinesthetic.

Activity 1

Figure 3 *Parachutes Book 1* (McGraw-Hill, 2001)

In the first activity, children listen to the words, point to the pictures, and say the words on the tape. This activity addresses their visual, auditory, and tactile learning styles. In the second activity (Figure 4), students count the fish and color them. This activity addresses their visual, tactile, and kinesthetic learning styles. In addition to the activities in the student book, the teacher's edition offers numerous other activities. The *Mind Map* activities give students an opportunity to develop both analytic and global styles by giving them opportunities to work alone and work with other children. Some of the activities in the Teacher's Guide are step-by-step, while others are presented in context. These different activities address both field dependent and field independent learners and build on their strengths. Most of the activities expose students to a limited amount of information, thereby helping learners who are not comfortable with uncertainty and have a low tolerance for ambiguity. The collage activity supports left-brain dominant learners because it helps them analyze and reflect. *Awareness of Math* exercises help right-brain dominant learners by focusing on interactive, global, auditory activities.

Learning Strategies In *Quest Book 2*, the lesson on ancient Egypt focuses principally on reading and writing although speaking and listening are also developed through the variety of activities introduced. The first half of the chapter is devoted to reading and the second half to writing. Three readings on ancient Egypt are introduced. Each reading section is divided into *Before Reading, Reading,* and *After Reading*.

In the prereading activity in Figure 5 (page 281) students are asked to use the cognitive learning strategy— elaboration of prior knowledge and the socio-affective strategy of cooperating. Elaboration of prior knowledge asks students to relate new information to known information and to then make personal associations. Most students know something about Egypt already. The *Before Reading* activity asks students to think about what they already know about Egypt and relate the knowledge to a wall painting of the Pharaoh Nakht and his wife. There are no wrong answers to the questions. Students are encouraged to use their prior knowledge. Students are also asked to work together to complete a task, thereby using the socio-affective strategy of cooperating.

Activity 2

Figure 4 *Parachutes Book 1* (McGraw-Hill, 2001)

Part One Rules of Egyptian Art

Before Reading

Discussion.   Look at the following wall painting. In small groups, examine the details of the painting and answer these questions.

1. Which people are Nakht and his wife? Why do you think so?

2. Who might the other people be?

3. What are the people doing? Describe as many activities as possible.

4. Do these figures look realistic? Why or why not? What seems strange about them?

Nakht and His Wife. Copy of a wall painting from the tomb of Nakht, c. 1425 BC, Thebes, Egypt. The Metropolitan Museum of Art, New York

Figure 5 *Quest: Reading and Writing in the Academic World Book 2* (McGraw-Hill, 1999)

In the next *Before Reading* activity (Figure 6), students are asked to once again make inferences and use the information given in the text to guess the meaning of words. They are also asked to use the cognitive strategy of deduction/induction to see if the information they are given in the pictures is consistent with a set of rules introduced earlier in the unit. Finally, they are asked to evaluate their answers by comparing their answers with a partner and develop the ability to determine how well they have accomplished the task.

In summary, the *Before Reading* activities in this section of *Quest Book 2* help learners develop strategies in each of the major categories–metacognitive (evaluating), cognitive (deduction/induction, making inferences, grouping, and elaboration of prior knowledge), and socio-affective (cooperating).

. : ┊ ┊ ┊ **Part Three** Reading in the Academic World

Before Reading

A. Vocabulary Preparation. The following textbook passage has some words that will be new to you. You can understand something about many of them from the context. What can you guess about each underlined word that follows? Write your guess for each of these words. Then compare your answers with another student's.

1. There was a <u>succession</u> of wars—one after another after another.

    My Guess: _____

2. The <u>ruler</u> who sat on the throne of Egypt was not always a great leader, but in the eyes of his people, he was both pharaoh and god.

    My Guess: _____

3. King Tutankhamen's tomb was filled with <u>magnificent</u> art—gold and silver, paintings, statues, and beautiful furniture.

    My Guess: _____

4. After 4,000 years, the wall painting was in poor condition, but art experts at the museum were able to <u>restore</u> it. Now it looks almost exactly as it looked when it was new.

    My Guess: _____

5. They made the <u>journey</u> from Memphis to the new capital, Thebes. When they finally arrived, they were hot and tired.

    My Guess: _____

6. He walked <u>aimlessly</u> through the old city. He had no purpose, no idea of where to go or what to do.

    My Guess: _____

7. Ancient Egyptians <u>went to great lengths</u> to protect the body of the pharoah. They were prepared to do anything necessary to keep his body safe.

    My Guess: _____

B. Thinking Ahead. Before you read, briefly review the Rules for Artists (page 110). Then look over the pictures in the textbook passage (pages 119–121). Do all of these pictures appear to follow the rules?

Figure 6 *Quest: Reading and Writing in the Academic World Book 2* (McGraw-Hill, 1999)

In the *Reading* sections, students are introduced to the concept of summarizing—identifying the key or main idea. Students focus on summarizing by thinking about the main idea as they read and underlining the interesting and surprising information.

Reading

As you read the following passage, think about the answer to this question.

- Why did the style of Egyptian art stay almost the same for 3,000 years?

Reading

As you read the textbook passage, think about the answer to this question

- How was art a mirror for the three periods in ancient Egyptian history?

Egyptian Civilization: A Brief History

It is usual to divide the long history of Egypt into three periods: the Old Kingdom, the Middle Kingdom, and the New Kingdom. These are further divided into dynasties. A dynasty was a period when a single family provided a succession of rulers. When one pharaoh died, a successor was chosen from the same family. It was important to keep the blood of a royal family pure; therefore, the pharaoh was not allowed to marry outside of the immediate family.

The Old Kingdom

The earliest dynastic period began around 3100 BC when Upper and Lower Egypt were united by a powerful pharaoh named Menes. Menes established his capital at Memphis and founded the first of the thirty-one Egyptian dynasties.

It was during the Old Kingdom that the pyramids were built. These massive tombs were an attempt to keep the body of the pharaoh safe. The Egyptians believed that the soul, or *ka*, remained with the body until death. At death, the ka left the body for a time, but it later returned and united with the body again for the journey to the next world. If the body was destroyed, the ka had to travel aimlessly for all eternity. For this reason, the Egyptians went to great lengths to protect the body—especially the body of the pharaoh, for he was both a king and, in the eyes of the people, a god.

Often, however, thieves broke into the pyramids. They stole the gold and other treasures and destroyed the pharaoh's body. Consequently, sculptors began to create statues of the pharaoh, such as the portrait of Khafre on his throne. They put these statues inside the tomb so that the ka could enter this stone statue for the journey to the next world.

Khafre, c. 2600 BC, Egyptian
Museum, Cairo, Egypt

Figure 7 Reading activities from *Quest: Reading and Writing in the Academic World Book 2* (McGraw-Hill, 1999)

In *After Reading, Part One,* students again work with summarizing. In addition, they work with advance organization. They use a graphic organizer to help them identify the key elements in the reading. In *After Reading, Part Two,* students have a chance to work again with elaboration of prior knowledge and guessing from context when they work with new idioms. In addition, they get a chance to develop metacognitive strategies by evaluating their performance on the activities and self-checking comprehension. They develop the socio-affective strategies of clarifying and cooperating when they are asked to cooperate in working with a partner and to ask questions. In summary, students are given opportunities to develop all three types of strategies in the *After Reading* activities—metacognitive, cognitive, and socio-affective.

After Reading

A. Main Ideas.   Go back to the reading. When you find the answers to these questions, mark them with a felt-tip pen.

1. If Egyptian art didn't change much for 3,000 years, was there a problem with the ability of the artists?

2. Why didn't Egyptian art change much for a such a long time?

B. Application.   Look back at the wall painting of *Nakht and His Wife.* Fill in the chart with examples from this painting. Then add the number of the rule (from Rules for Artists) that told the artist what to do.

Elements	Examples from the Wall Painting from the Tomb of Nakht	Rule #
space		
animals		
people: color		
size		
activity		
style		
actions of people (besides Nakht)		

C. Response Writing.   For ten minutes, write as much as you can about the wall painting *Nakht and His Wife.* Describe it and explain in your own words why the artist used these elements.

Figure 8 After Reading activities from *Quest: Reading and Writing in the Academic World Book 2* (McGraw-Hill, 1999)

What do you think would be the main challenges in introducing either the *Parachutes* lesson or the *Quest* lesson in the classroom?

6. Conclusion

This chapter introduced the concepts of learning styles and strategies, explained how they are different, and how they are linked together. In addition, useful taxonomies were provided to help teachers work with styles and strategies in their classrooms. This chapter also focused on five principles to help guide you in applying learning styles and strategies in your classroom, two specific techniques that include a perceptual learning inventory and an interactive activity, and two sample lesson plans from commercial texts to show you how to identify and work with learning styles and strategies. The information collected in this chapter should provide you with tools necessary for accomplishing the goals outlined at the beginning of the chapter. If your goal is to better meet the individual needs of your students, address the diversity you see in your classroom, and to better prepare your students for their classroom language learning experiences, then working with learning styles and strategies and applying the concepts presented in this chapter is a worthy endeavor.

Further readings

Chamot, A.U. and J. M. O'Malley 1994. *The CALLA Handbook*. Reading, MA: Addison Wesley.

This handbook was written for public school teachers who are responsible for teaching core curriculum subjects to language minority children. The handbook integrates the latest research on learning strategies with actual classroom-tested activities.

Christison, M. A. 1998. An Overview of Learning Styles and Their Application to the L2 Classroom. *Sunshine State TESOL Journal*.

This article provides a fairly comprehensive overview of learning styles, identifies student classroom behaviors associated with each learning style, and offers suggestions for practical activities.

Oxford, R. L. 1990. *Language Learning Strategies: What every teacher should know.* Boston, MA: Heinle & Heinle.

Based on current research, this text provides English language teachers with practical recommendations for developing their students' second language learning strategies. Detailed suggestions for strategy use in each of the four language skills are included, as well as case studies and models for setting up similar programs.

Reid, J. (ed.) 1995. *Learning Styles in the ESL/EFL Classroom*. Boston, MA: Heinle & Heinle.

This book is a collection of practical articles on learning styles edited by Joy Reid. It is now out of print, but can be accessed at <http://www.humanities.byu.edu/faculty/andersonn.html>

Reid, J. (ed.) 1997. *Understanding Learning Styles in the Second Language Classroom*. Englewood Cliffs, NJ: Pearson ESL.

This book is a collection of articles on learning styles and multiple intelligences. It is specifically directed to English language teachers and focuses on both theory and research and practical application.

Silver, H. F. and R. J. Hanson 1996. *Learning Styles and Strategies*. Woodbridge, NJ: The Thoughtful Education Press.

This manual is designed to increase one's understanding of learning styles and strategies and is based on Jung's Theory of Personality Types. It also enables teachers to help students become more responsible, autonomous learners.

Helpful Web sites

LD Pride, The Vancouver Island Invisible Disability Association (http://www.ldpride.net/learningstyles.MI.htm)

Learning Strategies Corporation (http://www.learningstrategies.com)

References

Chamot, A. U. and J. M. O'Malley 1994. *The CALLA Handbook.* Reading, MA: Addison-Wesley.

Cohen, R. 1969. Conceptual Styles, Culture Conflict, and Nonverbal Tests of Intelligence. *American Anthropologist,* 71:828–56.

Cummins, J. 2001. *Negotiating identities: Education for empowerment in a diverse society.* 2nd Edition. Los Angeles: California Association for Bilingual Education.

Dunn R., K. Dunn and G. E. Price 1975. *The Learning Style Inventory.* Lawrence, KS: Price Systems.

Dunn, R., K. Dunn and G. E. Price 1979. Identifying Learning Styles. In J. Keefe (ed.) *Students' Learning Styles: Diagnosing and prescribing programs.* Reston, VA: National Association of Secondary School Principals.

Dunn, R., K. Dunn and G. E. Price 1989. *Learning Styles Inventory: An inventory for the identification of how individuals in grades 3 through 12 prefer to learn.* Lawrence, KS: Price Systems.

Jung, C. G. 1976. *Psychological Types.* Princeton, NJ: Princeton Press.

Kachru, Y. 1988. Cognitive and Cultural Styles in Second Language Acquisition. *Annual Review of Applied Linguistics,* 9:149–63.

Kinsella, K. 1995. Understanding and Empowering Diverse Learners. In J.M. Reid (ed.) *Learning Styles in the ESL/EFL Classroom.* Boston, MA: Heinle & Heinle.

Nelson, G. 1995. Cultural Differences in Learning Styles. In J. Reid (ed.) *Learning Styles in the ESL/EFL Classroom.* Boston, MA: Heinle & Heinle.

Oxford, R., M. Ehrman, and R. Lavine 1991. Style Wars: Teacher-student style conflicts in the language classroom. In S. S. Magnan (ed.) *Challenges in the 1990s for College Foreign Language Programs.* Boston, MA: Heinle & Heinle.

Oxford, R. 1990a. Styles, Strategies, and Aptitude: Connections for language learning. In T. Parry & C.W. Stansfield (eds.) *Language Aptitude Reconsidered.* Englewood Cliffs, NJ: Prentice-Hall.

Oxford, R. 1990b. *Language Learning Strategies: What every teacher should know.* Boston, MA: Heinle & Heinle.

Oxford R. L. and N. J. Anderson 1995. A Cross-Cultural View of Learning Styles. *Language Teacher.* Cambridge University Press. 28:201–215.

Piaget, J. and B. Inhelder 1969. *The Psychology of the Child.* New York, NY: Basic Books.

Reid, J. M. (ed.) 1995. *Learning Styles in the ESL/EFL Classroom.* Boston, MA: Heinle & Heinle.

Reid, J. M. (ed.) 1997. *Understanding Learning Styles in the Second Language Classroom.* Englewood Cliffs, NJ: Prentice Hall/Regents.

Silver H. F. and J. R. Hanson 1996a. *Learning Styles & Strategies.* Woodbridge, NJ: The Thoughtful Education Press.

Silver H. F. and J. F. Hanson 1996b. *Teaching Styles & Strategies.* Woodbridge, NJ: The Thoughtful Education Press.

Chapter Fourteen

Learner autonomy in the classroom

Phil Benson, University of Hong Kong (China)

At the end of this chapter, you should be able to:

Goals

 define autonomy and explain what fostering autonomy in the language classroom means to you.

 say how you would organize a project or series of classroom activities so that the students make choices and decisions about their learning.

 evaluate how textbook units and classroom activities offer, or fail to offer, opportunities and support for autonomy.

1. What is autonomy?

In a definition that has stood the test of time, Holec (1981, p. 3) defined **autonomy** as "the ability to take charge of one's own learning." More recently, I have defined it as "the capacity to control one's own learning" (Benson, 2001, p. 47). Although these definitions do not differ substantially, autonomy is perhaps best described as a capacity, as Holec has often described it, because various kinds of abilities can be involved in control over learning. Researchers generally agree that the most important abilities are those that allow learners to plan their own learning activities, monitor their progress and evaluate their outcomes. In my own research, I have also suggested that different kinds of abilities may be needed for control over the day-to-day management of learning, control over the mental processes involved in second language learning and control of the content of learning (Benson, 2001, p. 50). But these ways of talking about autonomy only describe the areas of learning over which autonomous learners need to exercise control.

No matter how we divide up the language learning task, the abilities that allow learners to control each area are clearly many and varied. It is also difficult to specify exactly what they are. Little (1991, p. 49), for example, tells us that autonomy is a capacity for "detachment, critical reflection, decision-making and independent action," but Candy (1991, pp. 459–466) lists more than a hundred abilities associated with autonomy in learning! This tells us that autonomy can never be an all or nothing matter (Nunan, 1997). There are degrees of autonomy, and autonomy may also take different forms. From the classroom teacher's point of view, therefore, the important question is not how to produce autonomous learners, but how to build upon the autonomy that learners already possess. For this reason, we tend to say that autonomy can be fostered, but not taught. In order to foster autonomy in the classroom, we as teachers need to provide learners with the opportunity to make significant choices and decisions about their learning. We also need to help them develop abilities that will allow them to make these choices and decisions in an informed way.

Reflection

The best place to begin exploring your own understanding of autonomy may be your own experiences of learning:

1. Who were your favorite teachers and why? Did these teachers allow you to make choices and decisions? Is this one of the reasons that they were your favorites?

2. What is your attitude towards choice and decision-making in your own learning? Which choices and decisions do you think that you should make yourself and which would you prefer to leave to teachers?

2. Background to autonomy in the classroom

In the field of political philosophy, personal autonomy refers to our freedom and ability to "shape our own lives" (Young, 1986, p. 81). Advocates of personal autonomy see it as a basic human right—without autonomy our lives may be less than human. Preparing younger learners to exercise personal autonomy in adult life is a declared goal of many educational systems around the world, but advocating autonomy *in learning* means more than this. It means that students should be allowed and encouraged to shape their own *learning* as well as their own lives. Put somewhat differently, it means that learning should be seen as an integral part of life, and not as a preparation for it.

The idea of autonomy first came into language teaching in the late 1960s through the adult education movement in Europe and North America, and for many years it continued to be associated with adult learners who had left formal education. Many of the early autonomous language learning projects were carried out within the Council of Europe's Modern Languages Project in the 1970s. Henri Holec, who provided us with our first definition of autonomy in learning, played a key role in this project as the director of the *Centre de Recherches et d'Applications en Langues* (CRAPEL). This center continues to be a focal point for research and practice on autonomy in the present day.

At CRAPEL, autonomy was fostered through **self-directed learning,** or learning outside the classroom that was planned and executed by the learners themselves. Self-directed learning at CRAPEL was based on a **self-access center**—an open access resource center containing authentic print, audio and video target language materials. Self-directed learning also involved learner training, in which learners learned how to learn by experimenting with self-access materials with the help of language learning counselors. Many of the important concepts and practices associated with autonomy in learning today were established in this and other Council of Europe projects for adult learners. In the 1980s, however, the emphasis began to shift from the adult learner who was no longer receiving formal education to younger and older learners whose learning was mainly focused on the classroom.

One of the most influential classroom projects was carried out by Leni Dam and her colleagues in English language learning in Danish secondary schools (Dam, 1995). Their approach does not involve self-access or formal learner training. Instead, classroom learners are simply asked to take responsibility for the major decisions in their language learning throughout their secondary school years. The learners are also asked to take responsibility for ensuring that their learning meets national curriculum and examination requirements. The work of Dam and her colleagues has clearly demonstrated that teenagers can manage their own classroom learning without adverse effect on their proficiency. Although it is sometimes suggested that their situation is exceptional, similar projects elsewhere have also produced positive results. Johnson, et al. (1990), for example, have shown that primary school children are able to make significant decisions about their language learning and Holmes (1990) has reported similar results for young children with learning difficulties.

Early work on autonomy was mainly concerned with learners who were learning on their own. The experience of fostering autonomy in the classroom has, therefore, raised new questions concerned with the social relationships involved in autonomous learning. One of these questions concerns the role of the teacher in an autonomous classroom. If the learners make most or all the key decisions about their learning, what does the teacher do? Voller (1997) has argued that the teacher may act as a *facilitator* who initiates and supports decision-making processes, a *counselor* who responds to the ongoing needs of individuals, and a *resource* who makes his or her knowledge and expertise available to the learners when it is needed. Clearly, teachers who want to foster autonomy should not see themselves as directors of classroom learning or as founts of knowledge to be poured into the heads of the learners. Crabbe (1993, p. 208) also reminds us that fostering autonomy is not simply a matter of how we see our relationship with our students. It is also a question of how we interact with them. The important question, he argues, is "whether the minute-by-minute classroom practice indirectly *fosters* or discourages autonomy" by highlighting choices in the curriculum and challenging the learners' ideas about their own roles in the classroom.

A second important question concerns the social side of learner decision-making in the classroom. In earlier models of self-directed learning, it was largely assumed each learner would make decisions by and for themselves. But in recent years, emphasis has been placed on the ways in which the choices and decisions of one influence those of others. Important work on classroom decision-making has been carried out in the fields of collaborative experiential learning (Kohonen, 2001) and curriculum negotiation (Breen and Littlejohn, 2000). In both of these approaches, coming to terms with the needs and choices of other learners in the classroom is seen as a crucial aspect of the development of autonomy. Little (1996, p. 210), has also argued that autonomy implies interdependence, rather than independence, and that a "capacity to participate fully and critically in social interactions" is essential to it.

A third question concerns our own autonomy as teachers. In recent research on "teacher autonomy," our willingness and ability to model the autonomy that we would like to see in our students is seen as being of greater importance than any particular method or technique (Little, 1995; McGrath, 2000). All teachers are, of course, subject to institutional and curriculum constraints that limit the freedom they are able to grant their students. For this reason, the ways in which we foster autonomy will depend on our individual judgments of what is possible or reasonable in our own situations. But as

Little (1995, p. 178) argues, the starting point for teacher autonomy must be a recognition that we cannot help but "teach ourselves," because the curriculum that we present to the learners is our own. Even if the curriculum we present to the learners has been designed by others, it is our interpretation of it that counts most for the learners in our classroom. In this sense, autonomous teachers are those who are aware of the ways in which they interpret the curriculum and who look for areas within it where there may be room for negotiation with the learners. When we ask learners to make choices and decisions, we are also asking them to take risks. It is, therefore, reasonable that we should be prepared to take risks ourselves. This means that teacher autonomy also implies confidence in our own professional judgment of when and where it is appropriate to transfer control to the learners.

The ideological roots of autonomy in learning remain important because they can help us to understand why fostering autonomy in the language-learning classroom can be important to learners. Research on the effectiveness of autonomous learning projects suggests that learners who participate in them may well gain rather than suffer in terms of proficiency (Dam and Legenhausen, 1996; Dickinson, 1995). But for many teachers this may be less important than the personal and social benefits that can be gained through autonomous language learning. Fostering autonomy may simply mean helping students to learn languages in ways that are more relevant to their lives. Early work on individual self-directed learning also remains important. Self-access and learner training have now become important features of the language learning scene in general, and most teachers are likely to come across these ideas at some point in their careers. (See, for example, Gardner and Miller, 1999, on self-access and Cohen, 1998, on learner training.) These ideas also point to important considerations when we try to foster autonomy in the classroom. Although our school may not have a self-access center, providing learners with a choice of resources in the classroom will be important. Although we may not wish to have formal learner training sessions, helping learners to make choices and decisions will also be important. Thinking about the newer questions in autonomy—our roles as teachers, the social dimensions of classroom decision-making, and our own autonomy as teachers—will also be of value in our efforts to put autonomy into practice in the classroom.

Reflection

In their book on new methods of teacher education, Freeman and Cornwell (1993, p. xii) ask: "Is learning to teach a matter of replicating how other teachers do things? Or does it depend on coming to grips with ones own ways of thinking and doing things in the classroom?" How would you answer this question? How is your answer related to teacher autonomy in your view?

3. Principles for fostering autonomy in the classroom

Dam (1995, p. 6) suggests that fostering autonomy in the classroom is initially "a matter of getting started, of taking the first steps towards creating a learning environment where learners are encouraged to make decisions concerning their own learning, where the teacher dares to let go." The results of these first steps will largely determine the steps that follow, which means that there is no simple recipe for fostering autonomy in the classroom. In place of such a recipe, however, we can offer certain principles based on our knowledge of what tends to work well in classrooms and what doesn't.

1. Be actively involved in the students' learning.

In traditional classrooms, teachers plan the content of lessons and methods of presentation, organize practice or communicative activities during the lessons themselves, and evaluate learning outcomes through tests and other forms of assessment. In other words, they direct the students' learning. Teachers who want to foster autonomy try to avoid these kinds of direction as much as possible, but this does not mean leaving the students to get on with the job of learning by themselves. Instead, they try to help the students take greater control over their learning by becoming more actively involved in it themselves. Some of the ways in which this can be done through preparation, classroom management, and evaluation will be exemplified below. For the moment, however, let us say that the first principle for fostering autonomy is that both the learners and the teacher must be actively involved in everything that happens in the classroom.

2. Provide a range of learning options and resources.

Fostering autonomy begins with preparation, which often involves thinking about the different ways in which something can be learned. In order to offer choices and opportunities for decision-making, we will need to bring a range of learning options and resources into the classroom. For example, if we are using a particular textbook, we will need to think about how the activities can be modified or re-ordered according to the students' preferences. If we want to offer learners a choice between **inductive** and **deductive** ways of learning a grammar point (see, Nunan, Chapter 8, this volume), we will need to prepare tasks that support both approaches. This can, of course, represent a considerable burden for a busy teacher, which is one reason why a self-access center can be a useful complement to classroom learning. An alternative is to encourage learners to bring in their own learning resources.

Dam (1995, p. 14), for example, simply asked students to bring some English into the class. The things that they brought included a cap with English words on it, tourist brochures, advertisements with English phrases in them, a newspaper, and even a joke that one of the students had written. These objects were placed in a box labeled Our Own Materials and became resources for personally relevant language work in later lessons. This example shows how students can also be involved in lesson planning. Planning for the next lesson in an autonomous classroom often begins at the end of the last lesson with the teacher asking the students what they would like to do next.

3. Offer choices and decision making opportunities.

While it is important to build opportunities for choice and decision making into lesson plans, it also important to create and respond to such opportunities when they arise spontaneously. Decision making takes place in the language learning classroom at a number of levels. Later in this chapter, for example, we will see how decision making opportunities can arise or be inhibited by different styles of teacher talk. The physical organization of the classroom may also be important. If the furniture is laid out so that students can sit in groups, choose who they work with, and move around during the lesson, they are more likely to take initiative in the classroom. By moving around the classroom and sitting with groups of students, teachers can also create an atmosphere where the students are encouraged to make suggestions. Choices and decisions need to be made at various levels of the teaching and learning process, and many teachers prefer a gradual approach in which the learners progressively move from lower to higher levels (Nunan, 1997). But it is also important that the choices and decision making opportunities offered should be significant from the students' point of view. This calls for sensitivity on the teacher's part to what the students see as significant and what they see as trivial.

4. Support the learners.

In order for learners' choices and decisions to be meaningful they must also be informed. This means, for example, that if we are going to offer the learners a choice between inductive and deductive tasks in grammar learning, we will probably need to explain the rationale behind each approach, allow the learners time to experiment with each, and give them the opportunity to discuss and evaluate their experiences. Teachers who want to foster autonomy also often make themselves available as counselors to individual learners during and between classes. The line between support and direction, however, can be a fine one because both imply that we make our knowledge and expertise available. For example, it may be difficult to explain the differences between inductive and deductive tasks without implicitly directing the students to one or the other by communicating our own preference. Supporting, rather than directing, the learners in their choice of task would mean presenting the options in a way that encourages free choice and shows respect for the learners' final decision.

5. Encourage reflection.

Learner's choices and decisions ultimately become meaningful to them through their consequences. Many teachers feel that direction is justified because it makes learning more efficient. If students decide things for themselves, they will make mistakes and precious time that could otherwise be spent on learning will be wasted. The argument against this is that mistakes are an opportunity for learning. We know, for example, that the production of linguistic errors in speech and writing may be a form of hypothesis-testing that is important to language acquisition. Hypothesis-testing in the learning process may be equally important in development confidence in our own ways of learning. Students, however, do not always see things in this way and teachers need to actively encourage reflection, help students to draw conclusions, and help them to act upon them. Returning once again to our inductive/deductive grammar task choice in Principle 2, the teacher might organize a brief review at the end of a lesson where students who have tried each approach report on their experiences. A decision could then be made on whether the whole class should continue with one of these approaches, whether each individual should continue with their own preference, or whether more time is needed for experimentation. A decision could then be made on what the teacher and the students should do in order to prepare for the next class.

Reflection

What are your feelings about classroom decision making? What kinds of decisions do you think can safely be left to the learners, and which do you think the teachers should make?

Write a proposal for a series of classroom activities focussed on past tense verb forms and designed to foster autonomy. Your proposal should specify: (a) areas for learner choice and decision making, (b) the resources you would make available and those that are to be provided by the learners, (c) your role as the project teacher, and (d) opportunities for reflection.

4. Classroom techniques and tasks

The ways in which teachers put the principles described in the previous section into practice vary a great deal and depend largely upon the teaching and learning situation and the teacher's creativity. In this section, I will describe some of the techniques and tasks used by one teacher in one situation in order to exemplify how these principles were put into practice in the context of one short experimental course. The situation is a university classroom, but the techniques and tasks described could be used in any classroom where grammar is the focus. The course is described in greater detail by Littlejohn (1983).

Littlejohn's students were English language learners at the University of Bahrain, who had failed their preparatory English course in the previous year, and were required to take an additional 84-hour course. Littlejohn first demonstrated his own active involvement by deciding not to repeat the previous year's course or draw up a syllabus before the course began. Instead, he planned a sequence of activities designed to involve the students in the selection of learning content and in the management of day-to-day classroom activities.

Littlejohn began by asking the students to complete a questionnaire in English on their learning experiences and preferences. The results were compiled on the board and discussed in class. This activity was teacher-directed but designed to demonstrate that the learners' experiences and opinions would be drawn upon during the course. One of the outcomes of this activity was a collective awareness that grammar, which became the focus of the remainder of the course, was particularly important to the learners.

Littlejohn next divided the students into small groups, which were each allocated a different unit from the previous year's grammar textbook. The groups were asked to assess exactly what each section in their unit asked them to do and to rate each section in terms of difficulty (see Figure 1). Based on the results of this task, a list of grammar topics in order of their difficulty for the class as a whole was compiled on the board. Again, this activity was teacher-directed, but the learners had taken a first step towards active involvement in the planning of the course, because these topics determined the content of much of the remainder of the course.

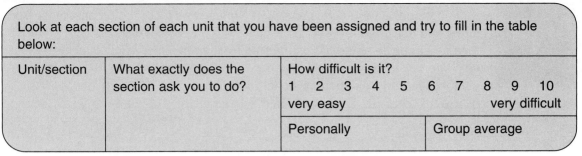

Unit/section	What exactly does the section ask you to do?	How difficult is it? 1 2 3 4 5 6 7 8 9 10 very easy very difficult	
		Personally	Group average

Figure 1 Textbook assessment sheet (Littlejohn, 1983)

The next step was to allocate the grammar topics to groups of volunteers, who then researched their chosen topic in order to present their findings and provide exercises, tasks, games, and other activities for the whole class. During the research phase, the learners began to make choices and decisions that were meaningful because they would determine what each group would present to the class. In order to help the learners make these choices and decisions, the teacher brought resources into the classroom (grammar books, dictionaries, and other textbooks). He also supported the learners by providing initial guidance and by sitting among the students during the classroom research sessions, giving advice when called upon.

Towards the end of the course, Littlejohn also introduced student-directed lessons in which small groups of students planned and carried out learning activities of their own choice. In order to prepare for these lessons, the groups first compiled a list of all the activities that they had done in class before, those that they had found enjoyable and useful, and their ideas about what they wanted to learn. The activities they chose were thus based on reflection upon their earlier experiences and current needs. The teacher again supported the students with resources and by being available for assistance. He also followed up these student-directed sessions with teacher-led sessions in which he introduced other possible activities and approaches and initiated discussions on problems in learning without teacher direction.

Littlejohn reports that the students who took this course did well in their final examinations. He also reports that, although they were both weak in English and came from traditional learning backgrounds, after some initial resistance they responded well, displaying a sense of responsibility for their learning and playing an active role in class. One point to note about this example is techniques and tasks were creatively designed and sequenced. Because the development of autonomy is a gradual and unpredictable process, techniques and tasks tend to "work" only when they build upon each other and are responsive to the immediate needs of the learning situation. It is also worth noting how Littlejohn retained overall control over the structure of the course, but skillfully used techniques and tasks to progressively transfer control over the content and methods of day-to-day learning to the learners.

5. Autonomy in the classroom

The techniques used by Littlejohn illustrate how autonomy can be fostered in the classroom through creative design and sequencing of techniques and tasks. But in order to use techniques and tasks of this kind, a teacher must already have some freedom in relation to the implementation of the curriculum. There is also much that can be done to foster autonomy within more restrictive situations, however, and in this section we will consider three examples of how the ways in which we talk to and interact with our students can create or inhibit opportunities for choice and decision-making.

Teachers' instructions

Even in an autonomous classroom, it is often the teacher who provides the tasks and activities. The ways in which we present these tasks and activities, however, can be significant. Crabbe (1993) recorded classroom task instructions during a course for adult immigrant learners in New Zealand. The following is an extract of an instruction for a reading task on the theme of social customs:

> **Extract 1**
>
> OK, well, I've got another piece of reading here. Some of you may have heard of Guide for New Settlers. There's a section on specific social events—what you should do in situations. What I want you to do is not to read it in detail but to scan it for the questions I have given you. There are headings that will help you find where the information is. I'll ask you to do this as quickly as possible and finish in fifteen minutes. (Crabbe, 1993, p. 449)

As Crabbe notes, the teacher does not explain why the learners should scan rather than read in detail or what the *purpose* of the scanning activity is in the context of the lesson. While the students are reading, the teacher also notices that one of the students is not following the task instructions, and says:

> **Extract 2**
>
> Excuse me J, you don't need to read the whole thing from start to finish. You look at the questions first and then try to find the answers. (Crabbe, 1993, p. 449)

Again, the teacher does not explain why the learner should not read from start to finish, but simply reminds him of the instruction in order to keep him on task. This teacher may well have been following a tried-and-tested strategy of revealing the stages of the lesson step-by-step—a strategy that can both simplify the lesson for the student and create a certain amount of suspense. Teachers who wish to foster autonomy, however, might choose to act otherwise, by first explaining the lesson plan as a whole and the purposes of each task. When they encounter learners who have gone off task, they might begin by asking why they have done so and, if it seems important that they go back to the task as it was originally designed, explain the purpose of the task again. This example illustrates how important the ways in which we interact with learners can be if we want to foster autonomy. It is essentially by talking and listening to students that we become actively involved in their learning and create opportunities for them to be more actively involved in what happens in the classroom.

Action

1. How would you rephrase the instructions in Extract 1 so that they might be more supportive of the learners' autonomy?

2. Take a unit from any general language teaching coursebook—for example, a unit that begins with a text or dialogue and goes on to provide language input and tasks. Evaluate this unit in terms of the degree to which the task instructions are likely to inhibit or support autonomy.

3. Imagine that you were to teach this unit over a lesson or two. What additional instructions or explanations would you give, and how could you modify the tasks so that they would be more supportive of autonomy?

Teacher-learner dialogue

Language teachers often engage in dialogue with learners, not for the purpose of organizing classroom work, but for the purpose of teaching new language and engaging the learners in communicative practice. In her book on classroom interaction, Johnson (1995) discusses two contrasting dialogues of this kind, which highlight how opportunities for choice and decision-making can be involved even in this kind of talk. In Extract 3 (which is taken from a much longer dialogue reprinted in Johnson's book), the teacher is discussing a newspaper advertisement for a clearance sale.

Extract 3

1. *T:* What is this advertisement about?
2. *Peersak:* Radio ... sale.
3. *Milo:* Cheap sale ...
4. *T:* What is the word that is used there?
5. *Suchada:* Clearance sale.

6. **T:** *Clearance sale. OK, in the first place, do you know the meaning of "clearance sale?"*

7. **Suchada:** *Clearance sale.*

8. **T:** *Clearance sale. Let's look at the word "clearance". What does it come from?*

9. **Peersak:** *Clear.*

10. **T:** *Therefore, "clearance" sale will mean what?*

11. **Suchada:** *To clear up.*

12. **T:** *To clear up, that's right. To clear up all the goods in the store...*

(Johnson, 1995, p. 94)

Johnson's comment on this extract, which continues in much the same vein, is that the talk follows a typical pattern in which the teacher initiates most of the exchanges with questions that aim to elicit specific short responses—usually a vocabulary item or its meaning. We can also note that in their answers, the students are essentially "filling in blanks" in the teacher's contribution, rather than making linguistic choices or decisions. In Extract 4, the teacher and student are discussing an article on Gay Pride week.

Extract 4

1. **T:** *So what other questions do you have about this (the article), or Gay Pride week in general?*

2. **Stan:** *What is this pin?*

3. **Rosa:** *Oh, I saw that too ...*

4. **Stan:** *I saw this on some people, but I didn't know. I thought it some politics or something...*

5. **T:** *OK. It says, "Straight, Secure, Supportive." Do you know what that means?*

6. **Stan:** *Maybe some politics.*

7: **T:** *You thought it had to do with politics? Well, you are sort of right, because Gay Rights has become a political*

*issue, but let's think about the words
on the pin; it says "Straight, Secure,
Supportive." Do you have any ideas
about what "straight" means in
reference to what we have been
talking about, in terms of Gay
Rights Week?*

8. **Rosa:** *Opposite, not gay.*

(Johnson, 1995, pp.102–103)

In Extract 4, the teacher also talks most of the time, but she begins with an open-ended question and her follow-up questions respond to a question initiated by one of the students. Although these follow-up questions are also concerned with the meanings of words, it is interesting to see how the interaction develops once the meaning of the word supportive has been established.

> ### Extract 5
>
> 24. **T:** *Yes, that we can support them as
>   people who have social and legal
>   rights, but we don't have to be
>   like them.*
>
> 25. **Stan:** *But maybe they think
>   you are gay too, maybe they
>   think you are because they
>   see your pin and that's what
>   they think.*
>
> 26. **Rosa:** *No, you're not like them
>   but it's OK.*
>
> 27. **Stan:** *What if they see this pin
>   on you, they might just think
>   you are too.*
>
> 28. **T:** *Well, what would you think if you
>   saw someone wearing this pin? …*

(Johnson, 1995, p. 104)

In Extract 5, the students not only begin to speak more, but also to exchange opinions with each other. The teacher's last question in the extract also responds to their exchange of opinions and to their feelings about the topic at hand.

These extracts illustrate teacher-student interactions of very different types and it is worth noting that the ways in which two teachers initiate and develop these interactions have an important influence on involvement of the learners in them. Teachers who wish to foster autonomy may favor interactions of the second type, because they leave space for learners to make not only linguistic choices and decisions, but also choices and decisions about the meanings that they express. Again, this example illustrates the importance of the ways in which we interact with students. Through classroom dialogues of this kind, we provide opportunities for language practice and acquisition, but we also communicate expectations of what we expect learners to contribute to the classroom. Students who are accustomed only to answering teachers' questions are far less likely to offer opinions about how their learning is organized than those who are accustomed to offering opinions during classroom dialogues.

Action

1. Choose a reading text from a general language teaching coursebook. How would you lead a discussion on the text that would give the students opportunities to make linguistic choices and express opinions?

2. How would you move on from this discussion to a task that the learners had contributed towards themselves? For example, you may think about how to develop the discussion of the topic of the text into a discussion of "how we can find out more about this topic?"

What an autonomous classroom looks like

These comments on teacher talk suggest that fostering autonomy in the classroom cannot really be reduced to techniques or tasks. Teaching styles, attitudes towards interaction, and the spaces that we create for learners to become actively involved in their own learning are important factors, which set the context for how well a particular task or technique will work. For this reason, we will conclude with an extract from Dam's (1995) account of her own efforts to create an autonomous classroom for secondary school learners of English in Denmark, which gives an impression of what an autonomous classroom might look like. Here, Dam (1995, pp. 67–9) reproduces her notes from a lesson with a class she had been teaching for four years. The students were working together on group projects.

Example ▸ **Tuesday, March 13—a single period**

There is no break before this lesson, so when the teacher arrives some groups have already started work while others haven't. The teacher passes her materials over to the different groups. For . . . (one) group she hasn't been able to find anything. They themselves, however, have been to the local library and have brought along some Danish books on the topic. The teacher reminds the class that today they will only have half an hour for their group work because of the presentation of the radio play "Little Red Riding Hood" which had been announced by one of the groups in the previous lesson.

Soon all the groups are at work, and there is time for the teacher to move around and observe what is going on. Have they gotten started? Are they following their plans? Have they managed to find materials? Are there any problems? Do they need help? There is also time to discuss why they chose the topic they did.

The following is an extract from one student's diary.

Example

Tuesday, March 13

1. *go on with our radio play*
2. *Homework: read in "The woman who disappeared." chapter 3 and 4.*
3. *presentation of "Little red riding hood" by Rasmus, Martin, Louise and Sandra.*

Presentation agenda:

a. *tell about how we decided to work*

b. *read a part from our roles*

c. *listen to the tape*

d. *comments: I think it was good, because they spoke in a funny way.*
   —they spoke clearly
   —it was funny

Example   Notes from the teacher's diary

- *Remember to support positive and "constructive" comments from the class when presenting projects.*
- *Think of ideas for "being better at reading and talking" for the radio-play group.*
- *Bring along some English poems.*
- *Sandra has improved her intonation.*

The work in the class continues like this for the next few weeks. Once a week there is a presentation of previous group projects. Apart from this, the groups continue undisturbed with their projects and with individual work, and they plan their time themselves. The teacher sees to it that she gets around the groups at least once a week.

Commentary Although incomplete, Dam's notes convey a vivid impression of the kinds of things that are likely to be happening in a classroom where the learners have become used to more autonomous ways of learning. Some of the things we may note are that the lesson appears to have no clear beginning or end. The students are working at their own pace on self-designed group tasks and their work is not bounded by the formal timetable. The natural development of these tasks also determines the schedule of whole class events, such as the performance of the radio play. Student's diary suggests that she is actively involved in planning and evaluating her own work (and the work of others!). The teacher is not "teaching" in the traditional sense, but is rather facilitating and supporting, although she also seeks opportunities to become actively involved in the students' work. Dam's diary also suggests that she is constantly reflecting upon the events and processes that are taking place in the class and planning ahead. Dam's account may give the impression of a chaotic classroom! But we should also note that it took her and her students four years to reach this point. By this stage the coherence of the students' learning lies not in her efforts to direct it, but in their own understanding of the relevance of what they are doing.

6. Conclusion

In this chapter, autonomy has been defined as the capacity to control one's own learning. At the most basic level, fostering this capacity in the classroom begins with the teacher's own decision to become more actively involved in the students' learning in order that the students may also become more actively involved in making choices and decisions. I have suggested some principles, techniques, and tasks that may help us to go further than this, but I have also emphasized that fostering autonomy is largely a question of talking and listening to students in ways that will help them feel that their involvement in classroom processes at every level is respected and valued. We cannot teach students to become more autonomous. We can, however, create the atmosphere and conditions in which they will feel encouraged to develop the autonomy that they already have.

Further readings

Benson, P. 2001. *Teaching and Researching Autonomy in Language Learning*. London: Longman.

This volume offers a comprehensive survey of theory and practice in the field.

Breem, M. P. (ed.) 2001. *Learner Contributions to Language Learning*. London: Longman.

Highly recommended as a collection of papers surveying recent thinking relevant to the issues discussed in this chapter in the field of second language acquisition.

Breen, M. P. and A. Littlejohn (eds.) 2000. *Classroom Decision-Making: Negotiation and process syllabuses in action*. Cambridge: Cambridge University Press.

A stimulating collection of accounts of experiments in classroom decision-making.

Dam, L. 1995. *Learner Autonomy 3: From theory to classroom practice*. Dublin: Authentik.

A practical account of autonomous work in the classroom.

Little, D. 1991. *Learner Autonomy 1: Definitions, issues and problems*. Dublin: Authentik.

A brief, cogent introduction to the theory of autonomy in language learning.

Helpful Web sites

Autonomy and Independence in Language Learning (http://ec.hku.hk/autonomy)

This Web site is maintained by the author of this chapter and includes a comprehensive bibliography on autonomy and related issues.

AILA Scientific Commission on Learner Autonomy in Language Learning (http://www.vuw.ac.nz/lals/div1/ailasc)

Less forbidding than its name might suggest, the AILA Scientific Commission is the main professional group concerned with autonomy in language learning. The AILA SC Web site is a good source for upcoming activities and publications.

References

Benson, P. 2001. *Teaching and Researching Autonomy in Language Learning.* London: Longman.

Breem, M. P. (ed.) 2001. *Learner Contributions to Language Learning.* London: Longman.

Breen, M. P. and A. Littlejohn (eds.) 2000. *Classroom Decision-Making: Negotiation and process syllabuses in action.* Cambridge: Cambridge University Press.

Candy, P. C. 1991. *Self-Direction for Lifelong Learning.* San Francisco, CA: Jossey-Bass.

Cohen, A. D. 1998. *Strategies in Learning and Using a Second Language.* London: Longman.

Crabbe, D. 1993. Fostering Autonomy from within the Classroom: The teacher's responsibility. *System, 21*(4): 443–452.

Dam, L. 1995. *Learner Autonomy 3: From theory to classroom practice.* Dublin: Authentik.

Dam, L. and L. Legenhausen 1996. The Acquisition of Vocabulary in an Autonomous Learning Environment: The first months of beginning English. In R. Pemberton, et al., (eds.) *Taking Control: Autonomy in language learning.* Hong Kong: Hong Kong University Press.

Dickinson, L. 1995. Autonomy and Motivation: A literature review. *System* 23(2):165–174.

Freeman, D. and S. Cornwell (eds.) 1993. *New Ways in Teacher Education.* Alexandria, VA: TESOL.

Gardner, D. and L. Miller 1999. *Establishing Self-Access: From Theory to Practice.* Cambridge: Cambridge University Press.

Holec, H. 1981. *Autonomy in Foreign Language Learning.* Oxford: Pergamon. (First published 1979, Strasbourg: Council of Europe.)

Kohonen, V. 1992. Experiential Language Learning: Second language learning as cooperative learner education. In D. Nunan (ed.) *Collaborative Language Learning and Teaching.* Cambridge: Cambridge University Press.

Holmes, B. 1990. First Steps Towards Autonomy for Pupils with Learning Difficulties. In I. Gathercole (ed.) *Autonomy in Language Learning.* London: CILT.

Johnson, J., H. Pardesi, and C. Paine 1990. Autonomy in our Primary School. In Ian Gathercole (ed.) *Autonomy in Language Learning,* London: CILT.

Johnson, K. E. 1995. *Understanding Communication in Second Language Classrooms.*

Cambridge: Cambridge University Press.

Little, D. 1991. *Learner Autonomy. 1: Definitions, Issues and Problems*. Dublin: Authentik.

Little, D. 1995. Learning as Dialogue: The dependence of learner autonomy on teacher autonomy. *System,* 23(2):175–182.

Little, D. 1996. Freedom to Learn and Compulsion to Interact: Promoting learner autonomy through the use of information systems and information technologies. In R. Pemberton, et al., (eds.) *Taking Control: Autonomy in Language Learning*. Hong Kong: Hong Kong University Press.

Littlejohn, A. 1983. Increasing Learner Involvement in Course Management. *TESOL Quarterly,* 17:4.

McGrath, I. 2000. Teacher Autonomy. In B. Sinclair, et al. (eds.) *Learner Autonomy, Teacher Autonomy: Future directions*. London: Longman.

Nunan, D. 1997. Designing and Adapting Materials to Encourage Learner Autonomy. In P. Benson & P. Voller (eds.) *Autonomy and Independence in Language Learning*. London: Longman.

Voller, P. 1997. Does the Teacher have a Role in Autonomous Learning? In P. Benson & P. Voller (eds.) *Autonomy and Independence in Language Learning*. London: Longman.

Young, R. 1986. *Personal Autonomy: Beyond negative and positive liberty*. London: Croom Helm.

Chapter Fifteen

Classroom-based assessment

Geoff Brindley, Macquarie University (Australia)

At the end of this chapter, you should be able to:

Goals

✔ **list** the reasons why assessment and evaluation are carried out in the ESL/EFL classroom.

✔ **describe** a range of methods and tools that can be used to assess language proficiency and achievement.

✔ **develop** classroom assessment tasks that are linked to learning outcomes.

1. What is assessment and evaluation?

Assessment

Chapelle and Brindley (2002, p. 267) define **assessment** as "the act of collecting information and making judgments on a language learner's knowledge of a language and ability to use it." Assessment is thus concerned with *individual student learning.* The term evaluation, on the other hand, is often used in the broader sense of *program evaluation,* and refers to the process of collecting information and making judgments on the quality of the *total language program.* This involves a consideration of a range of elements in addition to student learning, such as teacher and student attitudes, teaching methods and materials, as well as administrative systems and resources.

The two most important qualities of assessment are **validity** and **reliability.** A valid assessment is one which provides information on the ability we want to assess and nothing else. If we wanted to find out about a person's conversational ability in English, for example, we would not ask them to read out a list of English words, since reading aloud would not be considered by most people to be part of conversational ability. Validity also concerns the extent to which the *uses* that are made of assessment are appropriate. To continue the previous example, using the results of an assessment of reading words aloud as an indicator of conversational ability would be an *invalid* use of that test. Similarly, in the context of classroom assessment, if we wanted to find out how well learners had mastered the vocabulary that they had covered in class, it would not be appropriate to use a test containing vocabulary they had not been taught.

Reliability refers to the consistency with which our assessment tools measure language ability. An assessment is reliable when there is little difference in learners' scores or in judges' ratings across different occasions or different judges. If we use a test to assess a learner's ability on Monday, we would want it to yield similar results on Tuesday. Similarly, if two teachers were assessing the same piece of student writing, we would hope that they would be in fairly close agreement on the quality of the performance.

Reflection

1. In some educational settings, the quality of language programs is judged solely on the basis of students' test scores. Is this fair?

2. A teacher wants to assess the listening comprehension of her advanced ESL/EFL class. She plays them a radio news bulletin and asks them to write a short paragraph outlining the main points. Is this a valid assessment of listening ability? Why or why not?

Evaluation

Evaluation is a broader concept than assessment. It involves collecting and interpreting information (which will usually include assessment data) for making decisions about the effectiveness of a particular program. Language program evaluation may be carried out for a variety of reasons. Often the government or an external funding body will want to know whether the program is providing "value for money" and will commission a team of consultants to conduct an evaluation. Sometimes an institution might conduct its own internal evaluation in order to identify any problems with its administrative and educational systems, with a view to improving them. However, teachers are usually concerned not so much with system level concerns such as these, but rather with the question of whether or not their course was successful on its own terms. In particular they will want to find out learners' opinions of the course.

Action

Imagine you were a teacher and you were asked by the school you work in to provide evidence of the quality of the program you were teaching. Write down a list of the information that you would want to collect.

Quality, like proficiency, can be defined in many ways and for this reason it is not easy to list indicators of quality. Nevertheless, if we think about the elements that might contribute to a program's success from teachers' and learners' perspectives, then we can begin to identify some of the factors that we would need to take into account in determining whether our course worked. These might include:

<u>Student factors</u>

• Student learning outcomes

<u>Course factors</u>

• Content
• Atmosphere
• Materials and learning activities
• Assessment
• Teaching/classroom management

<u>Institutional factors</u>

- Facilities
- Resources

The evaluation could also include a self-evaluation element for students and teachers which provides the opportunity for them to reflect on the extent to which the course has met their own goals and expectations.

Action

Turn each of the factors on pages 311-312 into a question. For example: "Were student learning outcomes satisfactory?" How would you go about answering these questions?

2. Background to assessment and evaluation

Beliefs about the nature of language proficiency have changed somewhat over the years and language tests have reflected these changes. From the 1950s to about the mid-1970s, it was thought that language proficiency involved mastery of separate parts of the linguistic system such as the sound system, grammar, and vocabulary, so these were the elements that were tested. Typical test items that test candidates encountered might have looked something like the following:

Discriminating between sounds

Choose the word that contains the same sound as that underlined in the first word.
<u>glove</u>   a. t<u>o</u>p   b. m<u>o</u>ve   c. b<u>u</u>s   d. <u>o</u>ver

Grammar

I've been living here.................ten years
a. since   b. during   c. for   d. while

Vocabulary

Choose the word which is closest in meaning to the word on the left:
apprehensive   a. obvious   b. worried   c. near   d. ready

The tests that were used during this period were known as discrete-point tests because they tested one linguistic item at a time. In order to make them as reliable as possible, the designers included large numbers of items and used machine-scorable "objective" types of items such as multiple choice.

Although these kinds of tests were highly reliable and efficient to administer, they could only assess a person's knowledge of isolated elements and thus did not provide much useful information about the test-takers' ability to use the language in the real world. Applied linguists and language test developers, therefore, began to reassess the notion of language ability and to try to spell out explicitly what happens when people use language for communicative purposes. One of the first attempts to do this in a systematic way was by Canale and Swain (1980) who proposed a model of communicative competence that identified the different kinds of abilities that were required to communicate appropriately in a particular social context. More recently, Bachman and Palmer (1996) have proposed a detailed framework for describing communicative language ability that includes language competence (including grammatical knowledge as well as knowledge of how to use language appropriately in context) and strategic competence (strategies that enable language learners to create and understand discourse). Bachman and Palmer (1996, p. 57) provide a detailed guide for describing the characteristics of the language tasks that learners have to carry out in real life so that assessment tasks can be designed to reflect these characteristics.

This principle of matching assessment tasks to real-world language use has been increasingly applied to language test construction in recent years. In contrast to the rather artificial items that were used in earlier tests, many tests nowadays include authentic-looking texts and present the learner with tasks similar to those they would encounter in using the language for communication. Thus, some of the commonly used tests of English for academic purposes (EAP) require candidates to demonstrate the language skills they would need as a student in an English-speaking university, such as writing an essay in which they present and defend their opinion, or listening to a lecture in which they have to identify the lecturer's main points. Similarly, the assessment procedures that are used for certifying foreign language teachers' proficiency in the United States include an oral interview in which candidates have to converse with a native speaker of the language they are preparing to teach. In the interview, candidates might have to carry out a range of language functions that could include giving personal information, describing people or activities, telling a story, giving opinions, and speculating about future events. This emphasis on real-life language is also evident in classroom assessment. Assessment activities used by teachers today will typically include a range of performance tasks that require learners to engage in purposeful communication that is relevant to their needs. We will look at some of these later in this chapter.

3. Principles of classroom assessment and evaluation

1. Make sure that the kind of assessment you use is appropriate for its intended purpose.

In language programs, assessment is used for a variety of purposes. The main ones are:

- to give learners feedback on their progress and to motivate them to study
- to certify a person's ability or determine their suitability for selection
- to demonstrate achievement to external parties such as parents, school boards or government funding authorities

(Broadfoot, 1987)

It is very important to ensure that the type of assessment you use is appropriate for its purpose. The misuse of assessment can have quite detrimental effects on learners. Consider these comments from students, quoted by Shohamy (1985, p. 9):

> We spent ten lessons conjugating the past tense but on the test there were only two conjugations.

> I don't see the connection between the test and my knowledge. Otherwise how can I explain the fact that I get good grades on English tests, but last week, when I met an American, I couldn't say anything in English? How come we never get to speak on tests?

These students cannot see the relationship between what they are supposed to be learning and what they are being tested on. Thus, these tests, which are intended to be motivational tools, are having quite the opposite effect.

Reflection

Think of the tests you have taken during your educational career. Can you remember ever taking a test that was not appropriate for its intended purposes or target group? If so, what effect did this experience have on you?

2. Make sure your assessment tasks are based on an explicit statement of the ability you are assessing and are clearly related to learning outcomes.

Before we can assess something, we have to be able to describe it, so the starting point for any language assessment is a statement that describes the ability we want to assess. If we want to assess something called speaking ability, for example, we have to be able to specify what the components of this ability are. This is called **construct** definition. A construct is an abstract concept (in this case speaking proficiency) that cannot be observed directly.

When they are designing a proficiency test, the first thing that test designers do is to write what are called test specifications which define the construct that is to be tested and describe the kinds of tasks that will be used. Making the construct explicit in this way gives the designers a means of verifying that the tasks they construct actually test what they are supposed to be testing.

The same principle applies in the case of classroom assessment. However, the starting point for planning classroom assessment will usually be a statement of student learning outcomes rather than a theoretical construct definition. Since the main aim of assessment is usually to establish the extent to which outcomes are achieved, it is very important to ensure that assessment tasks are clearly related to the course or unit outcomes. An example of how this can be done is shown in Figure 1. You can see how the broad learning outcome (here it is called a "profile sentence"), *greet someone*, is broken down into more specific behaviors that are involved in greeting someone *(performance criteria)*. To determine whether or not someone has achieved the outcome, the teacher needs to devise an assessment task that requires learners to demonstrate these abilities.

PROFILE SENTENCE: Greet someone

Performance criteria (the student has demonstrated the ability to:)
Use appropriate forms of address
Use a range of greetings and responses
Recognize and convey relationship and attitude in a short encounter

Consistency
Demonstrate ability in at least three contexts with variables such as time, place, relationship.

Constraints
Greetings should be both initiated and responded to.

Examples of contexts
As member of a group, with neighbors, shopkeepers, friends, colleagues, officials, teachers

Examples of appropriate evidence
Oral demonstration

Figure 1 Performance criteria for a proficiency exam (Royal Society of Arts, 1988)

3. Involve learners in assessment.

Classroom assessment is part of the learning process, so it should be done with learners, not to them. Before assessment takes place, it is important to make sure that learners know why they are being assessed, what the results of the assessment mean, and how the results are going to be used. In addition, the instructions for doing the task need to be made clear. In some cases it might be necessary to provide these in the learners' first language. The criteria that will be used to assess their performance also need to be explained. If different levels of achievement are possible for a particular task, learners should be told what these levels mean and what is considered to be a satisfactory level of performance.

If the purpose of an assessment is to provide diagnostic feedback, then this feedback needs to be provided in a form—either verbal or written—that is easy for the learners to understand and use. For example, learners often want explicit feedback on their written errors and advice on how to proceed in order to address the problems they are having. Conferences involving either one-to-one or group discussion between teacher and students are one way in which this can happen.

4. Use a variety of assessment methods.

In recent years, teachers have become increasingly dissatisfied with using "one-off" tests to assess classroom achievement. A test is a finite event that happens in a short time and by definition, the type and amount of material that can be included is limited. In addition, some learners simply do not like taking tests and perform below their real ability. For these reasons, assessment researchers in recent years have stressed the importance of using a variety of assessment methods in addition to tests. Not only does this show development over time, but it also gives the teacher a richer picture of learners' abilities in a range of different contexts.

4. Classroom techniques and tasks

Different types of assessment are used at various points throughout a language program for various purposes. These are summarized below. Specific examples will be given in the next section.

Precourse assessment

At the beginning of a course of instruction, we will usually want to ascertain the learners' ability to use a language for particular communicative goals, regardless of any instruction they may have had previously. For this purpose we would use a **proficiency test** which would give us a general idea of their level of ability so that the course can be pitched at the appropriate level of difficulty. This could be either a commercial test or one that is developed "in-house" by a particular institution. A proficiency test may also be used as a **placement test** to sort learners into groups of similar proficiency level or as a **selection test** to ascertain whether a person has sufficient language proficiency to begin a particular course of study or to practice a given profession or occupation. Even though most teachers will not be responsible for the construction of proficiency tests, it is important that they are able to interpret and act on the information that such tests provide.

The results of proficiency assessment may be interpreted in two ways. First, learners' scores or grades can be compared with each other (e.g., "Maria scored 90 out of 100/in the top 10 percent"). This is known as a **norm-referenced** interpretation. Alternatively, their performance may be compared with an external standard or criterion which has already been defined, such as a particular course objective or descriptor of a performance (e.g., "can give simple personal information"). This is known as a **criterion-referenced** interpretation. Criterion-referenced reporting provides test users with qualitative information about what a test taker can do with the language. For example, a learner who is assessed at Threshold Level on the framework used by the Council of Europe for describing language proficiency:

> Can understand the main points of clear standard input on familiar matters regularly encountered in work, school, leisure, and so on. Can deal with most situations likely to arise while traveling in an area where the language is spoken. Can produce simple, connected text on topics that are familiar or of personal interest. Can describe experiences and events, dreams, hopes, and ambitions and briefly give reasons and explanations for opinions and plans.

> (North, 2000, p. 28)

In-course assessment

Once learning is under way, we will want to find out how much a student has learned in a particular unit of instruction. For this purpose, we would use some form of **achievement assessment**. Achievement assessment may be based either on the specific content that has been covered or on the course objectives. Hughes (1989) considers that the latter approach is greatly preferred since he believes that assessing mastery of specific content may not tell us whether the objectives have actually been achieved. As we have seen, the major advantage of basing assessment on the course objectives is that there is a very close link between assessment and instruction: what is taught is what is assessed and what is assessed is what is reported. This allows teachers, learners, and external parties such as parents or school administrators to see to what extent the intended outcomes of the course have been achieved.

An informal way of keeping track of progress over a period of time is by giving *progress achievement* tests such as short weekly tests based on the topics, themes, or structures that have been covered during that week. The results of these tests can be used to give students feedback on their progress in relation to the course objectives and to help them identify any areas where they might need to do more work. Used in this way, the tests have a **diagnostic** function. Another important purpose of progress achievement tests is to motivate learners by allowing them the opportunity to demonstrate what they have learned. For this reason, they tend to be designed so that learners achieve high scores.

In addition to tests, there are a variety of other non-test procedures that can be used to gather ongoing information on learners' progress and achievement, including systematic observation, conferences between the teacher and the student, and self- and peer assessment. One method that has been shown to be particularly useful is the **portfolio**. A portfolio contains a collection of student work selected by the student that demonstrates their efforts, progress, or achievement over a period of time. Portfolios may contain samples of classroom tests, samples of writing, audiotapes, or videotapes of oral performances.

End-of-course assessment

At the end of a period of instruction teachers will usually need to report on learners' achievement to external authorities (for example at the end of a school term). This is known as **summative assessment**. For this purpose, *final achievement tests* would be used. These usually resemble formal tests and may be constructed by external educational bodies or by teachers within an institution with special responsibilities for assessment.

5. Assessment and evaluation in the classroom

In this section we will look at some examples of ways in which students' proficiency and achievement can be assessed at various points throughout the program for the range of purposes that we have identified. We will also consider how learners themselves can be involved in the assessments.

Proficiency assessment at course entry

As we have seen, the results of some proficiency tests are reported in the form of criterion-referenced descriptors of different levels of ability. Although these descriptors are a useful indicator of a learner's overall proficiency, they tend to be rather broad and general and thus are of limited value in course planning. However, general proficiency descriptors can be helpful in sensitizing learners to what is involved in learning a language, particularly if they are couched as self-assessment (SA) statements, as in the following example from Oskarsson (1980):

SPEAKING	
☐ I speak the language as well as a well-educated native.	5
☐	4.5
☐ I speak the language fluently and for the most part correctly. I have a large vocabulary so I seldom have to hesitate or search for words. On the other hand I am not completely fluent in situations in which I have had no practice with the language.	4
☐	3.5
☐ I can make myself understood in most everyday situations, but my language is not without mistakes and sometimes I cannot find the words for what I want to say. It is difficult for me to express myself in situations in which I have had no opportunity to practise the language. I can give a short summary of general information that I have received in my native language.	3
☐	2.5
☐ I can make myself understood in simple everyday situations, for example asking and giving simple directions, asking and telling the time, asking and talking about simpler aspects of work and interests. My vocabulary is rather limited, so it is only by a great deal of effort that I can use the language in new and unexpected situations.	2
☐	1.5
☐ I can just about express very simple things concerning my own situation and my nearest surroundings, for example asking and answering very simple questions about the time, food, housing and directions. I only have a command of very simple words and phrases.	1
☐	0.5
☐ I do not speak the language at all.	0

Figure 2 Self-assessment statements for speaking skills

Action

If you speak another language, rate yourself on the speaking scale (Figure 2, page 319). To what extent do you feel your proficiency was adequately represented by the descriptions on the scale? Add any features of your proficiency that you think are missing.

Asking learners at the beginning of the course to self-assess where they are on this type of scale and the level they wish to achieve can be a useful way of involving them early in the specification of their own language learning goals and objectives, thus encouraging self-direction.

SA can also be used as a placement tool. Learners can be asked to say how well they can carry out the types of tasks that they will encounter in the syllabus. This provides information that the teacher can use in course design and also encourages learners to reflect on their learning needs, goals and objectives.

Commentary The notion of SA may be unfamiliar and even threatening to some learners, and in some cases, it may take some time before they understand the rationale for self-assessment. In this regard, one of the clear messages that emerges from research into SA is that it needs to be introduced in a carefully staged way so that learners know why it is being used and how it can help them learn better. Before asking learners to use SA tools, then, the teacher needs to spend some time discussing the aims of self-assessment, its advantages, and ways in which learners might become involved. This could be done at the beginning of a course in conjunction with proficiency assessment using a SA scale such as the one above. The learners also need to have the opportunity to develop skills in organizing their learning, reflecting on their achievements, describing their own and their peers' performances, and making assessment decisions. Some people maintain that a parallel learner training program is necessary if SA is to be systematically incorporated into the program. Given the need for this supplementary component, it may be difficult to incorporate SA into language programs in which hours of instruction are limited.

Reflection

1. "Self-assessment is a waste of time. Learners will just cheat." What do you think of this statement?

2. If you were asked to justify the use of self-assessment to a language learner, what would you say?

Ongoing achievement assessment

Observation

Observation is one of the most widely used methods of keeping track of learners' progress in the classroom. Teachers commonly observe learners' performance in the classroom on a day-to-day basis and follow this up with some kind of diagnostic feedback, either verbal or written, which alerts the learner to his or her strengths or weaknesses. Used in this way, observation is an important part of **formative assessment,** the purpose of which is to inform and improve the learning process.

One of the most commonly used formats for observation-based assessment and monitoring is the checklist. In its most basic form, this consists of a grid containing the learner's name, the task or objective which is to be attempted, and a series of boxes which allow the teacher to note whether or not the task has been successfully achieved. In some cases, rather than a simple yes/no judgment on achievement, there is a simple rating scale describing different levels of attainment in relation to the task or objective that is the object of instruction. Some formats also allow for the inclusion of the learner's and/or their peers' assessment of their own achievement in addition to the teacher's.

Reflection

Study the checklist (Figure 3, page 322) that was developed for monitoring learners' achievement of English language competencies in a workplace program in the U.S. (U.S. Department of Health and Human Services, 1985). Imagine you are a teacher who is discussing the checklist with a student after it has been filled in. Is there anything you would want to change?

Action

Design a similar checklist for monitoring learners' achievement of language competencies in a beginning level unit on shopping (you will need to think about what competencies are involved). Include five competencies.

Name		**Class**	
TEPR Entry Date		Social Security No.	

Key :   0 - Needs Improvement
       1 - Communicative/Satisfactory
       2 - Good
       3 - Very Good			

		Date	Date
1. State previous occupation(s) in simple terms.			
2. Ask and answer basic question about work shifts, starting date, specific hours and pay day.			
3. Read want ads and identify skills needed for a job.			
4. Describe previous work experience, job skills, qualifications, and training in detail, including degree of ability.			
5. State own ability to use tool, equipment, and machines.			
6. Follow simple step-by-step oral instructions to begin and perform a task which is demonstrated, including simple classroom instructions.			
7. Ask if the task is done properly.			
8. Ask simple clarification questions about routine job task and instructions.			
9. Ask supervisor/co-worker for help.			
10. Respond to simple oral warning/basic commands about safety.			
11. Interpret common warnings/safety signs at work site.			
12. Give simple excuses for lateness or absence in person.			
13. Report work progress and completion of tasks.			
14. Follow simple two-step oral instructions on the job.			
15. Find out about the location of common materials and facilities at the work site.			
16. Follow simple oral instructions which contain references to places or objects in the immediate work area.			
17. Modify a task based on changes in instructions.			
18. Respond to supervisor's comments about quality of work on the job, including mistakes, working too slowly, and incomplete work.			
19. Give specific reasons for sickness, absence, or lateness.			
20. Report specific problems encountered in completing a task.			

Figure 3 Student competency checklist

Commentary The checklist format, although obviously fairly basic, is simple to use and allows for achievement of tasks or objectives to be informally and rapidly monitored by the teacher either on an individual or group basis. Developing strategies and skills can also be noted and monitored. In addition, it serves as a record which can be used by learners to keep track of their own learning progress and difficulties and to demonstrate achievement of objectives to other people. The performance levels that are used, however, tend to be rather vague and impressionistic (e.g., "good") and might need to be made more precise if the information had to be conveyed to other people.

Developing tasks for assessing achievement: rating scales

As we have seen, assessing language production requires the elicitation of a performance and then a judgment on that performance. In the case of speaking and writing skills, this judgment will often be carried out using a **rating scale** that describes and quantifies the key features of the performance, as in the previous example from Oskarsson (1980). The scale descriptors may be quite general (e.g., "Can handle most social situations with facility.") or they may relate to a particular area of language use (e.g., "Can write a wide range of business correspondence with confidence and competence."). Scales can even be developed to describe a specific task (e.g., "Provides all/most/some information."). It is generally inappropriate to use a scale that has been designed for one purpose (e.g., a general proficiency scale) for another purpose (e.g., to describe achievement of a particular classroom objective).

Now look at the cartoon in Figure 4.

Figure 4 Prompt for picture description task

Study the Extracts 1 and 2 below which were collected from two adult ESL learners doing a picture description task. Which learner do you think is the more proficient? Why?

Extract 1   Learner 1

Ze boy gives ze...money ze man who selled ze balloon...and ze man...give him ze change...and ze balloon..and ze boy...runs with three balloons to his mother. He's very exciting about zis...and ze boy gives ze rest of ze money his mother. But he...ze boy is too light for ze balloon and he goes up in the air.

Extract 2   Learner 2

Dey boy wants a balloon...so...de boy...told to grandma "I want a balloon" so you gave me some money and...er...de baby went to...er...er...salesman ...and...de boy told him "I wanna three balloon" and den..."How muchee?... er...um...um...de salesman gave him some changee...and den...balloon. He's got a balloon now...and...he came back here...um...and den...he gave grandmother some changeee...give...um...gave her...have her...er...de boy flew...flew up.

Commentary Interestingly, when I gave a group of ESL teachers this exercise, they did not agree in their rankings. Some of them thought that Learner 1 was more proficient because she was able to explain precisely why the boy flew away ("the boy is too light for the balloon"). However, others thought that Learner 2 was better because in their view she provided more detail, had a wider range of vocabulary and better control of grammar (note her consistent use of the past tense, even though in this case the historic present would normally be used).

What criteria would we use, then, to rate these performances? The ones that this group of teachers came up with were as follows:

- Overall communicative effectiveness (task fulfillment)
- Fluency
- Vocabulary
- Grammatical accuracy
- Pronunciation, intonation and stress

If you look at the criteria, it becomes clear that the reason for the disagreement between the teachers can be traced back to the emphasis that they give to the different features of performance. Some teachers were focusing on the first criterion, overall communicative effectiveness (also called task fulfillment), which concerns the learner's ability to get the message across, while others were more concerned with the learner's mastery of the language code in terms of grammar and vocabulary.

Once the key features of the performance have been identified, it is relatively straightforward to turn them into a rating scale. But in order to be able to quantify the performances we need to add a scoring system. The scale might then look like this:

Overall communicative effectiveness	5	4	3	2	1	0
Fluency	5	4	3	2	1	0
Vocabulary	5	4	3	2	1	0
Grammatical accuracy	5	4	3	2	1	0
Pronunciation, intonation and stress	5	4	3	2	1	0

Figure 5 Criteria scale for rating speakers

If some criteria are deemed to be more important than others, different weightings can be given to each of the criteria. If the teachers were able to agree that communicative effectiveness was more important than, say, pronunciation, this could be reflected in the marking scheme by giving the former a weighting of, say, 30 percent and the latter a weighting of 10 percent.

Because rating is quite a subjective process, it is important to ensure that people who use rating scales regularly are provided with training in how to interpret and use them. This is particularly necessary when the results of the assessment carry high stakes (such as selection or entry).

Reflection

Of the performance criteria in the rating scale above, which do you think would be the most difficult for raters to agree on? Why?

Action

Using the model on page 325 (Figure 5), try to create a similar rating scale for the outcome statement: *Can give an oral presentation.*

You may need to change some of the performance criteria.

6. Conclusion

In this chapter, I have briefly traced the development of language assessment from the time when it was concerned with people's mastery of isolated elements of the language to its present focus on using language to communicate in the real world. We have looked at the different purposes for which language assessment is carried out in language programs and the kinds of tools that can be used to assess proficiency and achievement. One of the main themes running through the chapter has been the need for a close link between assessment and teaching. Classroom assessment is a means of informing and improving learning—if you teach what you assess and you assess what you teach, then both learners and teachers know what has been achieved and where they need to go next.

Further readings

Bailey, K. 1998. *Learning about Language Assessment*. Boston, MA: Heinle & Heinle.

This book is a good introduction to assessment issues, and is firmly based in practice, with many examples of actual tests and assessment tasks used by teachers, accompanied by helpful commentaries from the author. It provides clear explanations of assessment tools and techniques for test analysis.

Brown, J. D. (ed.) 1998. *New Ways of Classroom Assessment*. Alexandria, VA: TESOL.

Brown has compiled a very useful compendium of teacher-developed classroom assessment activities that can be integrated with teaching. It contains numerous examples of assessment that do not involve formal testing, such as observation, self-assessment, portfolios, journals, and conferences.

Cohen, A. D. 1994. *Assessing Language Ability in the Classroom*. Second Edition. Boston, MA: Heinle & Heinle.

This is a comprehensive overview of assessment theory and practice, firmly grounded in research, containing numerous examples of tools for assessing language proficiency and achievement.

Genesee, F. and J. Upshur 1996. *Classroom-Based Evaluation in Second Language Education*. Cambridge: Cambridge University Press.

For the development of both formal and informal assessment tools for classroom use, this clear, nontechnical guide includes numerous examples of techniques that can be used for a range of assessment purposes.

O'Malley, J. M and L. Valdez-Pierce 1996. *Authentic Assessment for English Language Learners*. New York, NY: Addison-Wesley.

This volume provides a detailed and accessible introduction to ways of integrating teaching and learning in ESL classrooms through the use of "authentic" assessments such as observations, checklists, interviews, and portfolios. It contains many exemplars of assessment tools that can be adapted to local needs.

Helpful Web site

Resources in Language Testing (http://www.surrey.ac.uk/ELI/ltr.html)
Run by Glenn Fulcher from the University of Surrey, this site is a very useful "one-stop shop" that offers a rich variety of resources relating to language assessment. It contains links to a large number of assessment sites, both in general education and language learning. As well, there are downloadable articles on assessment, video interviews with experts in the field, examples of tests, and a wide range of other information on aspects of language assessment. The site is regularly updated.

References

Bachman, L. F. and A. S. Palmer 1996. *Language Testing in Practice*. Oxford: Oxford University Press.

Broadfoot, P. 1987. *Introducing Profiling*. London: MacMillan.

Canale, M. and M. Swain 1980. Theoretical Bases of Communicative Approaches to Second Language Teaching and Testing. *Applied Linguistics,* 1(1):1–47.

Chapelle, C. and G. Brindley 2002. Assessment. In Schmitt, N. (ed.) *An Introduction to Applied Linguistics*. London: Arnold.

Hughes, A. 1989. *Testing for Language Teachers*. Cambridge: Cambridge University Press.

North, B. 2000. Defining a Flexible Measurement Scale: Descriptors for self and teacher assessment. In G. Ekbatani and H. Pierson (eds.) *Learner-directed assessment in ESL*. Mahwah, NJ: Lawrence Erlbaum.

Oskarsson, M. 1980. *Approaches to Self-Assessment in Foreign Language Learning*. London: Pergamon.

Royal Society of Arts 1988. *English as a Second Language: Dual certification*. London: RSA.

Shohamy, E. 1985. *A Practical Handbook in Language Testing for the Second Language Teacher*. Tel Aviv: Tel Aviv University.

United States Department of Health and Human Services 1985. *Mainstream English Language Training Project*. Washington DC: Office of Refugee Resettlement, United States Department of Health and Human Services.

Glossary

academic vocabulary – vocabulary that is more frequent and widely occurring in academic text than in other types of text

accuracy – the ability to produce grammatically and phonologically well-formed words, phrases, and sentences

achievement assessment – an assessment of what has been learned in a particular course or unit of instruction

acquisition orders – the chronological order in which learners acquire the grammatical items in a second language

adapted – a text that has been simplifiied in terms of its grammar and vocabulary

adjacency pairs – two bits of language that fit together appropriately

adjunct program – a course that focuses on second language writing in support of a "content" course, such as psychology or chemistry: these courses teach the style and vocabulary expected in the content course

altered – a text in which the wording is the same as the original, but that has been altered in terms of visuals, typesetting, glossing, etc.

approaches – general, philosophical orientations to language teaching

assessment – collecting information and making judgments on a learner's knowledge

audience – readers for a piece of writing

audiolingual technique – drill-based techniques based on behaviorist psychology

audiolingualism – a drill-based method based on behaviorist psychology and structural linguistics

authentic texts – spoken and written language which is created in the course of genuine communication rather than being specially created for the purposes of language learning and teaching

autonomy – the capacity to control one's own learning

behaviorism – a theory of learning associated with the use of repetitive drills; learners are considered to be empty vessels into which the teacher pours knowledge

blended learning – Web-based study combining independent learning with teacher-mediated instruction in a chatroom environment

bottom-up processing – using component parts: words, grammar, and the like, to process meaning

brainstorming – a learning strategy involving generating as many ideas, words or concepts related to a given topic as possible

branching computer program – a program in which learners face more difficult questions if their answers were correct or undertake remedial training and/or questions if their answers were wrong

CALL – computer-assisted language learning

channel – the medium of the message (aural/oral or written)

clause – a group of words with a subject and a verb marked for tense that form a grammatical unit

cloze – a listening or reading based completion activity where every fifth word in a text has been replaced by a blank

cognitive code learning – a method based on the notion that second language learning involves reasoning rather than habit formation

cognitive overhead – refers to the learning that must take place before a student is able to use a program; for example, for primary school students, the odd arrangement of letters on a computer keyboard presents considerable cognitive overhead to completing a task that requires them to write

cognitive learning strategies – learning strategies that apply directly to learning

cognitivism – a teaching approach that believes writing is part of a process of critical thinking and problem-solving

communicative language teaching – a language teaching method based on the concept that interaction is the key to language learning and that students must have opportunities to communicate during lessons

comprehensible input – challenging language that is slightly above the current linguistic level of the learner

concordancing – a process of looking at the relationship between words to reveal rules about language use in the real world

construct – an abstract concept that cannot be observed directly

constructivism – a theory of learning which builds on the knowledge of individual learners and allows them to organize their own learning

contact assignment – a task in which learners have contact with other people and use the target language to speak with them

content – the "what" of a language syllabus (topics, themes, grammar, vocabulary pronunciation), as opposed to the "how" (pedagogical tasks and activities)

content-based instruction (CBI) – the teaching of language through exposure to content that is interesting and relevant to learners

context – the situation in which language occurs

contrastive rhetoric – the comparison of writing styles and processes from different languages

core meaning – the meaning that is the common part of the various senses of a word

coursebook – a published book used by the students and teacher as the primary basis for a language course

criterion-referenced – the interpretation of assessment results in relation to an external standard

curriculum development – processes and procedures for selecting, sequencing, and justifying program content, learning procedures, and evaluation

declarative knowledge – knowledge that allows one to state a rule or principle

deductive learning – a procedure in which learners are give a rule or principle, and then find examples of the rules in samples of language

descriptive grammar – grammars based on what people actually say and write as opposed to what they should say and write according to prescriptive grammarians

diagnostic test – assessment that identifies learners' strengths and weaknesses

discourse – the study of the relationship between language and its contexts of use

discourse community – a group of language users with a common purpose, for example, physicists, who use language in a similar way

dispreferred sequence – when two pair-parts of speech do not fit together

distinctive feature – a particular quality of a speech sound which distinguishes it from another speech sound (e.g., voicing); usually related to where in the mouth a sound is produced and how it is produced

editing – improving writing through correcting mistakes in grammar, spelling, and punctuation

evaluation – the collection and interpretation of information for making decisions about the effectiveness of an educational program

explicit – in explicit teaching, the learner's attention is deliberately drawn to a principle or rule

expressivism – a teaching approach that encourages self-expression through journal writing, personal narratives, and so forth

extensive reading – reading silently for extended periods of time

fluency – the ability to speak the language with relative ease while focused on getting one's meaning across: fluency includes the ability to produce connected, continuous streams of speech without causing communication breakdowns

fluent reading – reading smoothly at an appropriate rate with adequate comprehension

foreign language (FL) context – a situation where the language being learned is not the society's language of communication (e.g., learning English in Japan or studying French in Australia)

format shift – switching to a different skill or grouping than the one proposed in the textbook

formative assessment – assessment that is carried out in order to inform the learning process

freewriting – an unstructured writing exercise in which grammar, spelling, or other formal elements are not important

gap-fill drills – exercises in which the learner has to provide information expected by the program, rather than demonstrating what he or she knows

genuine – an authentic text that has been created for the real world, not the classroom

global/gist listening – listening for the main idea, topic, situation, or setting

grammar dictation – a technique where the teacher dictates a passage containing target language forms at normal speed while students take notes and then work together to reconstruct the passage

grammar-translation – a language teaching method based on the explication of grammatical rules and extensive practice in doing translations from the first to the target language and vice-versa

graphic organizers – drawings, pictures, or outlines that show how reading material is organized

high frequency words – the most frequent 2000 words of a language

holistic – paying attention only to the whole piece of writing, and not giving attention to one detail over another

holistic rubric – a rubric which describes in general terms the qualities of excellent, good, fair, and unsatisfactory assignments

implicit – in implicit teaching, the learners are left to infer principles or rules for themselves

inductive learning – a procedure whereby a learner studies samples of the target language and devises rules and principles based on those samples: it contrasts with deductive learning, in which the rules are presented and then applied

information gap activity – an activity in which one learner has information that another lacks and they must use the target language to convey that information

input – spoken or written language that is made available to learners as a basis for learning

input enhancement – a technique for getting students to notice the grammar item that the teacher wants to introduce

input hypothesis – Stephen Krashen's theory stating it is necessary for the learner to understand input language that is slightly beyond the learner's present linguistic competence

intensive reading – reading a short passage to develop specific reading skills

interactive models – the processing of top-down and bottom-up data at the same time

interactional speech – speech for the purpose of establishing or maintaining social relationships

jigsaw activity – a bi-directional or multidirecitonal information gap situation, in which each person in a pair or group has some information the other person(s) must have in order to complete a task: they must use the target language to share that information

keyword technique – a mnemonic technique which involves using a first language word to link the form and the meaning of a foreign word

knowledge domain – an organized collection of information on a topic, including processes

learner-centered education – an approach that uses information about learners' needs and preferences in selecting learning content and procedures; also refers to programs in which learners are actively involved in learning through doing

learning burden – the amount of effort needed to learn a word, depending largely on how much the aspects of the word relate to previous knowledge

learning contract – a way to help teachers and students share responsibility and provide constructive feedback for learning through increased accountability: learners agree on goals to be met but are usually quite free to decide the ways in which they meet those goals

learning (pedagogical) tasks – classroom work which has an outcome other than the production of a piece of language and in which the focus is principally on meaning rather than form

learning strategies – characteristics teachers want to encourage in students to enable them to become more proficient learners

learning styles – a learner's natural, preferred ways of absorbing, processing, and retaining new information

linear computer program – a program where all learners follow the same path

low frequency words – words not in the most 2000 frequently used words of a language

metacognitive learning strategies – learning strategies where students control their own learning process

method – integrated set of classroom procedures, usually based on beliefs on the nature of language and learning

methodology – the development of principles and procedures for selecting, sequencing, and justifying learning tasks and activities

morpheme – a meaning unit in a language, which is either a *free morpheme* (a word) or a *bound morpheme* (a prefix or a suffix)

morpheme order studies – a series of studies conducted in the 1970s which showed that learners acquire certain grammatical morphemes in a set order regardless of their first language background

negotiation for meaning – the processes, during interaction, of checking, clarifying, asking for slower speech and/or repetition, which enables speakers to understand and make themselves understood

non-weighted rubric – a rubric which provides descriptions of writing quality by level across other writing criteria

norm-referenced – the interpretation of assessment results in terms of the performance of the group that is tested

notional-functional approach – an approach to syllabus design based on concepts such as time, duration, quantity, as well as a specification of the things that people do through language such as ordering, inviting, and complaining

phonemes – meaning-bearing units of sound in a particular language; phonemes can be *segmental* (the consonants and vowels) or *suprasegmental* (stress, rhythm, and intonation)

phonics approach – an approach to the teaching of reading in which students are taught to match the sounds to letters

phrase – two or more words functioning together but without a verb marked for tense

placement test – a test that is used to place learners into a group or class

portfolio – a collection of student work selected by the student that demonstrates their efforts, progress, or achievement over a period of time

practicality – the extent to which a test or assessment can be feasibly implemented with available resources

prescriptive grammar – rule-based grammars specifying what people should say and write

principled eclecticism – a combination of approaches to teaching, choosing the most appropriate elements from each to suit the population or situation

procedural knowledge – being able to apply a rule or principle to practice

process writing – a teaching approach that places importance on different aspects of the cycle of writing, including invention, drafting, and revision, and not just the final product produced

productive – producing language, as in speaking and writing, going from meaning to form

proficiency test – an assessment of a person's ability to use a language for a particular purpose regardless of any previous instruction

programmed instruction (or programmed learning) – a behaviorist approach to teaching at the computer in which incremental achievements or failures at different tasks govern the student's learning path

quickwriting – similar to freewriting, but typically with a given topic

rating scale – a scale containing a series of ordered categories indicating different levels of ability

receptive – receiving language, as in listening and reading, going from form to meaning

reliability – the consistency with which an assessment measures language behavior

revision – the rethinking improvement of a piece of writing through clarification, development, and reorganization

role-play – a speaking activity in which the learners take on someone else's identity and act out a situation in order to practice using the target language

rubric – a written form or checklist to assist in the evaluation of a writing assignment

schema – the interrelated knowledge patterns in our minds

schemata – background knowledge

second language (SL) context – a situation where the learners' target language is the language of communication in the society (for example, when studying English in the UK or learning Spanish in Mexico)

segmentals – a language's inventory of individual consonant and vowel sounds: most analysis of the English sound system include at least 24 consonant sounds and 15 vowel sounds

selection test – a test that is used to determine whether a person is accepted into an educational program

self-access center – an open access resource center containing authentic print, audio, and video target language materials

self-directed learning – learning outside the classroom that was planned and executed by the learners themselves

silent way – a method designed to maximize student self-responsibility and minimize student dependence on the teacher

simulation – a role-play activity which attempts to approximate realistic conditions by using props, documents, settings, etc.

skills – unconscious awareness of strategies while reading a passage with understanding

social constructionism – a teaching approach that focuses on the context of writing and the influence that context has on the product

socio-affective factors – emotional aspects of language learning such as anxiety, motivation, and self-esteem

strategic reading – choosing the appropriate strategies to be a successful reader

strategies – conscious steps that readers take to improve their reading ability

structural linguistics – an approach to linguistics based on the notion that language consists of sets of hierarchical units, from sounds to morphemes to words to clauses to sentences

sustained-content language teaching (SCLT) – a version of content-based instruction in which learners acquire language in the course of intensively studying a single subject

suggestopedia – a method based on the use of relaxation techniques to make students more receptive to the target language

summative assessment – assessment that takes place at the end of a course or unit of instruction

suprasegmentals – a dimension of the sound system that extends over more than individual consonant and vowel sounds: suprasegmentals include patterns of word stress, sentence stress, rhythm, and intonation (including the rhythmic and melodic characteristics of speech)

sustained content language teaching (SCLT) – language development course in which course content is drawn exclusively from one academic discipline

syllabus – a document setting out language content (topics, themes, grammar, vocabulary and pronunciation features) in a sequenced and integrated way

tango seating – a seating arrangement in which two students are facing opposite directions but their right shoulders (or their left shoulders) are together, so that they can hear one another but not see what is on their partner's desk

target language – the language which learners are attempting to learn

task-based language teaching – an approach to pedagogy in which the point of departure is an inventory of things that people do with language rather than a list of grammatical items

text – a stretch of spoken or written language of undetermined length

top-down processing – using background knowledge to process meaning

transformational-generative grammar – a theory that attempts to describe a finite set of abstract rules for generating all grammatical utterances in a language; the theory explicitly rejected the notion that language acquisition was a matter of habit formation

transactional speech – communication for the purpose of getting something done, typically the exchange of goods and/or services

unequal power discourse – discourse in which one party has more social status and/or power than the other(s) and therefore has certain privileges (delegating turns, nominating topics, changing topics, asking questions, etc.) that the other speakers don't have

utterance – something someone says

validity – the extent to which an assessment is appropriate for its intended purposes

voicing – the question of whether or not the vocal chords are vibrating when a sound is made

weighted rubric – a rubric which breaks the writing skills into categories and sub-categories and assigns a specific point value to each

word family – a base word and its closely related inflected and derived forms

wordmapping – the process of creating a visual representation or 'map' of the relationship between topic-related vocabulary

Index

academic vocabulary, 134, 136
Academic Word List, 136
accuracy, 55, 76, 161, 180
achievement assessment, 318, 321-326
  observation, 321-322
  rating scales, 323-326
Acklam, Richard, 226, 230, 234
ACTIVE Skills for Reading, Book 1
  (Anderson), 82-83
ACTIVE system, 79-81, 82-83
activity charts, 238
activity repertoires, 233-234
adjacency pairs, 177, 188-189
adjunct instruction, 202, 204, 206
adjunct programs, 91
Aebersold, J. A., 78
affective issues, 116, 117
Alexander, L. G., 227
Allington, R. L., 69
Allwright, D., 60-62
Anders, P. L., 78
Anderson, N. J., 76, 82, 269
Anderson, T. G., 251
anticipation guides, 79-80
approaches, 5
Arens, K., 7
Arsenic and Old Lace (Kesselring), 119
assessment, 310-326
  background, 312-313
  classroom examples, 319-326
  classroom techniques/tasks,
    317-318
  defined, 310
  principles, 314-316
  reading, 77
audience, 88, 101
audiolingualism, 5-6, 7
  and coursebooks, 226-227
  and grammar, 155-156, 165
  and listening, 25
  and speaking, 49
authenticity. *See* task authenticity; text
  authenticity
autonomy, 290-305
  background, 291-293
  classroom examples, 299-305
  classroom techniques/tasks,
    297-298
  defined, 290
  principles, 294-296

Bachman, L. F., 313
background knowledge, 74, 79-80, 82.
  See also bottom-up vs. top-down
  processing; schema theory
Bailey, K. M., 60-62
balls, 118

Bamford, J., 33
Bartlett, F. C., 251
Beck, I. L., 75
behaviorism
  and computer-assisted language
    learning, 249-251
  and coursebooks, 226
  and methodology, 5-6
  and pronunciation, 113
  and speaking, 49
Benson, P., 290
Berlitz, Charles, 25
bits and pieces listening activity, 37
Bizzell, P., 89
bottom-up vs. top-down processing
  and listening, 26-30, 35, 37
  and reading, 70-71, 72-73
brainstorming, 97, 100, 101, 276, 278
branching programs, 250
Breen, M. P., 292
Brindley, G., 310
Brinton, D. M., 202, 203, 204, 206,
  207, 209, 211
Broadfoot, P., 314
Brown, H. D., 5
Brown, S., 28, 30, 33, 33-34, 36, 39
Buck, G., 24, 29
Burt, M., 156

CA (conversation analysis), 177-178
CALL. *See* computer-assisted language
  learning
CALLA (cognitive academic language
  learning approach), 271
CALP (cognitive academic language
  proficiency), 271
Canale, M., 313
Candy, P. C., 290
Cantoni-Harvey, G., 202
capacity hypothesis, 32
Carpenter, P., 32
Carrell, P. L., 74
Carter, 183
Cassidy, D., 78
Cassidy, J., 78
CBI. *See* content-based instruction
Celce-Murcia, M., 115, 154
*Centre de Recherches et d'Applications en
  Langues* (CRAPEL), 291
Chamot, A. U., 76, 271
Chandler, D., 254-255
channels, 48
Chapelle, C., 310
Charles (Jackson), 81
chatlines (IM discussions), 256
Chaudron, C., 26
checklists, 321-322

Chomsky, Noam, 6
clarifying, 35
classroom arrangement, 184, 253, 295
classroom context mode of classroom
  discourse, 181-182
clauses, 52
cloze exercises, 36, 37, 142, 249
CLT. *See* communicative language
  teaching
cognitive academic language learning
  approach (CALLA), 271
cognitive academic language proficiency
  (CALP), 271
cognitive code learning, 6, 7
cognitive learning strategies, 269, 272
cognitive learning styles, 270
cognitive psychology, 6, 91
Cohen, A. D., 293
Cohen, R., 269
collaboration, 15-17, 254, 292. *See also*
  group work; pair work
communicative language teaching
  (CLT), 5, 6-7
  and content-based instruction, 207
  and grammar, 157
  and listening, 25
  and pronunciation, 114-115, 126
  and speaking, 50
companion Web sites, 256-257
comprehensible input, 26, 201
comprehension, reading, 75, 81, 83
computer-assisted language learning
  (CALL), 248-265
  background, 249-252
  classroom examples, 258-264
  classroom techniques/tasks,
    254-257
  defined, 248-249
  principles, 252-254
concordancing, 255-256, 260
Connor, U., 74, 90
consciousness-raising grammar
  activities, 157, 161
construct definition, 315
constructivism, 252, 261
contact assignments, 58
content-based instruction (CBI),
  200-201
  background, 202-205
  classroom examples, 211-219, 224
  classroom techniques/tasks,
    209-211
  principles, 205-209
content schema, 26
context, 54, 58, 106, 200-201
contrastive rhetoric, 89-90
conversation, 63, 64, 177-178. *See also*

discourse; speaking
conversation analysis (CA), 177-178
core meaning, 132-133, 145
Cornwell, S., 293
Corson, D. J., 134
Coulthard, 175
Council of Europe, 227, 291, 317
coursebooks, 226-245
    background, 226-228
    classroom examples, 239-245
    classroom techniques/tasks,
      234-238
    companion Web sites, 256-257
    defined, 226
    principles, 228-234
    See also modifying coursebook
      material
Coxhead, A., 136
Crabbe, D., 131, 292, 299
Crandall, J., 202
CRAPEL (*Centre de Recherches et
    d'Applications en Langues*), 291
"Creating Inventories" activity,
    275-277
criterion-referenced assessment, 317
*Cultural Thought Patterns in Intercultural
    Education* (Kaplan), 89
Cummins, 271
curriculum development, 4

Dam, Leni, 291, 293, 294, 295,
    303-305
Day, R., 33
debate activities, 210
decision making, 295
declarative knowledge, 160
deductive methods, 158-159
deliberate learning, 133, 134, 138, 142
descriptive grammars, 154
diagnostic assessment, 318
dialogue, 300-303
Dickinson, L., 293
dictation, 35-37, 41, 161-162
dictionaries, 139
Dictogloss, 161-162
direct method, 25
discourse, 174-193
    background, 175-182
    classroom examples, 190-192
    classroom techniques/tasks,
      185-189
    defined, 174
    principles, 182-185
    teacher-controlled, 58-60
    transcription system, 193
discourse communities, 91, 134
discourse markers, 175, 184, 187-188
discrete-point tests, 313
discussion activities, 210
dispreferred sequences, 177, 188-189

distinctive features, 53
doctor/patient listening activity, 41-42
Dörnyei, Z., 178
Doughty, C., 157, 161
drafting, 98
drama, 119, 183
Duffy, G. G., 78
Dulay, H., 156
Dunn, K., 276
Dunn, R., 275

EAP (English for Academic Purposes),
    227, 313
editing, 91, 98-99
Ehrman, M., 269
Elbow, Peter, 90
elicitation, 237
Elley, W. B., 148
Ellis, R., 157
e-mail penpals, 256
emotional issues, 116, 117
English 900, 227
English for Academic Purposes (EAP),
    227, 313
English for Specific Purposes (ESP),
    227
EnglishTown, 257
ESP (English for Specific Purposes),
    227
evaluating (listening strategy), 35
evaluation
    as curriculum component, 4
    defined, 311-312
    writing, 94-96
    See also assessment
exchange structure analysis, 175-177
explicit techniques, 161
expressivism, 90-91
extensive reading, 72, 148

Farstrup, A. E., 77
feedback
    and assessment, 316
    and computer-assisted language
      learning, 253
    pronunciation, 116
    writing, 93, 98
    See also follow-up phase
Fehr, B. J., 177
Field, M. L., 78
final achievement tests, 318
FL (foreign language) context, 54, 58
fluency
    and assessment, 325
    and discourse, 180
    grammar, 161
    reading, 76
    speaking, 55
    and vocabulary, 131, 133, 134,
      143-144, 149

fluent reading, 68
focus on form, 157-158
follow-up phase, 11, 13-14
    classroom examples, 18-20
    and coursebooks, 233, 238
    and listening, 38, 41-42
foreign language (FL) context, 54, 58
formative assessment, 321
format shifting, 236, 242
Fotos, S., 157
Freeman, D., 293
freewriting, 90
Fullilove, J., 29-30

gadgets. *See* props
gap-fill drills, 249, 250-251
garden path technique, 162-163
Gardner, D., 293
Gardner, R., 177
gist (global) listening, 31, 38-39
GlobalEnglish, 257
global (gist) listening, 31, 38-39
Goodman, K., 70, 71
Gordon, D., 120
Gouin's series method, 25
Grabe, W., 68
graded readers, 70
    and vocabulary, 141-142, 144,
      146-147, 148
grammar, 154-171
    and assessment, 312, 325
    autonomy, 297-298
    background, 155-158
    classroom examples, 163-171
    classroom techniques/tasks,
      160-163
    and content-based instruction,
      214-217
    defined, 154
    and methodology, 5, 6, 7-8
    principles, 158-160
grammar translation approach, 5, 226
graphic organizers, 210
group work, 55, 209-210, 259-260

Hamilton, R. L., 75
Hamilton-Jenkins, A., 143
Handman, W., 119
Hanson, J. R., 269
Harper, A., 120
Helgesen, M., 30, 36, 39
Herzberg, B., 89
high frequency words, 135-136, 137,
    138, 139
    classroom examples, 144, 145, 147
Hoffman, J. V., 78
Holec, Henri, 290, 291
holistic rubrics, 95
Holmes, B., 292
Holten, C., 203, 209

Hu, M., 133
Huey, E. B., 69
Hughes, 318
Huizenga, Jann, 100
humanism, 6
Hutchings, G. A., 261
Hutchinson, T., 208, 227

IM discussions (chatlines), 256
immersion, 157-158
implicit techniques, 161
inductive methods, 158-159, 162-163
inference
        and listening, 31, 35, 39-40
        and reading, 81
information gap tasks, 12-13
        content-based instruction, 210
        grammar, 170
        speaking, 56-57
input. *See* input hypothesis; listening;
    reading; receptive language skills
input authenticity, 34
input enhancement, 161
input hypothesis, 25-26, 201
intensive reading, 71
interactional speech, 56
interactive models of reading, 72-73
interactive processing, 29
"Interactive Search and Find" activitty,
    277-278
International Phonetic Alphabet (IPA),
    114
Internet, 119, 255, 256-257
intonation, 53
inventories, 275-277
IPA (International Phonetic Alphabet),
    114
Iran-Nejad, A., 77
IRF sequences, 175-176, 179, 180, 183,
    185

Jackson, Shirley, 81
jigsaw activities, 56, 210
Johnson, J., 292
Johnson, K. E., 193, 300-302
Jung, Carl, 269
Just, M., 32

Kachru, Y., 269
Kamil, M. L., 70
Kaplan, Robert, 89
Kawai, Y., 77
kazoos, 118
Kennedy, G., 130
Kesselring, Joseph, 119
keyword technique, 142
Kinsella, K., 268, 269, 275
knowledge domains, 259
Kohonen, V., 292

Krashen, Stephen, 7-8, 25-26, 156, 157,
    201
Kroll, B., 96
Kucan, L., 75

language, units of, 51
language acquisition research
        and content-based instruction, 201
        and grammar, 7-8, 156-157
        and listening, 25-26
        and speaking, 50
        and vocabulary, 74
Language and Content (Mohan), 202
language laboratories, 25
Laroy, C., 117
Larsen-Freeman, D., 91, 157
learner-centered education
        computer-assisted language
            learning, 254
        content-based instruction, 207
        and methodology, 7, 8-9
        pronunciation, 117
        vocabulary, 140-141
learning contracts, 259, 261
learning strategies. *See* learning
    styles/strategies
learning styles/strategies, 268-285
        background, 269-272
        classroom examples, 279-285
        classroom techniques/tasks, 275-278
        defined, 268
        and listening, 35
        principles, 273-275
        and reading, 68, 76, 77, 81
Lee, J. F., 207
Legenhausen, L., 293
Levince, R., 269
Levine, A., 74
linear programs, 250
listening, 24-43
        background, 25-26
        bottom-up vs. top-down
            processing, 26-30, 35, 37
        classroom examples, 41-43
        classroom techniques/tasks, 35-41
        defined, 24-25
        strategies for, 35
        and task variety, 31-32
        and text characteristics, 32-34
        types of, 30-31
        and vocabulary, 133, 143
Little, D., 290, 292, 293
Littlejohn, A., 292, 297-298
Littlewood, W., 207
Long, D., 26
Long, M. H., 58-59
low frequency words, 136, 137, 138,
    139, 144, 145, 146
Lynch, T., 32

main idea, 39
managerial mode of classroom dis-
    course, 179
materials mode of classroom dis-
    course, 179-180
McCarthy, 183
McCarthy, M. J., 174
McGrath, I., 292
McKeown, M. G., 75
Meaning-based (Whole Language)
    approach to reading, 71
Mekler, E., 119
Meloni, C., 256
memory, 32
Menasche, L., 33-34
Merrill, P. F., 250
metacognition, 75
metacognitive learning strategies, 269,
    271
methodology, 4-20
        background, 5-8
        classroom examples, 14-20
        classroom techniques/tasks, 11-14
        defined, 4-5
        principles, 8-11
micro-listening, 37
Miller, L., 293
MIM/MEM (mimicry/memorization),
    25
minimal pairs, 117-118
mistake logs, 237-238
modifying coursebook material
        discourse, 183
        format shifting, 236, 242
        importance of, 230-231
        listening, 37, 38-39, 40
        personalization, 235, 237, 240
        props/visuals/realia, 236
        and stereotypes, 240
Mohan, Bernard, 202
Moir, J., 140
monitoring, 35, 233, 237-238
Morgan, M., 7
Morley, J., 117, 123
morpheme order studies, 7
morphemes, 52
motherese, 33
motivation, 252
Moulton, W., 5-6
multiword units, 130-131
Murphy, J. M., 205
Murray, Donald, 90
Murtagh, L., 72

Nation, I. S. P., 74, 131, 133, 138,
    140, 143
National Council of Teachers of
    English (NCTE), 89
negotiating for meaning, 15-18, 55
Nelson, G., 269

non-weighted rubrics, 94-95
norm-referenced assessment, 317
North, B., 317
notional-functional approach, 227
Nunan, D., 7, 8, 9, 38, 56, 207, 251, 257, 290, 295

observation, 321-322
The Odd Couple (Simon), 119
Olshtain, E., 154
O'Malley, J. M., 76, 271
O'Neil, R., 228
oral reading, 69
Ortony, A., 26
Oskarsson, M., 319, 323
Our Town (Wilder), 119
output. *See* productive language skills; speaking; writing
overall communicative effectiveness (task fulfillment), 325
Oxford, R. L., 76, 77, 268, 269, 271, 275

pair work, 55, 57, 209-210
Pally, M., 205
Palmer, A. S., 313
Palmer, H. E., 130
pattern practice, 120-121
Pawley, A., 130
peer pressure, 116
penpals, 256
personality learning styles, 270
personalization, 235, 237, 240
personal methodology, 10-11
Peterson, P. W., 29
phonemes, 52, 123-125
phonics approach, 70, 114
phrases, 52
Piaget, Jean, 269
placement tests, 317
Platt, J., 112, 154
Pomerantz, A., 177
portfolio assessment, 318
practice writing, 92-93
prediction, 35
prelistening activities, 29, 41
prescriptive grammars, 154
pretasks, 11, 12, 15-16, 240
Price, G. E., 276
principled eclecticism, 91
prior knowledge. *See* background knowledge
problem solving, 210
procedural knowledge, 160
process writing, 96-99
    classroom examples, 100, 101
    and content-based instruction, 210
productive language skills, 24, 48
    and vocabulary, 133, 134, 142-143, 148-149

See also speaking; writing
professional development, 77-78. *See also* teacher self-evaluation
proficiency tests, 317, 319-320
profile sentences, 315-316
programmed instruction (programmed learning), 249-250
programmed learning. *See* programmed instruction
progress achievement tests, 318
pronunciation, 112-126
    and assessment, 312, 325
    background, 112-115
    classroom examples, 120-125
    classroom techniques/tasks, 117-119
    defined, 112
    principles, 115-117
proofreading, 91, 98-99
props, 118, 236

Questioning the Author technique, 75
quickwriting, 97

ranking activities, 211
rating scales, 321, 323-326
reading, 68-84
    background, 69-73
    classroom examples, 82-83
    classroom techniques/tasks, 79-82
    defined, 68-69
    and listening, 24
    principles, 74-78
    and vocabulary, 74, 80, 133, 141-142, 144, 146-148
reading journals, 81
reading rate, 76, 81
realia, 236
real-world language use. *See* task authenticity; text authenticity
receptive language skills, 24, 48
    and vocabulary, 133, 141-142, 146-148
    See also listening; reading
recordings, 119, 183. *See also* listening
reflection, 13-14, 296. *See also* follow-up phase
Reid, J. M., 269, 275
reliability, 310
repeated reading, 81
responding, 35
Reves, T., 74
revising, 98
Reynolds, N., 89
rhythm, 53
Rice, Alison, 234
Richards, J. C., 4-5, 25, 26, 112, 120, 154, 207
Rodgers, T., 25, 207
role-plays, 57, 183, 210

Rost, M., 33, 35
Royal Society of Arts, 315
rubber bands, 118
Rubin, J., 33
rubrics, 94-96
Rumelhart, D. E., 26

SA (self-assessment), 319-320
Sacks, 177
Samuels, S. J., 70
SARS method, 230
Sato, Y., 231
scanning, 83
Schegloff, 177
schema theory, 11, 26, 28, 251-252
Schulman, M., 119
SCLT (sustained-content language teaching), 205
screenplays, 119
second language (SL) context, 54, 58
segmental phonemes, 52
selection tests, 317
self-access centers, 291
self-assessment (SA), 319-320
self-confidence, 117
self-directed learning, 291
Self-Evaluation of Teacher Talk (SETT), 178-182, 184, 192
sensory learning styles, 270
sequencing activities, 211
series method, 25
SETT (Self-Evaluation of Teacher Talk), 178-182, 184, 192
Shaughnessy, M. P., 91
sheltered content instruction, 202, 203, 206
Shetzer, H., 256
Shohamy, E., 314
sign listening activity, 39-40, 42
silent reading, 69
silent way, 6
Silver, H. F., 269
Simon, Neil, 119
simulations, 57, 183
Sinclair, 175
skills
    integration, 206
    reading, 77
    See also specific skills
skills and systems mode of classroom discourse, 180-181
Skinner, B. F., 249, 250
slow motion speaking (SMS), 118-119
SL (second language) context, 54, 58
SMS (slow motion speaking), 118-119
Snow, M. Ann, 202, 204, 206
social constructionism, 91
socio-affective learning strategies, 269, 272
Sommers, N., 98

speaking, 48-64
    background, 49-53
    classroom examples, 58-64
    classroom techniques/tasks, 56-58
    defined, 48
    and listening, 41
    principles, 54-56
    and vocabulary, 142-143, 148-149
    See also discourse
specific information, listening for,
    30-31, 35-37
speed, 33, 33-34
speed reading, 144
speed writing, 144
spontaneous speech, 115
spot-the-mistake activities, 168
Stanovich, K. E., 70, 72
Stevens, V., 250
Stevick, E., 6
Stoller, F. L., 205
strategic reading, 68, 76, 77, 81
stress, 53
structural linguistics, 5-6, 155, 227
substitution drills, 156, 165
suggestopedia, 6
summarizing, 283, 284
summative assessment, 318
support, 295-296
suprasegmental phonemes, 53
survey tasks, 210, 238
sustained-content language teaching
    (SCLT), 205
Swaffar, J., 7
Swain, M., 134, 313
Swan, M., 227
Syder, F. H., 130
syllabus design, 4

tango seating, 57
target language, 49
task authenticity
    and assessment, 313
    and content-based instruction,
      208-209
    and discourse, 181, 184
    and listening, 34
    and writing, 101
    See also content-based instruction
task-based language teaching (TBLT),
    7, 114-115, 227
task fulfillment, 325
task instructions
    and assessment, 316, 320
    and autonomy, 299-300
    and coursebooks, 231-232, 237
tasks, 11, 12-13
task variety
    and autonomy, 294-295
    and learning styles/strategies, 273
    and listening, 31-32

TBLT (task-based language teaching),
    7, 114-115, 227
teacher autonomy, 227, 292-293
teacher roles. *See* learner-centered edu-
    cation; teacher talk
teacher self-evaluation
    discourse, 178-182, 184, 192
    and learning styles/strategies,
      273-274
    reading, 77-78
teacher's guides, 234
teacher talk
    and autonomy, 295, 300-303
    and discourse, 58-60, 183, 190
    self-evaluation, 178-182, 184, 192
    and speaking, 55
Terrell, T., 7
text
    defined, 51
    difficulty, 32-33
    and listening, 24, 30, 32-34
    See also text authenticity
text authenticity
    and computer-assisted language
      learning, 253
    and content-based instruction, 208
    and listening, 33-34
textual schema, 26
theater. *See* drama
theme-based language instruction,
    202, 203
thesauri, 256
Thomas-Ruzic, Maria, 100
Thurrell, S., 178
Titone, 25
tokens, 130
top-down vs. bottom-up processing.
    See bottom-up vs. top-down pro-
    cessing
Torres, E., 227
tracking, 119
transactional speech, 56
transcription system, 193
transformational-generative grammar,
    6
Tsui, A., 29-30

unequal power discourse, 58
Ur, 161
U.S. Department of Health and
    Human Services, 321
utterances, 48, 51

validity, 310
values clarification activities, 211,
    217-219
Van Ek, J. A., 227
van Lier, L., 48, 51, 176, 193
VanPatten, B., 207
visual instructions, 237

visuals, 236
vocabulary, 130-150
    and assessment, 312, 325
    background, 133-135
    classroom examples, 144-149
    classroom techniques/tasks,
      141-144
    and content-based instruction,
      212-213
    defined, 130-133
    principles, 135-141
    and reading, 74, 80, 133,
      141-142, 144, 146-148
Voller, P., 292
vowels, 123-125

WAC (Writing Across the
    Curriculum), 91
waiting time, 184
Wajnryb, Ruth, 161, 162
Walsh, S., 175, 178
Warschauer, M., 256
Waters, A., 208
webbing activities, 80
Weber, H., 112, 154
weighted rubrics, 95
Wesche, Mari B., 202, 204, 206
"What do I want to know" listening
    activity, 37
"What is the order?" activity, 39
"Which picture?" activity, 39
Whole Language (Meaning-based)
    approach to reading, 71
Wilder, Thornton, 119
Williams, J., 157, 161
word cards, 138
word families, 131, 135-136
wordmapping, 97
word origins, 138
word parts, 138, 142
word webs, 80
working memory, 32
writing, 88-106
    background, 88-91
    classroom examples, 99-105
    classroom techniques/tasks, 96-99
    and content-based instruction, 210
    defined, 88
    principles, 92-96
    vs. speaking, 48
    and vocabulary, 142-143, 144
Writing Across the Curriculum
    (WAC), 91

Young, R., 291
"Your story" activity, 41

Credits

PHOTO CREDITS

p. v Chan Lee/Advivum Design (www.advivum.com). **p. 214** photo on left Paul A. Souders/CORBIS, **p. 214** photo on second from left CORBIS, **p. 214** photo in middle Claudia Kunin/CORBIS, **p. 214** photo on second from right CORBIS, **p. 214** photo on right CORBIS. **Reflection Icon:** EyeWire/Getty Images. **Action Icon:** David Buffington/Getty Images.

TEXT CREDITS

p. 27 Excerpt from *Active Listening: Building Skills for Understanding Student's Book* by Marc Helgesen and Steven Brown. Reprinted with the permission of Cambridge University Press. **p. 29** Figure from *Active Listening: Introducing Skills for Understanding Student Book* by Marc Helgesen and Steven Brown. Reprinted with the permission of Cambridge University Press. **p. 36** Excerpt from *Listen In* by David Nunan, 1998. Reprinted by permission of the author. **p. 48** From *Introducing Language Awareness for Education* by Leo van Lier, on Web site http://maxkade.miis.edu/Faculty_Pages/Ivanlier/language.html. Reprinted with permission from Leo van Lier. **p. 51** Excerpt from *Interaction in the Language Curriculum: Awareness, Autonomy and Authenticity* by Leo van Lier, 1996. Reprinted by permission of Pearson Education Limited. **p. 82** From *Active Skills for Reading, Book* 1, Text 1ˢᵗ edition by Anderson, © 2002. Reprinted with permission of Heinle, a division of Thomson Learning: www.thomsonrights.com. **p. 90** Figure from Robert Kaplan, *Language Learning 16*, 1966. Reprinted by permission of Blackwell Publishing UK and the author. **p. 100** Excerpt from *Writing Workout: A Program for New Students of English, 1ˢᵗ edition* by Huizenga and Thomas-Ruzic. © 1990. Reprinted with permission of Heinle, a division of Thomson Learning: www.thomsonrights.com. **p. 101** Excerpt from *Ready to Write: A First Composition Text* by Karen Blanchard & Christine Root, 1994. Reprinted by permission of Pearson Education Inc., White Plains, New York. **p. 102** Excerpt from *Tapestry Writing* 4, 2ⁿᵈ *edition* by M.E. Sokolik, © 2000. Reprinted with permission of Heinle, a division of Thomson Learning: www.thomsonrights.com. **p. 147** Reproduced by permission of Oxford University Press from *Dracula* by Bram Stoker retold by Diane Mowat © Oxford University Press 2000. **p. 162** Figure reproduced by permission of Oxford University Press from *Resource Books for Teachers: Grammar Dictation* by Ruth Wajnryb, © Oxford University Press 1990. **p. 164, 166, 169** Excerpts from *Expressions I, Meaningful English Communication, 1ˢᵗ edition* by D. Nunan, © 2001. Reprinted with permission of Heinle, a division of Thomson Learning: www.thomsonrights.com. **p. 176** Excerpt from *Cancode Spoken Corpus* by Michael McCarthy. Reprinted with the permission of Cambridge University Press. **p. 186** Figure from *Gateways Student Book* 2 by Irene Frankel and Victoria Kimbrough. Copyright © 1998 by Oxford University Press. Used by permission. **p. 187** Excerpt from *English Vocabulary in Use, Upper Intermediate, New Edition* by M.J. McCarthy and F. O'Dell, 2001. Reprinted with the permission of Cambridge University Press. **p. 229** Excerpt from *SuperGoal 3* by Manuel dos Santos, 2002. Reprinted with the permission of McGraw-Hill/Contemporary. **p. 229** Excerpt from *Interchange 3: English for International Communication: Workbook 3, Vol.* 2 by Jack C. Richards et al, 1998. Reprinted with the permission of Cambridge University Press. **p. 231** From "Teacher and Student Learning in the Workplace" by Kazuyoshi Sato, 2002, presented at the annual conference of the Japan Association for Language Teaching, Shizuoka, Japan. Reprinted by permission of the author. **p. 241** Figure from *Transitions Student Book* 1 by Linda Lee. Copyright © 1998 by Oxford University Press. Used by permission. **p. 232** Illustations from the book *Men, Women and Dogs* © 1943 by James Thurber. Copyright © renewed 1971 by Helen Thurber and Rosemary A. Thurber. Reprinted by arrangement with Rosemary A. Thurber and The Barbara Hogenson Agency. **p. 232** Figure from *Crosscurrents 1* by Marcia Fisk Ong et al, 1992. Reprinted by permission of Pearson Education Limited. **p. 243** Excerpt from *Expressions I, Meaningful English Communication, 1ˢᵗ edition* by D. Nunan, © 2001. Reprinted with permission of Heinle, a division of Thomson Learning: www.thomsonrights.com. **p. 279** Excerpt from *Parachutes Book 1* by Patricia Buere, 2001. Reprinted by permission of McGraw-Hill/Contemporary. **p. 281** *Quest: Reading and Writing in the Academic World* by Pamela Hartmann, 1999. Reprinted by permission of McGraw-Hill/Contemporary. **p. 314** From *A Practical Handbook in Language Testing for the Second Language Teacher* by Elana Shohamy, 1985. Reprinted by permission of the author.

We apologize for any apparent infringement of copyright and if notified, the publisher will be pleased to rectify any errors or omissions at the earliest opportunity.